DEFEATING MR CO2

ENERGY SAVING GUIDE TO ACHIEVING NET ZERO

HOMES + BUILDINGS

ACKNOWLEDGEMENT & APPRECIATION

Sincere appreciation extended to:
Rose Mary Petrass – for editing the book
Mehmoona Khurshid – for the artwork of selected images
Rehana Weale – for encouragement & support
Amyn Nathwani – for encouragement & support

Ashak Nathwani c/- Intertype Publish and Print
Unit 45, 125 Highbury Road
BURWOOD VIC 3125 Australia
info@intertype.com.au

Ordering Information:

Discounts are available on quantity purchases by corporations, associations, and others. Contact the "Special Sales Department" at the address above for details.

Mr CO2/ Ashak Nathwani.

ISBN: 978-1-7636667-9-5

FOREWORD

MATTHEW KEAN

Chair – Climate Change Authority – Australia

The built environment provides the backdrop to our daily lives. It's the homes where we live, offices where we work, shopping centres where we buy goods and services, hotels where we stay - and of course the roads, bridges, footpaths and other infrastructure that helps us move around.

Carbon is used and embedded in the construction and operation of every building and piece of infrastructure that exists. However, the sheer scale of the built environment - with more than eleven million homes and one million commercial properties - reinforces the opportunity that exists to leverage the built environment in pursuit of Australia's emission reduction goals.

Governments are continuing to build the policy toolkit in support of those endeavours. Energy performance requirements, energy efficiency programs and construction codes that keep raising the bar are essential elements of progress.

We will need to continue to invest in policy solutions, technological advances and decarbonisation solutions that support the shift to a low-emissions built environment. Good urban planning, building design and a wholesale embrace of the circular economy also need to become common practice.

The Climate Change Authority - which I'm fortunate to Chair - continues to turn its mind to the solutions that will inform progress to decarbonisation in the built environment. It was one of six priority sectors identified for attention in our recent Sector Pathways Report.

We also know the appetite for homeowners, for example, to lower costs, reduce energy use and contribution to a clean energy future is real. Australia is one of the world's leaders for adoption of rooftop solar - which makes sense in a sun-blessed nation.

They've shown that where they are armed with information and can take practical, affordable steps to improve the energy efficiency of their home, they will.

Defeating Mr CO2 seeks to help further close the knowledge gap. It reinforces the opportunity that exists to use the built environment in support of our climate change objectives; that the right solutions don't require a trade off with comfort - in fact, they can add to it; and reducing energy use makes sense at a time of cost-of-living pressures.

The depth of work that goes into the book illustrates Dr Ashak Nathwani's passion for combating climate change, commitment to big ideas and passion for the country he adopted on his arrival in Australia over 50 years ago.

The race to combat climate change requires good ideas and collaboration from across governments, industry, academia, climate scientists and environmentalists - among others. *Defeating Mr CO2* is emblematic of those endeavours and should enrich the debate about the road to net zero.

CONTENTS

INTRODUCTION

In this book, I address the climate emergency pragmatically, focusing on carbon dioxide (CO_2) as the primary greenhouse gas (GHG) driving global warming and its severe impacts on our climate and planet. As the world becomes hotter and natural disasters become more commonplace, it is vital that we drastically curb GHG emissions – especially in the built environment, which makes up a staggering 40 per cent of emissions. At the same time, since we spend around 90 per cent of our time indoors, we need to be able to occupy our homes, offices, and other indoor environments at the right temperature and humidity that constitute a comfortable place to be. Comfort is not something that needs to be sacrificed in the journey to net zero. It is, in fact, more important than ever. Buildings are now more than simple shelters – they are safe havens from a climate that is fast becoming more and more threatening. Therefore, the book is a guide to both carbon reduction and climate adaptation. It will show you, step by step, how to achieve net zero in building operations while maintaining comfort.

The book has been a long time in the making. After graduating with a mechanical engineering degree from the University of Nairobi in Kenya in 1972, I came to Australia as a political refugee with just 20 cents in my pocket. I was one of the victims of the tyrannous dictator Idi Amin who expelled around 50,000 people of Indian origin from Uganda. The choice for me was to leave the country or potentially get killed. Together with Samim, my wife and Shiraz, my brother, we arrived in Sydney at 5.00 pm on the 10th of October 1972. Serendipitously, exactly 50 years (to the hour) later, I received my PhD from the School of Architecture, Design and Planning at the University of Sydney. Coincidently, through the University of Sydney, I secured my first job in the building industry as controls engineer with Honeywell. At Honeywell, I was excited to gain my first hands-on experience on an energy efficiency project in a small outback town called Warialda. But my journey was not over yet.

The White Australia Policy – officially abolished a year before in 1971 – was still very much alive in many rural towns across the country. This meant that, due to my skin colour, I could not represent the company when visiting sites. My experience facing racism as a refugee during that time taught me the importance of persevering excellence in whatever I did. That seemed to have paid off. In 2016, I was honoured in the Queen's Birthday nominations and appointed Member of Order of Australia (AM) for my services to the Ismaili Community, sustainability, and engineering.

The book includes various case studies and experiences from my career in both technical and non-technical languages. After three years at Honeywell, I spent thirty-three years as a consultant with the leading engineering firm, Norman Disney Young (NDY), advocating for energy-efficient buildings and a best practice approach to green engineering and sustainability. Upon my retirement from NDY, I joined the University of Sydney, where I was instrumental in co-designing the first of its kind in Australia, an Indoor Environmental Quality (IEQ) laboratory and a new degree - Master of Architectural Science, High Performance Buildings. I continue to lecture on an occasional basis at the University on Sustainability, Facilities Management, and Engineering. I also continue work as an energy and GHG minimisation strategist carrying out audits of buildings in developing and developed countries. Iconic buildings that I have been involved with include the Sydney 2000 Olympic venues, Pinewood (Iskandar) Film Studios, Malaysia, ABC and SBS Radio & TV Studios, 1 Bligh Street, Sydney, Ismaili Centres in Lisbon, Vancouver, Dushanbe, Dubai, London, Toronto, and Houston, to name a few. Selected ones are covered as case studies in the book.

In the book, I use a character Mr Co2– a personification of the gaseous chemical compound - to explain how fossil fuel-generated electricity is responsible for the mechanisms of climate change: "My existence begins with the flip of a light switch, tapping into electricity from a coal-fired power plant. My origins trace back to carbon, my mother, and oxygen, my father. Along with my kin of polluting gases – methane, nitrous oxide, and fluorinated carbons – we compose the greenhouse gases." The introductory chapters, seen through Mr CO2's eyes, detail GHG emissions from all sectors and confirm why the built environment must be a focus for energy and GHG reduction.

Subsequent chapters cover the basics of the built environment and energy-consuming systems like lighting, electrical devices, and heating, ventilation, and air conditioning (HVAC) systems. They also discuss simple methods for enhancing energy efficiency and encouraging behavioural changes among occupants to reduce energy use. HVAC systems, responsible for 65 to 75 per cent of a building's energy use, are essential for maintaining indoor comfort as global temperatures rise.

The book's content is also enriched by practical experiences and feedback from the online course, 'Facilities Management and Greenhouse Gas Minimisation', available to all at no cost through the AKDN Learning Hub, which also hosts other sustainability-related training courses. This course, consisting of 15 concise videos, is a step-by-step guide for reducing energy use and GHG emissions in existing buildings while ensuring optimal comfort for occupants. The positive feedback from participants, including architects and sustainability professionals, highlighted the value of simplified HVAC concepts and their relevance to indoor comfort and energy saving techniques, which were traditionally confined to academic textbooks.

As you read through the book, I invite you to apply the teachings to your own practice, whether as a professional or a concerned citizen. If each one of us were to save a minimum of 10 per cent to 20 per cent energy by adopting the appropriate energy conservation measures, we can make a significant reduction in GHG emissions. This would increase exponentially if governments were to provide incentives such as tax deductions for the purchase of energy-efficient equipment and for adopting renewable energies. For governments, this would reduce the demand side energy and hence require less power generation.

Opportunities to save energy and GHG in homes and buildings are enormous. Let us all work together to defeat Mr CO2.

1

UNPREDICTABLE TO UNBEARABLE CLIMATE

CO_2
Carbon dioxide

MEET MR CO2

My name is Mr CO2. I am a product of carbon, my mother, and oxygen, my father. My journey commences with the flip of a light switch, tapping into electricity sourced from coal-fired power plants. While it may seem intricate, the energy needed for that bulb to glow necessitates the combustion of coal in a power plant. Thus, voila, I emerge, with the power station as my birthplace.

As carbon emissions arise from various sources and deforestation claims CO2-absorbing trees, my extended family of polluting gases – namely methane, nitrous oxide, and hexafluoro carbons – grows. Together, we constitute the greenhouse gases responsible for the escalating global warming crisis and its dire consequences on climate and our planet.

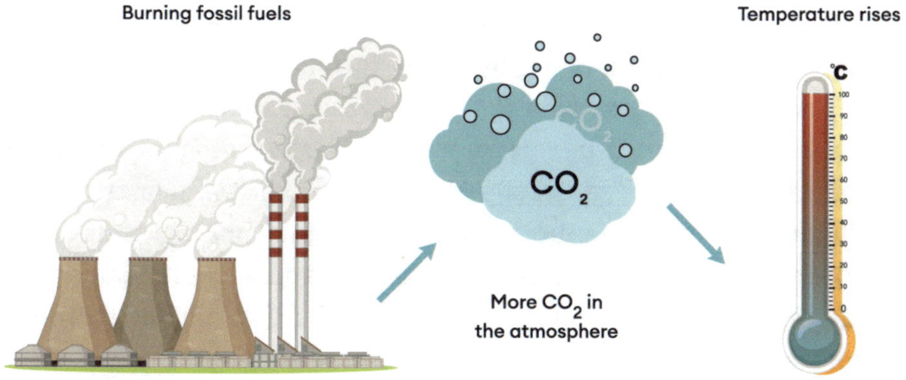

Looking Back

Most people are unaware of this surprising fact: the current level of CO2 in the atmosphere is like what it was about 4.3 million years ago. Back then, during a time called the mid-Pliocene epoch, the Earth looked significantly different to how it looks today. For instance, sea levels were approximately 20 metres higher, and the average temperature was about 3.9 degrees Celsius warmer than pre-industrial levels (when humans started to affect the climate). During this epoch, large forests covered parts of the Arctic that are now frozen tundra.

Sources of CO_2

CO_2 originates from diverse sources, both natural and human-induced. Let us examine each one.

Taking natural origins first, all organisms, including humans, exhale CO_2 during the respiratory process. Next, as the climate gets extreme, there is an increased frequency of wildfires, bushfires, or grassfires. whereby an extensive amount of CO_2 is released. Another source is when organic matter, such as deceased plants and animals, undergoes decomposition. There is also volcanic activity when significant quantities of CO_2 are emitted during volcanic eruptions, originating from deep within the Earth's crust. Finally, the Earth's oceans act as carbon sinks, absorbing CO_2 from the atmosphere and subsequently releasing it.

Looking at human-induced or anthropogenic sources, fossil fuel combustion takes the lead. This includes burning coal, oil, diesel, and natural gas for energy production in power plants and as standby power, industrial facilities, transportation (cars, trucks, aeroplanes, ships), and heating in buildings. This is followed by deforestation and land-use changes, where forests are cleared for agriculture, urbanisation, or other purposes, releasing CO_2 stored in trees and soil into the atmosphere. Certain industrial activities, such as cement production, chemical manufacturing, and metal smelting, emit CO_2 as a by-product. Another man-made activity responsible for increasing CO_2 is through waste management. Landfills and waste treatment processes produce CO_2 through the decomposition of organic waste. Lastly, biomass burning involving agricultural practices like burning crop residues releases CO_2 into the atmosphere.

Atmospheric Levels of CO_2

Atmospheric CO_2 is the second most abundant greenhouse gas after water vapour. Since time immemorial, CO_2 levels have varied widely, partly driving swings in our weather, especially average temperatures. CO_2 has become a proxy for measuring climate change.

Overall, the management of forests and other land like cropland and grassland acts as a net sink of CO_2, which means that CO_2 is removed from the atmosphere and stored in plants and trees. But as humans are producing more CO_2 than what is absorbed, CO_2 levels continue to rise. They are joined by other gases which also have been growing significantly.

As Figure 1 shows, scientists have been observing atmospheric CO_2 levels at the Mauna Loa Observatory in Hawaii since 1958.

FIGURE 1: MONTHLY MEAN CO2 – DATA: MAUNA LOA OBSERVATORY 2024

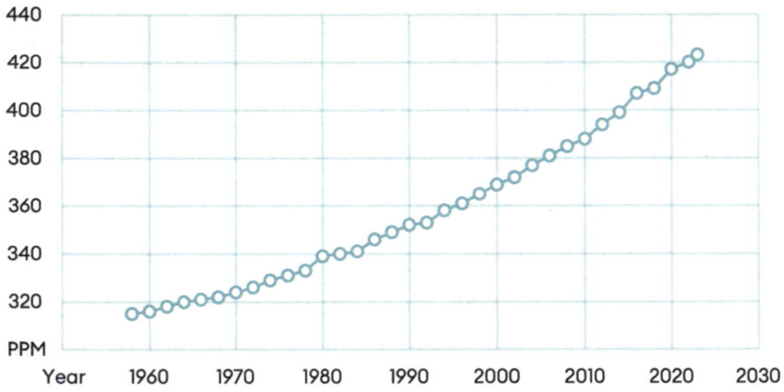

CO2 EQUIVALENTS

As Mr. CO_2, my extended family includes methane, nitrous oxide, and certain manufactured (fluorinated) gases—commonly termed 'carbon dioxide equivalents' or CO_2e. We are all considered the principal greenhouse gases. Once emitted into the atmosphere, most of us remain there for long periods, ranging from a decade to many millennia.

CO_2e serves as the standardised measurement for quantifying the prime contributors to climate change, known as the 'Triple C' – or climate change causes. Although these chemical compounds can originate from different sources and have different warming effects, they all influence climate change.

In my role as Mr CO_2, let me elaborate further on some of my colleagues and greenhouse gas partners.

Methane (CH_4)

Methane (CH_4) is naturally emitted from wetlands that are not managed or changed by human activity, where bacteria decompose organic materials in the absence of oxygen. Reservoirs and ponds with high organic matter and low oxygen levels produce CH_4 through the microbial breakdown of organic matter. Sporadic sources include termites, oceans, sediments, volcanoes, and wildfires.

The agriculture sector is a significant source of methane emissions in most countries. Methane gas is predominantly emitted by livestock such as cattle, pigs, sheep, and goats, as they produce CH_4 as part of their normal digestive process. Additionally, methane is released when their manure is stored or managed in lagoons or holding tanks.

Aside from agriculture, fugitive emissions produce a substantial amount of methane. 'Fugitive emissions' represent the unintentional gas leaks from processes such as fracking and more traditional oil and gas extraction and transportation. This happens when gas is transported through poorly maintained pipes, for example.

Natural gas and petroleum systems are the second largest source of CH_4 emissions in many countries, including the United Arab Emirates, the United States of America, Russia, and Canada. It is emitted during the production, processing, storage, transmission, distribution, and use of natural gas. It is also emitted through the production, refinement, transportation, and storage of crude oil. Coal mining is also a source of CH_4 emissions (US EPA, 2022).

Methane is also generated in landfills as waste decomposes and in the treatment of wastewater. Landfills are the third-largest source of CH_4 emissions in most cities.

Nitrous Oxide (N_2O)

Nitrous oxide (N_2O) is emitted from various agricultural soil management activities, including the application of synthetic and organic fertilisers to urban soils like lawns and golf courses, other cropping practices, manure management, and the burning of agricultural residues. Agricultural soil management is the largest source of N_2O emissions in the US, accounting for 75 per cent of total N_2O emissions in 2021.

Fluorinated Gases

Fluorinated gases have existed for a long time and have come to the forefront more recently. These gases are primarily used in various industrial applications, such as refrigeration, air conditioning, electronics manufacturing, and foam production. They are human-made and do not occur naturally in the atmosphere. Common types of fluorinated gases include hydrofluorocarbons (HFCs), perfluorocarbons (PFCs), and sulphur hexafluoride (SF_6). With the move to electrification in the building sector and the promotion of heat pumps, we will come across derivatives of these gases in the form of refrigerants more frequently.

Sulphur Dioxide

Sulphur dioxide is considered an indirect greenhouse gas, along with nitrogen oxides, carbon monoxide, and non-methane volatile organic compounds. This indirect greenhouse gas influences atmospheric warming through either chemical reactions or changing the Earth's capability to balance radiative energy. Sulphur dioxide is a contributor to aerosols, which can absorb solar radiation and warm the atmosphere or cool the atmosphere by creating cloud droplets that reflect sunlight. Power plants are the biggest global contributor to sulphur dioxide emissions. Data from satellites, checked against surface monitoring stations, found that much of Canada's sulphur dioxide emissions had also significantly decreased between 2005 and 2014. The same has been observed internationally. Investigators suggest that the decline followed the use of flue gas desulphurisation, fuel switches from coal to natural gas, and some older coal power plants shutting down. Market-based cap and trade programs, as well as state and federal regulations, have also encouraged emission control technologies.

THE GREENHOUSE GAS LAYER

As a result of human activities, greenhouse gases are increasing in concentration because they are entering the atmosphere more quickly than they are being removed. As part of the infamous 'layer' in the atmosphere called greenhouse gases (GHGs), each chemical compound has a part to play depending on its individual capability to add to the warming of the Earth. Each has what is called a 'global warming potential' (GWP).

Global Warming Potential (GWP)

GHGs warm the Earth by absorbing energy and slowing the rate at which the energy escapes to space; they act like a blanket insulating the Earth. Each GHG has a different capacity to contribute to climate change. This capacity depends on its radiative properties, molecular weight, and the length of time it remains in the atmosphere.

Scientists use the term global warming potential, or GWP, to measure how much different GHGs contribute to global warming. GWP is measured relative to carbon dioxide, so it is measured in CO_2e. CO_2 has a GWP of 1. The more that a given GHG gas warms the Earth compared to CO_2 over that time, the larger the GWP.

GWP considers both the direct and indirect effects that GHGs have over a specific period compared to the impact of carbon dioxide. By all accounts, CO_2 will remain in the atmosphere for a very long time, probably thousands of years – but for the purposes of the Kyoto Protocol of 1997, an international agreement on climate change, scientists use a period of 100 years.

Below are some relevant comparisons. Let us look at each one with respect to GWP.

- **Methane (CH_4):** Methane emitted from various sources, including agriculture, landfills, and natural gas production, has a GWP of around 28-36, meaning it has 28-36 times more warming potential than CO_2 (US EPA, 2022).
- **Nitrous Oxide (N_2O):** Nitrous oxide, mainly released from agricultural and industrial activities and combustion processes, has

a GWP of approximately 265-298, making it a significantly potent GHG (US EPA, 2022).

- **Hydrofluorocarbons (HFCs):** These are synthetic gases commonly used in refrigeration, air conditioning, and foam-blowing applications. As a result of some of the refrigerants having high ozone-depleting potential (ODP) – meaning they have a notable impact on the ozone layer, they are being phased out. The GWPs of HFCs vary depending on the specific type, but they can range from several hundred to several thousand (US EPA, 2022). A commonly used refrigerant in air conditioning units is R22, which has a GWP of 1810.
- **Perfluorocarbons (PFCs):** These industrial gases are used in various applications, including electronics manufacturing and aluminium production. PFCs have extremely high GWPs, ranging to over 12,000 (US EPA, 2022).
- **Sulphur Hexafluoride (SF6):** SF6 is primarily used in electrical equipment, such as circuit breakers and transformers. It has an exceptionally high GWP of 22,800, making it one of the most potent GHGs (US EPA, 2022).

It is worth noting that the GWP measurement of various gases is subject to scientific updates and refinements as research progresses. The values provided here are based on the Fifth Assessment Report of the IPCC from 2014. Newer studies or assessments may provide revised GWP values for these gases.

GWP values change depending on the timeframe considered for each GHG. For short-lived gases like methane, the GWP is more significant over short periods but decreases when considering longer periods. On the other hand, for long-lived gases like sulphur hexafluoride, the GWP is more substantial over longer timeframes but decreases when looking at shorter timeframes (US EPA, 2022).

An alternate way to measure the impact of greenhouse gases is the global temperature potential (GTP). It looks at how much the Earth's temperature changes over a specific time compared to the effect of CO_2. Calculating GTP is a bit more complex than calculating GWP because it involves using models to understand how the climate reacts to higher greenhouse gas concentrations. These models consider two main factors: climate sensitivity, which is how much the climate responds to increased greenhouse gases, and response time, which depends on how quickly the Earth's climate system absorbs heat, partly through the oceans (US EPA, 2022).

SOLAR RADIATION AND THE GREENHOUSE EFFECT

Solar Radiation

Figure 2 shows the direct and diffuse aspects of solar radiation.

FIGURE 2. SOLAR RADIATION

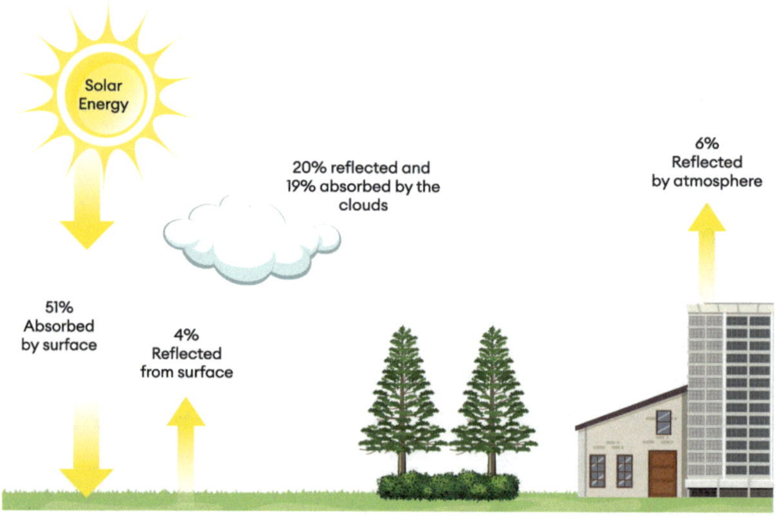

The Greenhouse Effect

The greenhouse effect is a natural process that helps keep the Earth warm enough for us to live on. Imagine the Earth as a big, cosy greenhouse. Just like a greenhouse, the Earth's atmosphere traps some of the heat from the Sun, keeping our planet's temperature just right for life.

FIGURE 3 GREENHOUSE EFFECT

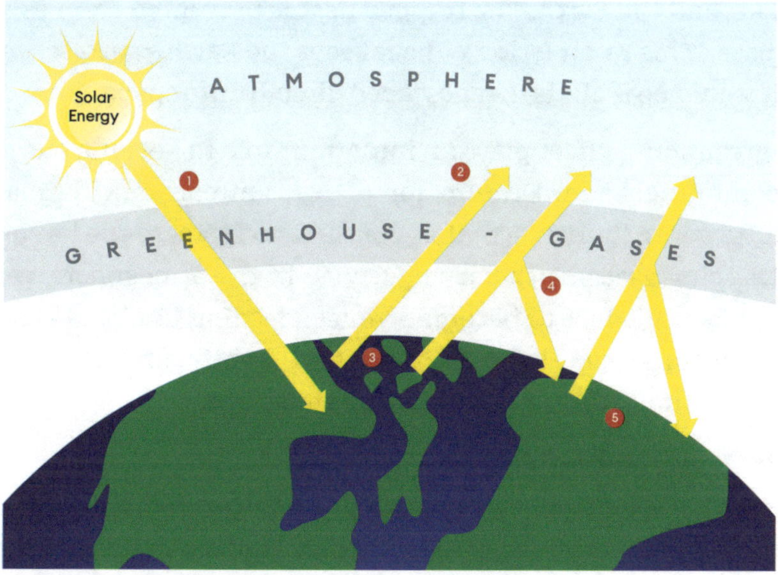

1. **Incoming solar radiation, on average, is 343 Watt per m2**
2. **Outgoing solar radiation @ 103 Watt per m2**
3. **Solar energy is absorbed by the earth's surface @ 168 Watt per m2 and is converted to longwave (infrared) back to the atmosphere.**
4. **Some of the infrared radiation is absorbed and re-radiate by the CO2 and CO2e molecules depending on the concentration of these greenhouse gases.**
5. **Earth surface gains more heat and re-radiates back to the atmosphere. The GHG layer keeps on re-radiating causing the earth's surface to keep on heating , causing global warming.**

This simple diagram in Figure 3 and the following information illustrates how greenhouse gases trap heat in the Earth's atmosphere, contributing to the warming of the planet.

When the Sun's rays reach the Earth, some of the energy is absorbed by the surface, warming it up. The Earth's atmosphere contains GHGs that allow most of the sunlight to pass through. The Earth's surface emits heat (infrared radiation) back towards space. Some of this heat is absorbed, and some is re-radiated by GHGs back to the Earth. The Earth radiates and re-radiates this heat back into the atmosphere in the form of infrared radiation. Normally, this heat would escape into space, but certain gases in the atmosphere, like CO_2 and CO_2es, act like a warm shield around the Earth. The trapped heat is prevented from escaping into space. This re-emission of heat keeps the Earth's surface warmer than it would be if all the heat escaped directly into space.

The greenhouse effect plays an important role in keeping our planet at a comfortable temperature for plants, animals, and humans to thrive. However, human activities continue to increase the levels of all heat-trapping gases (with varying GWPs) in the atmosphere, causing the greenhouse effect to become stronger, leading to global warming. Global warming needs to be limited to 1.5°C by reducing the GHG layer through minimisation of CO_2 and CO_2e emissions.

Climate Change and its Impacts

For decades, scientists have warned of the dangers of human-induced climate change. Public presentations at forums organised by the property industry and sustainability organisations in 1998 highlighted projections that are now becoming reality. Predictions of bushfires and floods from that time bear an uncanny resemblance to recent events worldwide. Forecasted insurance claims also have proven to be spot on.

On July 27, 2023, United Nations Secretary-General Antonio Guterres delivered a powerful message urging immediate radical action in response to the record-breaking July temperatures. He stated, "According to the science, the Earth has entered 'an era of global boiling,' surpassing the warming phase." Guterres described the intense heat across the Northern Hemisphere as a "cruel summer" and warned of impending disaster for the entire planet. He predicted that 2023 would break numerous temperature records, underscoring the urgency of the climate crisis. He has been proven absolutely correct.

Considering the likely consequences, the International Panel on Climate Change (IPCC) has set limits consistent with the goals of the Paris Agreement, a binding international treaty adopted at the UN Conference of Parties (COP 21) in 2015. The aim is to keep global warming well below 2 degrees Celsius (3.6 degrees Fahrenheit) above pre-industrial levels, with collaborative efforts to limit the increase to 1.5°C (2.7°F).

Scientists declared 2023 the hottest year on record, with scorching temperatures driven by climate change and further amplified by El Niño - this naturally occurring climate phenomenon that happens every two to seven years. European Union's Copernicus Climate Change Service analysis shows that 2023 was warmer than pre-industrial levels by more than 1.4 °C and was dangerously close to the warming limit of 1.5°C set by the Paris Agreement. Scientists and researchers believe that going beyond the 1.5°C benchmark heightens the risk of warming-related catastrophes (Ramirez, 2023).

In 2024, the impacts of global warming have been significant, with records indicating a continuation of a warming trend. The global average temperature for the period of June 2023 to May 2024 was the highest on record, with each month setting new temperature records. This marks a significant increase compared to previous years (NASA) (NOAA NCEI). The World Meteorological Organization (WMO) predicts that at least one year between 2024 and 2028 will likely exceed the critical 1.5°C temperature threshold set by the Paris Agreement. This temporary breach does not mean the long-term goal is permanently lost but indicates the increasing frequency and intensity of short-term temperature spikes (WMO). While most of the globe experienced above-average temperatures, some regions, such as the eastern United States and parts of Europe, saw cooler-than-average conditions during specific months. Additionally, January 2024 was notable for being the second-wettest January on record globally (NOAA NCEI).

These trends highlight the ongoing and escalating impacts of global warming, emphasising the urgent need for more ambitious climate action to mitigate long-term consequences (UN News)

EXTREME WEATHER EVENTS - 2024

UNPRECEDENTED FLOODING IN AFGHANISTAN, PAKISTAN, IRAN, AND BRAZIL

April and May 2024 saw large regions of central Asia hit by a series of storms resulting in heavy downpours and flash flooding. The worst affected country was Afghanistan, where 540 fatalities have been reported since March (WFP, 2024). In Pakistan, at least 124 people died in severe flooding in April (OCHA, 2024), while 18 people died in Iran in May (Iran International Newsroom, 2024). In addition, the heavy rainfall damaged thousands of homes and submerged agricultural lands.

In early May, floods and heavy rainfall in Kenya took the lives of more than 225 people. A further 160 people were injured, and over 212,630 people were displaced across the country. This came just a year after parts of Kenya experienced four consecutive seasons with little rain, creating one of Kenya's worst droughts.

SEVERE DRAUGHTS IN SOUTHERN AFRICA

From early 2024, large parts of Southern Africa experienced significantly below-average rainfall, with Zimbabwe, Zambia, Malawi, Angola, Mozambique, and Botswana receiving less than 20 per cent of the typical rainfall expected for February, with devastating consequences for the population largely depending on rainfed agriculture. Hence, the affected countries in Southern Africa continue to face an increased risk of severe food insecurity between rainy seasons.

DEADLY HEATWAVES

Kayes in Mali recorded 48.5°C on 3rd April (Bahati, 2024).

According to Saudi weather authorities, the holy city of Mecca hit 47-49°C during the day. According to ClimaMeter, a non-profit organisation, the temperature at Mecca's Grand Mosque peaked at 51.6°C.

DEVASTATING WILDFIRES IN CHILE

Extreme wildfires in coastal-central Chile, fuelled by intense and persistent fire-conducive weather conditions in the region since the beginning of the year, spread severe fires in Viña del Mar. The humanitarian impact was worse, with over 29,000 hectares burnt, 132 deaths, 300 missing, 7,200 houses destroyed, and 40,000 people affected.

RESEARCH

Researchers from affected countries and selected Western allies collaborated to assess to what extent human-induced climate change altered the likelihood and intensity of the weather conditions at the time of the most impactful floods, extreme rain and heat waves, and deadly wildfires. The research concluded that human activities were a significant factor in each case.

WAY FORWARD

All of this demonstrates the urgent need to continue to address climate change through adaptation and mitigation. Everyone has a role, from governments to companies and organisations to individuals. Sustainable practices, reducing GHG emissions, and climate adaptation strategies can significantly reduce the impacts, damages, and losses caused by climate change.

In the next chapter, we look at ways in which CO_2 is reduced and review sectors that contribute to CO_2 and CO_2e generation, together with strategies adopted by each sector towards GHG minimisation.

2

GREENHOUSE GAS MINIMISATION BY SECTOR

REDUCING CO_2

Global greenhouse gas emissions continue to rise at a time when they need to be rapidly falling. Nature plays a vital role in the CO_2 cycle. Trees release water vapour into the atmosphere through a process called transpiration, which cools the air. Trees provide shade, reducing the need for artificial cooling in urban areas and reduce the urban heat island effect, and thereby decreasing energy consumption and associated CO_2 emissions from power plants. Trees contribute organic matter to the soil through fallen leaves, branches, and roots. This organic matter enhances soil carbon storage, keeping carbon out of the atmosphere. Tree roots help stabilize soil and reduce erosion, which can prevent the release of stored carbon from soil into the atmosphere. In certain ecosystems, such as wetlands, trees and other vegetation can help regulate methane emissions by influencing microbial activity in the soil.

Most importantly, as we know, trees absorb CO_2 from the atmosphere during photosynthesis, using it to produce glucose and release oxygen. Let us examine how this phenomenon is harnessed through various human-initiated activities.

PLANTING TREES AND SEQUESTRATION

Carbon sequestration is the process of capturing and storing atmospheric carbon dioxide. It is one method of reducing the amount of CO_2 in the atmosphere with the goal of reducing global climate change. There are two major types of carbon sequestration: geologic and biologic.

Geologic

Geological carbon sequestration occurs when carbon is stored in places such as underground geological formations or rocks. This process is largely artificial or 'direct', representing an effective way of neutralising emissions put into human practices, such as manufacturing or construction. It is also largely technological, with recent innovations showing carbon being sequestered more effectively on larger scales.

They include:

Graphene Production

Graphene production requires CO_2 as a raw material. Although limited to certain industries, it's used heavily in the production of tech devices we use daily, such as smartphones or computer processors.

Engineered Molecules

In this new science, scientists are attempting to change the shape of molecules to form new compounds by capturing carbon from the air. In practice, this has the potential to create raw materials while reducing atmospheric carbon.

Carbon Capture and Storage (CCS)

CCS involves capturing carbon dioxide that's been produced by power generation or industrial activity, such as cement or steelmaking. This CO_2 is then compressed and transported to deep underground facilities, where it's injected into rock formations for permanent storage.

Biologic

The other form is biological carbon sequestration. Atmospheric carbon is absorbed and stored in vegetation, soils, woody products, and aquatic environments. As we know, trees and plants are natural carbon capture and storage machines, giving off oxygen and absorbing CO_2 during the day through the process we all learnt at school – photosynthesis. Trees store CO_2 in their biomass (trunks, branches, leaves, and roots). As a tree grows, it sequesters more carbon, which remains stored as long as the tree lives and even after it dies if the wood is used in long-lasting products.

Reforestation

Reforestation (planting trees in areas that have been subject to deforestation) and afforestation (planting trees in areas where no trees have stood in recent times) are forms of human-induced biological sequestration touted as key solutions to the climate crisis. As governments and businesses commit to large-scale tree-planting schemes to tackle climate change and restore biodiversity, there is a realisation that what and where you plant is just as important as the number of trees planted. A typical tree can absorb around 20 to 30 kilograms of CO_2 per year once fully grown. Saplings will absorb significantly less. Over 100 years, one tree could absorb around one metric ton of CO_2 (Science News, 2021).

However, planting trees to absorb carbon emissions will not even come close to solving the problem of climate change. According to Nafkote Dabi, climate change lead for Oxfam International: "Nature and land-based carbon removal schemes are an important part of the mix of efforts needed to stop global emissions, but they must be pursued in a much more cautious way. Under current plans, there is simply not enough land in the world to realise them. Around 1.6 billion hectares of new forests is required, which is approximately five times the size of India, or more than all the farmland in the world" (Oxfam, 2021).

Carbon credits are tradable credits representing a ton of carbon emissions reduced or removed from the atmosphere. Essentially, countries – or corporations – can pay for decarbonisation projects to account for their pollution ("pay to pollute" by some negotiators' standards). The market on which these credits are traded and the price at which they cost was heavily debated at the 2023 UN Conference of Parties (COP 28) held in Dubai, where experts, including the sector itself, discussed the scale of the problem.

Carbon markets have faced criticism for a lack of credibility in true environmental impact. As such, delegates at COP 28 discussed an organised UN-overseen carbon market on which emissions can be traded, and climate finance can be funnelled to developing countries. Negotiations, however, ultimately fell through. As a result, how the carbon market will function – and what role credits will ultimately play in global decarbonisation – is up in the air.

Carbon markets are essentially governed by Article 6 of the Paris Agreement, which allows countries to trade carbon credits bilaterally. Article 6.4 provides a framework for United Nations oversight of carbon markets. States are left to their devices without a clear consensus on how these articles should operate. Deals under Article 6.2 are continuing to be signed without UN oversight. At COP 28, while negotiations on carbon trading halted, bilateral agreements were announced: South Korea, Switzerland, Singapore, and the UAE are among the countries who agreed to the deals. It is unclear, however, whether these credits will be recognised under the Paris Agreement and whether any emissions reductions will count toward countries' nationally determined contributions.

Furthermore, countries are uncertain about what counts towards carbon credits generally. Article 6.4 determines that emissions removal and reduction factor into carbon credits, but many countries at COP 28 also pushed for emissions avoidance to count. This might include a project like Reduced Emissions from Deforestation and Forest Degradation (REDD+), which rewards forest owners for conserving their forests instead of cutting them down. Some argue that avoided deforestation does not meaningfully reduce emissions if the trees are not chopped anyway; others, however, argue that forest protection projects successfully prevent deforestation. Despite the initial progress of the Article 6.4 agreement, which would have allowed emissions avoidance in cases that can be treated as reduction or removal, the deal was ultimately not adopted. We must wait until COP 29 to be held in Azerbaijan in late 2024.

REDUCTION OF GHG BY EACH SECTOR

To effectively reduce emissions, we need to know where they come from – which sectors contribute the most? How can we use this knowledge to develop effective solutions and mitigation strategies?

FIGURE 4 GHG EMISSIONS BY SECTOR. DATA: (RITCHIE ET AL., 2024)

Energy is the largest contributor to global emissions. But there are some variations from country to country. In the US, for example, transport is a larger contributor than the global average, whereas, in Brazil, most emissions come from agriculture and land use change. (Ritchie et al., 2024)

Each sector is riddled with challenges. Amidst these challenges, humanity is trying to change course to counter the main drivers of climate change. The common objective of these efforts is to reduce GHG emissions. For each sector, a wealth of information is available outlining a range of initiatives underway to address this pressing issue.

Let us look at each sector and examine the respective sources and what measures are being taken to minimise GHG emissions.

ELECTRICITY GENERATION

Electricity is the main energy source for powering homes, business activities, factories, and the rapidly expanding infrastructure for EV charging. Different types of fuel used to generate electricity emit different amounts of CO2. Burning coal, for example, produces more CO2 than natural gas or oil.

As a general note, smart grid development is enabling more efficient and flexible power transmission and distribution. Smart grids integrate advanced sensors, communication networks, and control systems to optimise power flow, manage demand, and incorporate distributed energy resources. This improves grid stability and facilitates the integration of renewable energy sources, leading to reduced GHG emissions.

Another move gaining popularity internationally is the promotion of electrification of various sectors, such as transportation and heating. This is helping shift energy consumption from fossil fuels to cleaner electricity sources. Demand response programs are encouraging consumers to adjust their electricity usage during peak demand periods, allowing for better load balancing and maximising the utilisation of renewable energy resources.

Hydropower has historically been a prevalent renewable energy source, and some countries continue adding nuclear power to the mix. We are now witnessing the rise of many renewable energy sources, including solar, wind, ocean waves, and hydrogen. Renewable energy integration in the grid helps reduce GHG emissions by replacing fossil fuel-based generation. For example, wind turbines have increased in size and efficiency, enabling higher energy production, and micro-wind turbines are being marketed for domestic and small building applications. Continued research, innovation, and policy support are essential to further advance these technologies and accelerate the transition to a decarbonised power sector.

Solar Energy and Power Storage

Solar photovoltaic (PV) systems, too, have become more efficient and affordable, with improvements in solar panel design and manufacturing. Their prices have dropped, and they are being used extensively throughout the world.

Energy storage is becoming crucial for optimising renewable energy utilisation and enabling a more reliable and flexible power grid. Advancements in battery technologies, including lithium-ion batteries, have made storage systems more efficient and cost-effective.

More on solar energy and power storage in Chapter 5

Solar Panels

Nuclear

Nuclear power provides about 10% of the world's electricity. Countries like the United States, France, and China are leading producers. France, for instance, generates over 70% of its electricity from nuclear energy.

Nuclear power generation relies on nuclear fission, the process of splitting the nucleus of an atom. Uranium-235 is enriched to increase its fissile content. In some reactors, plutonium-239, generated from uranium-238, is used. Neutrons collide with the nucleus of a fissile atom causing the nucleus to split and release heat, more neutrons, and fission products (radioactive elements). The released neutrons trigger further fission in other nuclei, creating a chain reaction.

This energy is used to heat water into steam, which drives turbines connected to electricity generators. The most common types are Pressurized Water Reactors (PWRs) and Boiling Water Reactors (BWRs). In PWRs, water is kept under pressure to prevent it from boiling, whereas in BWRs, water boils directly in the reactor core. Control rods absorb neutrons and are used to regulate the fission process and maintain reactor safety.

The process produces radioactive waste, which remains hazardous for thousands of years. High-level waste includes spent nuclear fuel, which is stored in cooling pools and later moved to dry cask storage. Modern reactors have numerous safety systems to prevent overheating and accidents, but risks like meltdowns (e.g., Chernobyl, Fukushima) still concern the public.

It is interesting to learn that advanced nuclear power technologies, such as small modular reactors (SMRs) and advanced reactor designs, are being developed to provide low-carbon base-load power. Companies like NuScale are leading efforts to commercialise SMRs. These next-generation nuclear reactors are taking measures to enhance safety, efficiency, and sustainability while minimising waste generation and proliferation risks. They have the potential to contribute to low-GHG emission power generation if the stigmas of historical failures and 'not-in-my-backyard' can be overcome.

Hydrogen

The promising one is the use of green hydrogen. Hydrogen has gained attention as a clean and versatile energy carrier. Power generation technologies that utilise hydrogen, such as fuel cells, can produce electricity with zero GHG emissions when hydrogen is produced from renewable sources. Green hydrogen production has increased globally, with projects scaling up to meet climate goals. Countries like Australia, Germany, India, the U.S., and others are investing heavily in hydrogen production infrastructure. For example, Europe aims to produce 10 million tons of green hydrogen annually by 2030.

Although green hydrogen production is growing, it remains relatively expensive compared to fossil fuels due to the high costs of renewable electricity and electrolysis technology. However, prices are expected to drop as technology improves and economies of scale kick in.

Green hydrogen plays a critical role in energy storage. It can be produced when there's excess renewable electricity (like from solar or wind) and stored for later use. This makes it particularly attractive for balancing grids with a high share of intermittent renewable energy.

Some countries are beginning to test hydrogen as a fuel for electricity generation in power plants, either by blending hydrogen with natural gas or using 100% hydrogen in turbines. Companies like Siemens and GE are developing hydrogen-ready turbines to facilitate this transition. The European Union is leading in green hydrogen initiatives, with projects like the NortH2 in the Netherlands aiming to produce green hydrogen at scale using offshore wind energy. Other countries like Spain and Portugal are also advancing in hydrogen production linked to renewable sources.

Countries like Japan and South Korea are leading the way in developing hydrogen fuel cells and integrating hydrogen into their energy mix, including electricity generation. Australia is also positioning itself as a key exporter of green hydrogen and hydrogen-based generators.

Hydrogen Powered Generator.

Blue Diamond Machinery, Australia, has released the hydrogen-powered generator GEH2, which uses hydrogen with a Toyota fuel cell and a lithium-ion phosphate battery to produce 100kVA of instant power. The fuel cell and the battery work together to service whatever load it is providing or servicing at the time in the most efficient way. In line with information gathered from the supplier of GEH2, the only operating emission is 'a little hot water and filtered air'. It is a clean, consistent power source without diesel fumes or CO_2 emissions. The GEH2 recently powered LED screens, food stalls, lighting, and sound systems at the 2023 Australian Formula 1 Grand Prix.

Enhanced Geothermal Systems

Another environmentally friendly technology is Enhanced Geothermal Systems (EGS) involves extracting heat from the Earth's interior to generate electricity. Advancements in EGS techniques aim to access geothermal resources in previously considered unsuitable areas. These developments expand the potential for geothermal power generation, which offers a reliable and renewable energy source with minimal GHG emissions. In 2016, a survey confirmed that Pakistan is among the naturally gifted countries that have viable geothermal energy manifestations in places like the Hunza and Gilgit regions. (Younas et al., 2016). As a peer reviewer of designs, I have recently provided feedback on a few electricity generation projects in these regions.

TRANSPORTATION

For many people, commuting to and from work in their car is often seen as the 'bookends' of the daily grind. In Dhaka, Bangladesh, where I spent some time recently, the average commute time between my hotel and where I was working, the Aga Khan Academy School, averaged around one hour each way, depending on the ever-increasing traffic jams. Each journey was an adventure. It is incredible how all kinds of vehicles and pedestrians co-exist, utilising the unique 'language' of different beeps of the respective vehicle horns and the on/off flicking of headlights. During these traffic snarls, my head would go into overdrive in trying to estimate the amount of CO_2 emitted based on the average petrol or diesel car producing an equivalent of around 170 to 185 grams of CO_2e for every kilometre travelled. It is obvious that the larger the vehicle, the higher the emissions. Incidentally, the larger the vehicle, the higher the right it has to road use – with the unmistakable loud continuous horn beep signalling the message "I am bigger than you – get out of my way".

On the other hand, from an emissions perspective, it was pleasing to see the pedal-powered rickshaws. However, some rickshaws used for transporting materials are joining the electrification transformation.

Dhaka - 2023

Most forms of transport—whether by rail, air, or sea—are emission-intensive. A combination of strategies, including technological advancements and behavioural changes, is undoubtedly needed to achieve significant reductions in GHG emissions from the transport sector. Collaboration between governments, industries, and individuals becomes a crucial element for a sustainable and low-carbon future.

The transportation sector has changed noticeably over the past few decades. Let us examine key strategies and technologies being implemented.

Active Mobility

Promoting walking, cycling, and other forms of active transport decreases reliance on motorised transport, leading to lower GHG emissions.

Public Transportation

Encouraging the use of public transportation systems, such as buses and trains, helps reduce individual vehicle emissions.

Electric Vehicles (EVs)

Countries and organisations aim to reduce CO_2 emissions from the transportation sector by promoting the adoption of EVs. EVs produce zero tailpipe emissions, reducing the direct GHG emissions associated with conventional gasoline or diesel vehicles.

Recent developments in battery technology have focused on addressing key challenges such as energy density, cost, and sustainability. Solid-state batteries are emerging as a significant breakthrough in the field, especially for electric vehicles (EVs). Companies like Mercedes and Factorial have developed solid-state batteries that offer up to 80 per cent more range compared to traditional lithium-ion batteries. These batteries use a safer design and can extend EV ranges to 600 miles while also reducing the battery weight by up to 40 per cent. These innovations also aim to eliminate overheating issues and cut costs by removing the need for extensive cooling systems. In China, Tailan New Energy has developed solid-state battery cells with 720 Wh/kg, doubling the energy density of current cells in use. This development could lead to EVs with ranges over 1,300 miles on a single charge. Tailan's batteries use advanced composite materials and are designed to address common issues such as interface impedance, improving both performance and longevity.

MIT researchers are exploring cobalt-free alternatives due to the environmental and ethical concerns surrounding cobalt mining. They have developed organic cathodes for lithium-ion batteries, using materials like quinones, which can offer comparable performance to traditional cobalt batteries but at a fraction of the cost. These organic batteries also have the potential for faster charging and longer life cycles, making them a promising solution for future EVs.

Fuel Efficiency Standards

Implementing fuel efficiency standards for vehicles is a way to reduce GHG emissions. By designing vehicles with better aerodynamics, lighter materials, and advanced engine technologies, such as hybrid systems, manufacturers can achieve higher fuel efficiency, resulting in reduced CO_2 emissions per kilometre travelled.

Alternative Fuels

Exploring and adopting alternative fuels, such as biofuels, hydrogen, and renewable natural gas (RNG), can significantly reduce GHG emissions. Biofuels, for example, can be blended with conventional fuels to reduce CO_2 emissions. Hydrogen fuel cell vehicles emit only water vapour, offering a zero-emission alternative. The Commonwealth Scientific and Industrial Research Organisation (CSIRO), the Australian Government agency responsible for scientific research, has an increasing number of hydrogen-powered vehicles. I was privileged to learn through Rafiq Ali, an expert at CSIRO, how CSIRO was providing hydrogen charging stations for public use.

Hydrogen-powered CSIRO vehicle – Melbourne 2023

Intelligent Transportation Systems (ITS)

ITS technologies, such as traffic management systems, smart traffic lights, and real-time navigation systems, optimise traffic flow, reduce congestion, and minimise fuel consumption. These systems help improve overall transportation efficiency and reduce CO2 emissions.

Sustainable Urban Planning

Efficient urban planning is helping reduce the need for long-distance commuting and promote compact cities with shorter travel distances. By integrating residential, commercial, and recreational areas, cities minimise travel demand, leading to lower GHG emissions.

Freight Transport Efficiency

Improving freight transport efficiency is becoming crucial for reducing GHG emissions. This involves promoting a modal shift from road to rail or water transport, improving logistics and supply chain management, and optimising routes and loads to minimise energy consumption. As an example, Sydney Seaplanes intend to commence a thrice-daily route from Rose Bay in Sydney Harbour, with two of the round-trip flights touching down in and taking off from the west basin of Lake Burley Griffin, near the National Museum of Australia in Canberra.

Policy Measures and Incentives

Overall, Governments have a crucial role in minimising GHG emissions from the transport sector by implementing policy measures and providing incentives. These can include emission standards, carbon pricing, tax incentives for low-emission vehicles, subsidies for public transportation, and investment in sustainable infrastructure.

AGRICULTURE

Both livestock and various types of farming, including vegetable and grain farming, make this sector the largest source of methane emissions. In 2021, it was responsible for around 10 per cent of GHG emissions in the US (US EPA, 2022).

The agricultural sector also includes land-use changes. However, the sector is actively working to minimise GHG emissions in several ways. It is important to point out that agriculture's contribution to GHG emissions is multifaceted and varies across regions and farming systems. Implementing a combination of these strategies, tailored to local conditions and specific agricultural practices, must be the key to minimising GHG emissions while ensuring food security and sustainable agricultural production.

Let us examine some key strategies that are being adopted

+ Livestock, particularly cattle, produce methane during digestion. To reduce methane emissions from livestock, farmers are implementing techniques like improved feeding practices, better herd management, and dietary adjustments. These measures include optimising feed quality, managing grazing patterns, and utilising methane capture systems in livestock facilities.
+ Precision agriculture techniques utilise advanced technologies, such as GPS, sensors, and data analytics, to optimise crop production. This approach helps farmers apply fertilisers and water more efficiently, reducing GHG emissions associated with nitrogen fertiliser and water usage. It also enhances soil health and reduces the need for synthetic inputs.

- Conservation agriculture practices aim to minimise soil disturbance, maintain soil cover, and promote crop rotation. By reducing or eliminating tillage, farmers can sequester more carbon in the soil, enhance soil health, and reduce GHG emissions related to soil erosion and degradation. Practices like cover cropping and mulching also help retain soil moisture and improve nutrient cycling.
- Proper fertiliser management, including timing, application methods, and dosage, has the potential to significantly reduce GHG emissions from agriculture. Precision application techniques, such as split application and controlled release fertilisers, reduce nitrogen losses, nitrous oxide emissions, and environmental pollution. Efficient use of organic fertilisers, like manure, can also minimise emissions and enhance nutrient cycling.
- Integrating trees into agricultural landscapes through agroforestry systems helps sequester carbon, enhance biodiversity, and improve soil fertility. Planting trees on marginal or degraded lands (afforestation) can also contribute to carbon sequestration and mitigate GHG emissions as mentioned before.
- Efficient water management practices, such as drip irrigation and precision watering systems, minimise water waste and energy use, resulting in reduced GHG emissions. Proper drainage systems and water-saving technologies also reduce methane emissions from waterlogged or flooded agricultural fields.
- Farmers are increasingly adopting renewable energy sources, such as solar panels and wind turbines, to power their operations. Using renewable energy on farms reduces reliance on fossil fuels, decreases emissions associated with energy consumption, and can even generate surplus clean energy for the grid.
- Raising awareness and providing farmers with education about sustainable practices and technologies is crucial for reducing GHG emissions. Promoting knowledge-sharing platforms, farmer field schools, and extension services helps disseminate information on sustainable agricultural practices and their climate benefits.

INDUSTRIAL PROCESSES

Many industrial processes emit CO_2 either through the burning of fossil fuels or through chemical reactions that do not involve combustion, such as cement production, iron and steel production, and chemical manufacturing. Many industrial processes also use electricity and, therefore, can indirectly result in CO_2 emissions from electricity consumption.

It is important to note that each industry has unique challenges and opportunities for reducing GHG emissions. Implementing a combination of these strategies, along with industry-specific innovations and collaborations, is key to achieving significant emissions reductions in the industrial sector.

Below are some key strategies.

- Improving energy efficiency is a primary focus for the industrial sector. Industries are implementing energy-saving technologies, optimising processes, and adopting efficient equipment to reduce energy consumption and associated GHG emissions. This includes measures like upgrading machinery, improving insulation, implementing cogeneration systems (generating electricity and using process heat simultaneously), and utilising waste heat recovery.
- The industrial sector is increasingly shifting towards renewable energy sources to reduce reliance on fossil fuels. Industries are installing solar panels, wind turbines, and other renewable energy systems onsite to generate clean electricity. Power purchase agreements (PPAs) with renewable energy providers are also becoming common to ensure a sustainable and low-carbon energy supply.
- Utilisation and Storage (CCUS): CCUS technologies capture carbon dioxide emissions from industrial processes and store them underground or use them for various purposes. They are being implemented in power plants, cement production, and other industrial facilities to significantly reduce GHG emissions.

- Industries are continuously improving their manufacturing processes to minimise energy consumption and emissions. This includes optimising raw material use, streamlining production, and implementing cleaner technologies. Innovations such as advanced materials, efficient catalytic processes, and novel production techniques are being adopted to reduce the carbon footprint of industrial activities.
- Adopting a circular economy approach involves reducing waste generation, promoting recycling and reusing materials, and minimising resource consumption. Industries are implementing waste management practices, such as recycling programs, waste-to-energy technologies, and sustainable supply chain management, to minimise GHG emissions associated with waste disposal and resource extraction.
- Industries are focusing on promoting sustainability throughout their supply chains. This includes working with suppliers to reduce emissions, implementing green procurement practices, and assessing the environmental impact of raw materials. Collaborative initiatives and standards, such as carbon footprint labelling and responsible sourcing programs, help ensure sustainable practices across the supply chain.
- Industrial symbiosis promotes resource efficiency by fostering collaboration among neighbouring industries. By exchanging by-products, waste materials, and energy, industries can optimise resource utilisation and reduce GHG emissions. This approach creates a circular system where one industry's waste becomes another's valuable input.
- Governments are implementing policies and regulations to incentivise emissions reductions in the industrial sector. These include carbon pricing mechanisms, emissions trading systems, tax incentives for energy-efficient technologies, and stricter emission standards. Such measures encourage industries to adopt low-carbon practices and invest in clean technologies.

THE BUILT ENVIRONMENT

Buildings, which are the focal piece of this book, are estimated to account for around 35 to 40 per cent of total energy consumption globally and a similar proportion of GHG emissions. This is largely because we spend around 90 per cent of our lives within the confines of artificial indoor environments that require energy to keep us comfortable and safe. The amount of time we spend indoors does vary based on factors like lifestyle, occupation, recreational activities, and personal preference. Moreover, aspects such as climatic conditions, urbanisation trends, and the availability of indoor amenities all contribute to the inclination to spend more time indoors. The recent COVID-19 pandemic has further amplified this inclination due to its influence on our daily routines, as has the rise of working from home.

In 2019 the sum of all human-caused emissions was 59 gigatons. Emissions from the built environment vary significantly depending on factors such as the type of building, its location, energy sources used for heating and cooling, construction materials, and operational practices. Total emissions in the building sector reached 12 gigatons in 2019, of which 57 per cent were indirect CO_2 emissions from offsite generation of electricity and heat, followed by 25 per cent of direct CO_2 emissions produced onsite and 18 per cent from the production of cement and steel used for construction and/or refurbishment of buildings. If only CO_2 emissions were considered, the share of buildings' CO_2 emissions increase to 39 per cent of global CO_2 emissions.

FIGURE 5 GLOBAL ENERGY-RELATED CO2 EMISSIONS BY SECTOR (IEA, 2017)

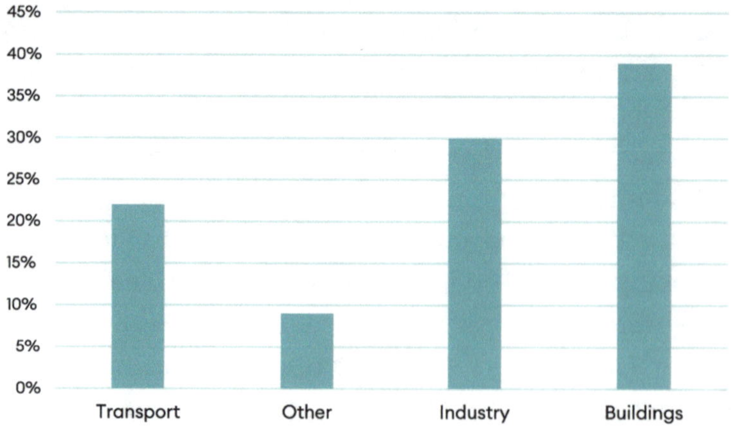

Embodied Vs Operational Energies in Buildings

As part of research on the topic 'Embodied versus Operational energies in residential and commercial buildings: where should we focus?' 100 case studies were conducted in 23 countries to evaluate data on embodied and operational energy in residential and commercial buildings. (Dilsiza, et al., 2019). The case studies included conventional, retrofit, low-energy, passive, and net-zero energy (NZE) 25 to 100 years old buildings. Using life cycle analysis (LCA), embodied energy (EE) values were estimated together with operational energy (OE). Results showed that operational energy significantly dominated the life cycle energy of the buildings by an average of 419 MJ/m2 per year and an average share of 72 per cent.

The share of the residential and non-residential buildings is shown in Figure 6.

FIGURE 6 RESIDENTIAL VS NON-RESIDENTIAL – EMBODIED VS OPERATIONAL

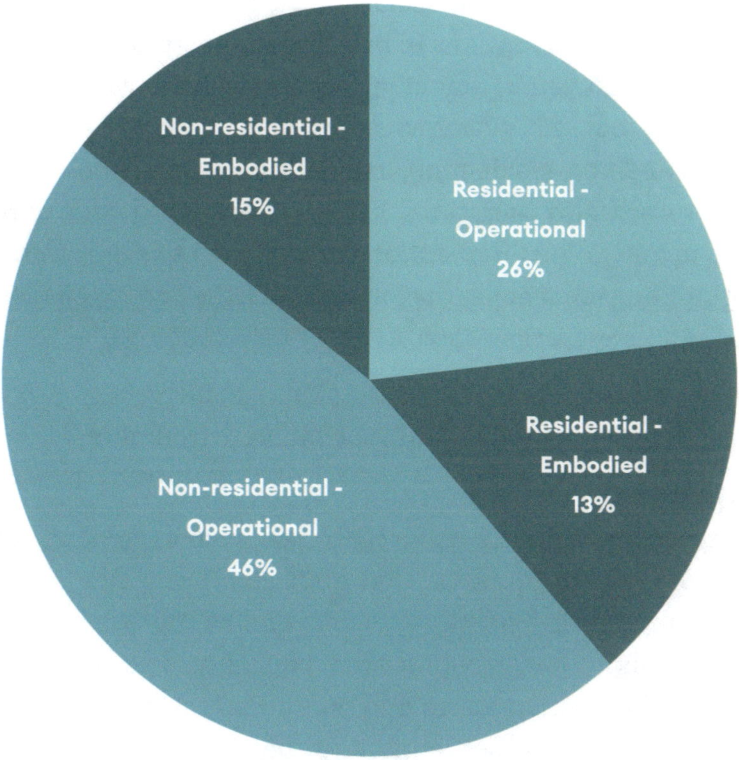

Based on the findings of this research, which I fully endorse, it can be concluded that the primary concern needs to be decreasing CO_2 by retrofitting existing buildings. It is acknowledged that changes in embodied energy are often obtained only through new construction or deep retrofit strategies. Therefore, if retrofitting conventional buildings is not an option, then new constructions should be either low-E or net zero energy to decrease overall life cycle energy. It was interesting to note that only about 14 per cent of the case studies yielded metered operational data. To create more accurate data, the metering of buildings is vital. Therefore, decreasing operational energy should be the primary focus to decrease GHG emissions from the existing building stock.

There is growing scientific evidence about the mitigation potential of the building sector and its contribution to the decarbonisation of global and regional energy systems and to meeting Paris Agreement goals and Sustainable Development Goals (SDGs) (IPCC, 2018; IEA, 2019c; IEA 2019). Mitigation interventions in buildings are heterogeneous in many different aspects, from building components (such as envelope, structure, and materials) to services (such as cooling and heating), to building types (residential and non-residential), to building size, function, and climate zone. There are also variations between developed and developing countries in mitigation interventions to implement, as the renovation of existing buildings challenges the former while the latter is challenged by the need to accelerate the construction of new buildings.

Some key contributors to GHG emissions can be broadly divided into static and dynamic aspects within the built environment.

Static Aspects

The production of construction materials, such as cement, steel, and glass, can be energy-intensive and emit significant amounts of CO_2 during manufacturing processes. Additionally, the transportation of these materials to construction sites contributes to emissions. The disposal of construction waste and operational waste from buildings can also contribute to GHG emissions, particularly if organic waste decomposes anaerobically, releasing methane (CH_4).

GHG emissions can be reduced by adopting sustainable building materials and construction practices together with enhancing urban planning to reduce transportation emissions and promoting circular economy principles to reduce waste.

Dynamic Aspects

Typically, heating and cooling systems account for approximately 35 to 40 per cent of the energy used by a whole commercial office building – or about 70 to 75 per cent of the base building, which comprises the whole building's services minus all the tenant-related lighting, IT equipment and any tenant-owned supplementary cooling and heating facilities (Harvey, 2013).

The design and efficiency of buildings play a crucial role in determining their energy consumption and GHG emissions. So do the building operations, including heating, cooling, lighting, and powering appliances. These often rely on fossil fuels such as natural gas and oil, which release carbon dioxide when burned. Actions to reduce electricity consumption, especially in regions where electricity generation are still heavily reliant on coal or other fossil fuels, can have a significant impact on reducing GHG emissions.

Focusing on the Built Environment

Whilst the building sector is a candidate for significant energy usage, it presents several energy and cost-saving potentials. Monitoring the buildings' energy consumption via monthly energy bills is the most visible way of observing ongoing GHG reductions.

Professionals can design and build new buildings that use less energy. Subsequent chapters elaborate on this.

Owners, tenants, and facility managers can operate existing buildings to ensure optimum comfort and minimise energy consumption and GHG emissions.

Chapter 15 is dedicated to how one can save energy bills at the domestic level.

Chapter 16 details step-by-step how to minimise energy and GHG in non-residential buildings.

Before we delve into the fundamentals of architecture, building services and the cost-effective ways to minimise energy and associated GHG for the built environment, we need to understand the comfort parameters and how they can be measured. After all, buildings need to provide the right level of indoor comfort to ensure occupant satisfaction and productivity.

3

QUALITY OF LIFE IN THE BUILT ENVIRONMENT

THERMOSTAT'S PERSPECTIVE

My name is L30NW-007. Sounds like a secret agent. But I am not – I am a thermostat. I am mounted at 1.7 metres on a column in the northwest corner of this prestigious building in Sydney on level 30.

What I am about to share with you involves information that could demystify the phenomenon of comfort.

Comfort is a complex issue and very personal. I see that every day. Very highly paid workers surround me, and you can be rest assured that, being a thermostat, I am blamed every day by a select few for not looking after their comfort needs.

I certainly try because my sole aim in life is to control the air-conditioning system serving this corner of the building during normal occupancy times. Most weekends, I am off, though that is changing as the lifestyle of office workers changes. I am starting to see more workers coming in on weekends. No rest for the wicked, as they say—I mean the workers, of course!

The absence of comfort triggers immediate and direct reactions. When discomfort arises, building occupants usually promptly communicate their discomfort.

This above is an excerpt reproduced with permission from the article I wrote in 2013 entitled 'The comfort factor, myths and myth busters' published in *The Fifth Estate*, an Australian online publication. Of the article, *The Fifth Estate's* founder and managing editor Tina Perinotto, whom I have known for over 25 years, wrote: "Ashak has ironically revealed the human side of the indoor air comfort dilemma that plagues so many building owners and managers by stepping into the imagined mind and feelings of the thermostat."

COMFORT – MYTHS AND FACTS

The formal definition of thermal comfort is 'the state of mind indicating satisfaction with the thermal environment', evaluated subjectively according to international standards like ASHRAE Standard 55 and ISO 7730.

Buildings, often regarded as a third layer of our environment, significantly influence our health and overall quality of life. Achieving high levels of well-being is crucial for optimal performance at home or work. Naturally, numerous factors, including our well-being and biological rhythms, exert varied and significant influences.

Ensuring occupant comfort is a multifaceted endeavour that necessitates balancing diverse factors, encompassing both personal preferences and the principles of architectural and engineering design. For instance, while one may find a particular level of lighting comfortable, they may prefer a different colour temperature (such as warm versus cool light). Similarly, individuals have varying thresholds for sound comfort. Over time, other factors may also influence comfort levels. It's essential to recognise that what is comfortable for one person may not be for another. Among building service professionals, discomfort often gives rise to the highest number of complaints and grievances.

FIGURE 7: DISCOMFORT

Indoor Environment Quality

Various factors collectively determine the indoor environment quality (IEQ) of air within a building or enclosed space.

These involve:

+ **Pollutants:** These can be both particulate matter (PM), such as dust, pollen, and smoke particles, as well as gases and volatile organic compounds (VOCs) emitted from building materials, furniture, cleaning products, and other sources.
+ **Airborne microorganisms:** These include bacteria, viruses, and fungi, which can affect IAQ and potentially lead to health issues.
+ **Temperature:** The thermal comfort of indoor spaces is crucial for occupant well-being. Temperature extremes can affect comfort and productivity.

- **Humidity:** Both high and low humidity levels can impact IAQ and comfort. Excessive moisture can lead to mould growth, while very dry air can cause respiratory irritation.
- **Ventilation:** Adequate ventilation is essential for diluting indoor pollutants and maintaining oxygen levels. It also helps regulate humidity and control indoor temperatures.

Outdoor infiltration is when outdoor air enters a building, whether through a window or door or via mechanical means. This infiltration can significantly influence indoor air quality in several ways:

- **Pollutant intake:** Outdoor pollutants such as vehicle emissions, industrial emissions, pollen, and dust can enter indoor spaces through infiltration, impacting indoor air quality levels.
- **Temperature and humidity:** Outdoor air temperature and humidity levels can affect indoor conditions when outdoor air infiltrates. In cold climates, outdoor air may need heating before entering, affecting indoor temperature and potentially lowering humidity levels. In warmer climates, outdoor air infiltration can increase indoor humidity levels.
- **Ventilation rates:** Outdoor infiltration can affect the ventilation rates of a building. Buildings designed for natural ventilation rely on outdoor air entering through intentional openings, which can be controlled to optimise IAQ.
- **Energy efficiency:** Uncontrolled infiltration can affect energy efficiency. Excessive outdoor air infiltration, depending on the outdoor conditions, has the potential to increase energy for heating or cooling.

Overall, managing outdoor infiltration is crucial for maintaining good indoor air quality. Properly designed ventilation systems, air filters, and building envelope strategies can help control the impact of outdoor air on IAQ and ensure occupants' health and comfort.

Human Body – Energy Exchanges

The forms of energy exchanges are shown in Figure 8.

FIGURE 8 ENERGY EXCHANGES IN A HUMAN BODY

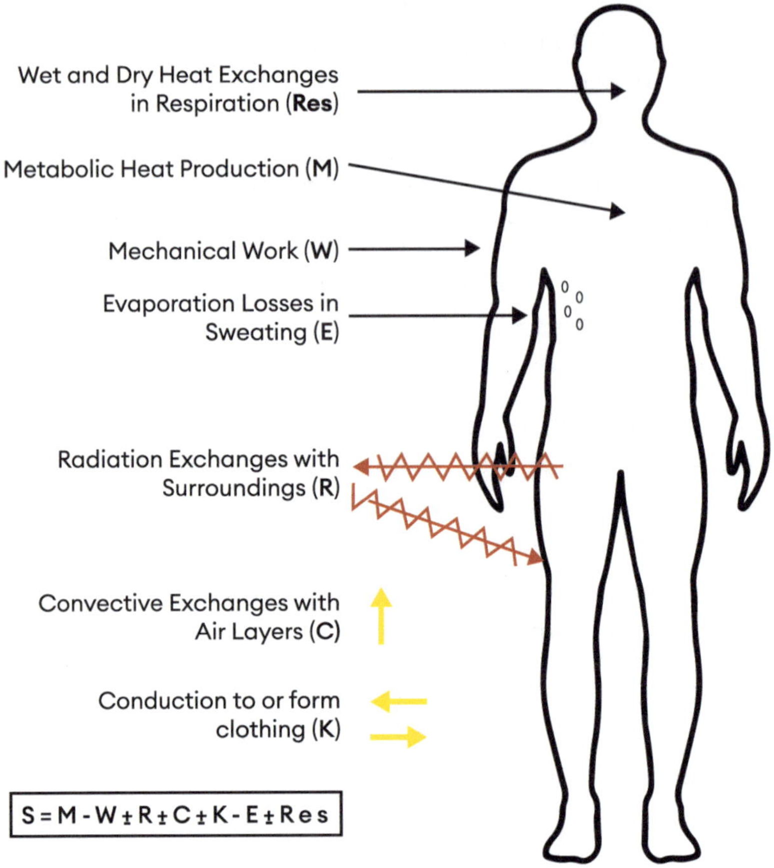

The subjective thermal comfort sensation of a human being is determined by the heat flows that run through the body. The heat generated inside the body must be completely emitted to the surrounding environment to maintain thermal balance.

FIGURE 9 BALANCING COMFORT

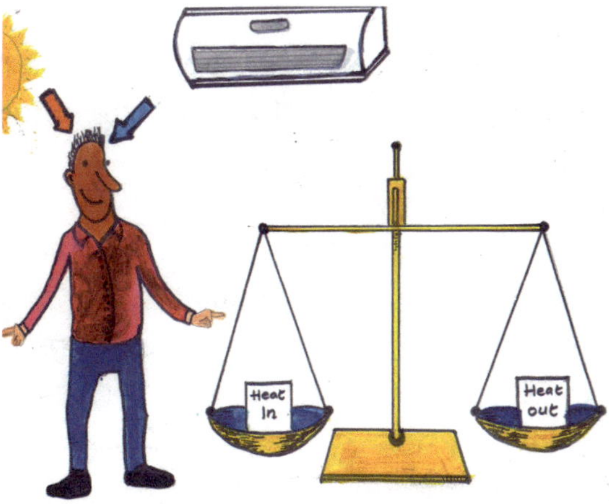

THE COMFORT BALANCE

The human body is equipped with the ability to maintain a relatively constant inner core temperature level, including minor fluctuations, independent of environmental conditions and during different physical activities. Under harsh climatic conditions, the human regulating mechanism can become overloaded when trying to adapt body temperature to its surrounding environment. Comfort balance is also related to physical aspects of a biological nature, like age and state of health or ethnically different adaptability levels. For thermal comfort, it is also important to note the type of clothing worn – and during which activities. For example, in 2016, I attended a conference on comfort, where a reference paper entitled, 'Which is Hotter–Sari or Bikini?' was presented by Lhendup G Bhutia. The paper found that Sari, with a higher 'clo' value, provided higher warmth. More about clothing later in this chapter

Both building owners and tenants know that comfortable indoor climate levels are decisive factors when it comes to upholding occupant productivity. Survey-based analysis shows that if a company suffers from an unacceptable indoor climate for around 10 per cent of work time, it leads to a noticeable decrease in work performance levels. When spread over 200 hours or 25 days per annum per staff member, this can result in a significant negative financial impact. As you can see, comfort makes for a happy and productive worker. But the risk goes beyond the moment – an absence of comfort can have long-term health consequences, often manifesting as vague symptoms over time.

SICK BUILDING SYNDROME

The 1970s and 80s saw a surge in legal cases associated with Sick Building Syndrome (SBS) in many countries. SBS is a term used to describe a set of symptoms that typically arise because of poor indoor air quality. Symptoms include headaches, irritation of the nose and throat, fatigue, nausea, difficulty concentrating, and respiratory discomfort. The primary culprit behind this phenomenon was, to a large extent, the inadequate upkeep of buildings and lack of regular maintenance of their services. Fortunately, cases of SBS have become increasingly rare. Building proprietors and managers are now acutely aware of their legal, contractual, and professional responsibilities regarding the provision of secure and comfortable environments for occupants. While indoor air quality, lighting conditions, and ergonomic considerations all play significant roles in creating a conducive, safe, and healthy indoor environment – especially in office buildings – thermal comfort stands out as having the most significant impact on occupants' day-to-day activities. Since we are spending a disproportionate amount of time in artificial environments, a very high number of complaints are related to discomfort, primarily attributed to issues with heating, cooling, and ventilation.

Food serves as the source of input energy for the human body. Excess heat generated by the body is released into the environment to enable normal functioning. The rate of heat transfer is directly proportional to the temperature difference. In cold environments, the body loses more heat to the environment, while in hot environments, it struggles to release enough heat. Both situations lead to discomfort. Thermal neutrality is achieved when the heat generated by human personal activity can dissipate, thus maintaining thermal equilibrium with the environment.

To elaborate further, I go back to my impersonation of being a thermostat. *"Rhonda, who sits in the workstation closest to me, seems to be happy. She also dresses sensibly – summer clothing in summer and often a sleeveless sweater during the cooler months. Shaukat on the other, who sits at the next workstation, always complains. He looks at me all the time as if it is my fault. He does not dress according to the seasonal changes. His complaints range from conditions being too hot or too cold or airflow too 'drafty'. The most interesting observation was when we had the hottest day in Sydney in January 2013 when the temperature rose to 43 degrees Celsius; Shaukat put on a cardigan because he reckoned that it was too cold inside. To be fair to Shaukat, there are indoor environments that are kept at higher temperatures in winter months and lower conditions in summer, requiring occupants to compensate by wearing respective types of clothing".*

I have witnessed such scenarios walking through numerous office spaces where a facility manager sets the temperature too low during warmer days or too high during cooler days, resulting in occupant attires heading towards those shown in Figure 10.

FIGURE 10 INCONSISTENT INDOOR ENVIRONMENTS

On the other hand, many temperature set-points are often set too high in summer and too low in winter. It is my observation that the level of complaints of the zones being hot or cold has increased since the commencement of the environmentalist movement in the '90s, leading to indiscriminate tampering of set-points to save energy. There is no doubt that the focus on minimisation of energy use, and hence reduction of GHG emissions, has been beneficial – considering that air conditioning, as an entity, contributes significantly to the generation of greenhouse gases. But has this been at the expense of compromising occupant comfort conditions? So, the obvious question is, what are the vectors that contribute to indoor thermal comfort?

COMFORT VECTORS

Various scholars have researched this important topic and have come up with the following vectors:

Activity

Activity is what generates heat in our body, such as walking around a shopping mall, sitting in the office, or exercising at the gym. Our level of physical activity determines the energy released by metabolism in an hour, measured in metabolic equivalent of task (Met) values. The equation used to calculate Met is 1 Met = 58.15 W/m2 body surface. The intensive activity attracts a higher Met value. Typically, the average body surface for a normal adult is 1.7 m2. A sedentary person in thermal comfort loses around 80-100 W of heat. The average activity level for the past hour is normally used when evaluating a person's metabolic rate due to the body's heat capacity. This means that a person exercising would have a higher Met value than a sedentary person.

Clothing

We can also measure comfort by assessing the thermal insulation of different types of clothing. For example, a sweater has more insulation than a swimming costume. This is called the Clo value.

Clothing must be light to provide comfort when activity is high, like when working out at the gym. This is the same reason people dress differently according to the season. The daily question of "What shall I wear today?" is largely determined by the weather forecast.

FIGURE 11 CLO VALUES

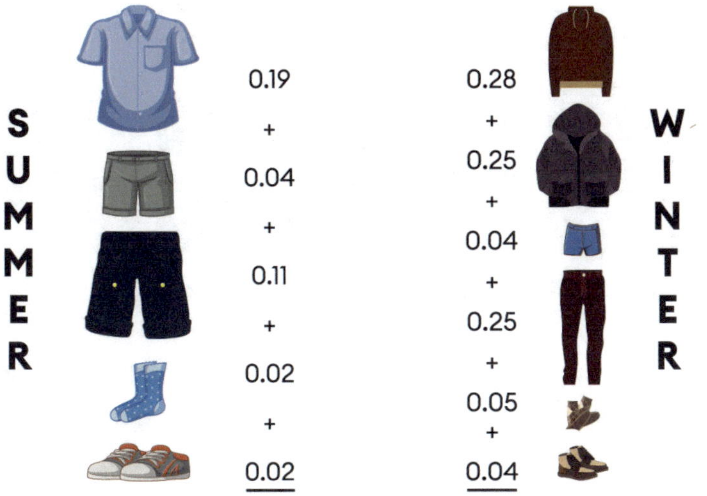

Clothing provides the required insulation over the body, and each item has an assigned clo value, which is tabulated in international standards such as ISO 7730 and ASHRAE Standard 55. An example is shown in Figure 11, comparing summer and winter attires.

During the experiments I was conducting as part of my PhD research, I needed to determine the Clo values for shawls since some female subjects were wearing them during my experiments in the laboratory, and these values were not listed in international standards. Therefore, I established these values by carrying out experiments using a thermal manikin at the unique Indoor Environmental Quality (IEQ) Laboratory at the University of Sydney (a building which I co-designed and project managed the construction of).

Laura, the thermal manikin, was dressed in a skirt and a shirt and different types of shawls were draped on her to determine the respective clo values. Five different shawl types from my dear wife's collection, namely pashmina, light wool, silk, embroidered wool, and heavy wool, were evaluated.

FIGURE 12 CLO VALUES - SHAWLS

Pashmina (0.05) **Silk (0.08)** **Embroidered Wool (0.15)** **Heavy Wool (0.18)**

The experiment found that a heavier shawl material reflected the increase in Clo value resulting in PMV improvement ranging from 32 to 39 per cent. Interestingly, whilst shawls have been used as fashion statements, this experiment justifies using appropriate shawls for indoor or outdoor conditions.

Note that most female theatre attendees do not put on a shawl immediately when going to the theatre. They tend to put it on a few minutes after sitting down. This is because the Met value is higher while walking into the theatre, and once the Met value normalises, as the occupant adjusts to the indoor environment, is when there is generally a need for the shawl.

Other environmental parameters that influence human comfort are temperature, radiant temperature, humidity, and airflow for any given activity and clothing.

Temperature

This is the one that most people relate to. Temperature sensing is a vital part of the thermostat. Since it is an important measure, every thermostat requires frequent recalibration to make sure that we are sensing the correct temperature.

FIGURE 13 DRY AND WET BULB 'SLING' THERMOMETER

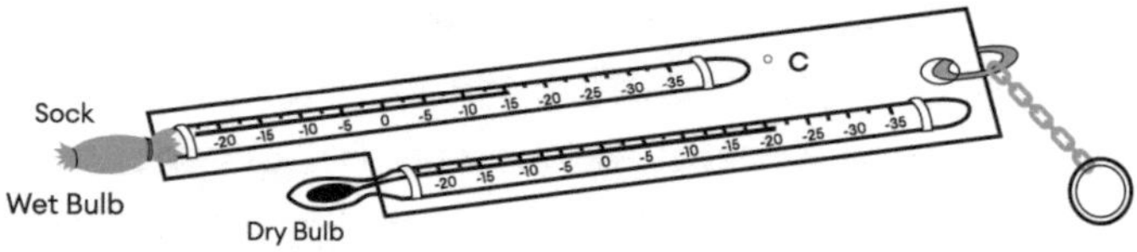

This is the most important environmental variable affecting thermal comfort. We commonly express our discomfort by saying, "It is hot" or "It is cold," often with a preceding adverb describing the extent. Air temperature, measured in degrees Celsius or Fahrenheit, consists of two components: dry bulb temperature, measured by a standard thermometer, and wet bulb temperature, measured by a thermometer with a damp cloth on the end due to its sensitivity to evaporation.

Under specific conditions, wet bulb temperature readings are equal to or lower than dry bulb temperature readings. The difference between dry and wet bulb temperatures allows us to determine relative humidity—the amount of moisture in the air. Generally, what we hear in the weather forecasts are dry bulb temperatures, and occasionally, humidity levels are mentioned. Room temperatures are adjusted in indoor settings with mechanical systems to maintain the respective dry bulb temperature. It is very rare to have humidistats except in specialised rooms.

Radiant temperature

One experiences this as energy radiating from objects, such as sitting next to a hot glass window on a sunny day or a cold window on a chilly day. The radiating energy can also be felt when sitting in front of an open fire, a radiant electric heater, or a gas-fired outdoor radiant heater in cold conditions. The impact of radiant heat or coolth depends on the type of heat-generating equipment and its distance from you. It is measured in watts per unit area, although there are other ways the impact can be measured – such as using the 'globe temperature' technique.

Humidity

It appears that variations in humidity are not as pronounced as they are for temperature in the comfort evaluation. Most commercial air conditioned spaces try to maintain between 40 per cent and 60 per cent relative humidity through the design of cooling equipment. Generally, there are no humidistats installed in normal offices. It is interesting that humidity variations impact electronic equipment more, so it is important to maintain close humidity conditions in data centres.

Airflow

This certainly impacts comfort, including air circulation and movement. Air velocity is measured in metres per second (m/s), and indoor air velocity is typically kept below 0.15 m/s. Recent research suggests that increased airspeed can provide improved indoor conditions through a concept termed 'adaptive comfort', which also relates to clothing and metabolism.

If the air velocity is high, one may feel cooler, mainly due to the evaporation of sweat from the skin. However, high velocities could lead to drafts. The most common complaint is the cold draft on one's neck. On the other hand, insufficient airflow could lead to a feeling of 'stuffiness'.

No wonder there were 'pankavallas' in the olden days, who provided air movement, using manual mechanisms, for the Maharajas and the Maharanis

The modern-day version of this phenomenon is the ceiling and other ventilation fans that can provide some relief from hot conditions. Almost at the cost of putting myself and the air conditioning industry out of business, I must agree that there is nothing like a cool breeze – especially a cool change after some of the scorchers that prevailed during the summer months.

Predicted Mean Vote

When applied to a specific activity and level of clothing, the above key attributes result in a comfort measure called Predicted Mean Vote (PMV). This index has a range of comfort in the centre. At minus three, humans feel the most uncomfortable—very cold or very dry. At plus three, humans also feel intolerably uncomfortable—very hot or too humid.

The ideal level of comfort is a PMV of zero (neutral).

FIGURE 14 PMV SCALE AND VECTORS – (FANGER, 1970)

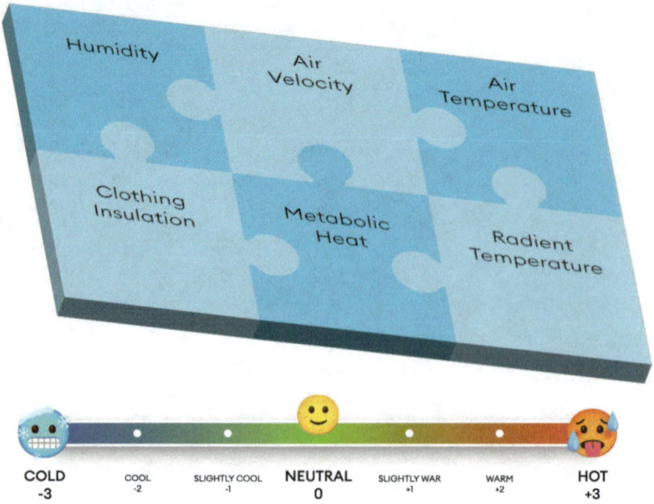

Olli Fanger, widely considered the father of comfort studies, concluded that the variation of the PMV index can be approximated by an analytic hyperbolic curve when it comes to predicting the percentage of people dissatisfied (PPD) in a thermal environment. An analytic hyperbolic curve is a particular kind of curved line that you can describe using math. In this case, it shows us the sweet spot at which we feel the most comfortable.

The PMV-PPD relationship is very simple: when the PMV is either plus or minus three, 100 per cent of any group of people will be dissatisfied. This occurs when conditions are either too hot, too cold, too humid, or too dry. As the PMV value approaches zero, the percentage of people dissatisfied improves.

FIGURE 15 PMV VS PPD – (FANGER, 1970)

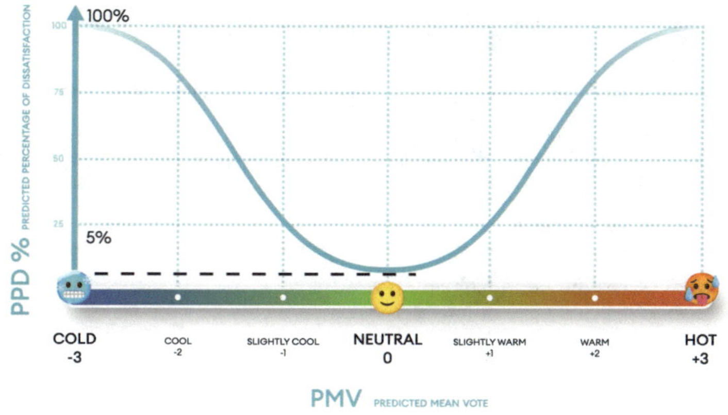

When the temperature, humidity and airflow are ideal for a given activity and clothing value, there will still be around 5 per cent of any group dissatisfied. This is human nature. You may have noticed this in your own experiences. Some estimate the percentage of people dissatisfied to be greater than 5 per cent during those ideal comfort conditions. From a facility management point of view, this is an important concept to understand. It means that it is not possible to satisfy all occupants of a building. There will always be some (around 5 per cent of any group) who will express dissatisfaction concerning thermal comfort, as conditions acceptable to the majority may not suit them for various reasons.

Many office spaces manage to attain PMV range of 0.5 to 0.75 – which is very good – bearing in mind PMV closer to zero is ideal. However, as outlined earlier, the level of occupant complaints may still be high. The more one researches in this area of comfort complexities the more one realises that only the surface has been scratched.

HEALTH, WELLBEING AND PRODUCTIVITY

In 2016, I represented Australia as a participant on an expert panel assembled by the World Green Building Council, where I contributed the chart shown on the next two pages.

Health, Wellbeing & Productivity:
Contribution by Dr. Ashak Nathwani AM –

The physical office environment
The office environment is made up of several factors, which can be measured or evaluated in numerous ways

Indoor air quality & ventilation
- Pollutants, Including VOCs
- CO_2
- Aroma
- Ventilation rate or fresh air
- Moisture control

Thermal comfort
- Indoor air temperature
- Mean radiant temperature
- Air velocity
- Relative humidity
- Clothing
- Activity

Lighting & Daylighting
- Quantity
- Quality
- Glare
- Day Light
- Task type

Noise & acoustics
- Background noise
- Privacy & interference
- Vibration

Interior layout & active design
- Workstation density
- Task based spaces & ergonomics
- Breakout spaces & social features
- Active design

Bibliophile & views
- Connections to nature
- Views outside

Look & feel
- Design character & brand ethos,
- including colour, shape, texture & art
- Cultural, gender & age sensitive Design

Location & access to amenities
- Access to amentites
- Transport
- Quality of public realm

Occupant health outcomes
The physical office factors influence the health of occupiers health outcome which can be measured or evaluated
Health
- Headaches
- Dye strain/damage
- Skin irritation
- Infections
- Fatigue
- Seminal Affective Disorder
- Stress & depression
- Other physical complaints i.e. back ache
- Other serious disorders, including cardiovascular etc.

Occupant wellbeing and perception outcomes
Health is an important element of wellbeing but an occupants sense of wellbeing is also comprised of their perception of numerous factors, including how productive they think they are:
- Perceived physical health
- Perceived psychological heath
- Perceived productivity
- Perceived office environment
- Perceived organisational culture

Organisational or financial outcomes
The office environment can have a direct impact on occupant productivity in which health and wellbeing is often a compounding factor This 'outcome for the organisation can be measured or evaluated in the following ways hoc exhaustive, all of which have financial implications for the employer
Productivity
- Absenteeism
- Presenteeism
- Staff turnoveriretention
- Revenue
- Medical costs
- Medical complaints
- Physical complaints
- Task efficiency & deadlines met

Flow chart

The University of Sydney, Australia

Ultimate aims

Maximised Return on Investment: financial evaluation based life cycle costing - capital & operational for all strategies designed to benefit occupants and improve productivity

- Lower employment cost per employee, including reduced absence costs
- Higher staff retention and reduced costs of staff turnover
- Greater ease of high quality recruitment, lowering recruitment costs and adding value Greater productivity of staff on core tasks, e.g. deadlines met, sales made etc.
- Optimised green building ratings resulting in higher value/lower risk/ improved reputation
- Reduced occupant complaints via "Help Desk' and other similar feed-back systems, leading to reduced costs
- Increased company revenue

Design, refurbishment or fit-out strategy

With the aim of enhancing or incorporating

- Indoor air quality & ventilation
- Thermal comfort
- Lighting & daylighting
- Noise & acoustics
- Interior layout & active design
- Basophilic design & quality views
- Look & fool
- Access to amenities

Strategies to maximise beneficial outcomes for office occupants will have a capital cost implication ranging from negligible to high depending on the strategy and the stage in the building lilfecycle.

Examples

- Following active design principles in a new build office - additional cost
- Reconfiguring an exiting office to maximise task-based spaces- medium cost
- Retrofitting an existing occupied office with new facade to improve daylighting - very high cost

4

ARCHITECTURE, BUILDINGS AND CO2

QUALITY OF LIFE

"Architecture is not simply about buildings, but about the quality of life of those who inhabit the built environment."

His Highness the Aga Khan made this statement in a speech at the 2016 Aga Khan Award for Architecture in the UAE. This perspective resonates deeply with me. Architecture plays a fundamental role in enhancing the quality of life for occupants in several significant ways. To start with, A well-designed space promotes efficiency, comfort, and convenience. Effective spatial planning considers the flow of movement, accessibility, and the integration of functional areas, which provide the platform to improve productivity and satisfaction for occupants.

Architecture shapes the aesthetic experience of occupants and contributes to a sense of place and identity. Thoughtfully designed spaces can evoke positive emotions, foster creativity, and provide a sense of pride and ownership. Buildings designed with health in mind promote physical activity through accessible stairs, attractive walking paths, and encouraging social interaction in shared spaces. Additionally, biophilic design principles that integrate natural elements into architecture have been shown to reduce stress, enhance cognitive function, and accelerate healing processes.

Importantly, architectural design influences thermal comfort by considering factors such as building orientation, insulation, shading, and materials. Well-insulated buildings with efficient heating, cooling, and ventilation systems can ensure comfortable indoor temperatures throughout the year.

In summary, architecture significantly influences the quality of life for occupants by creating functional, comfortable, and aesthetically pleasing environments that support physical health, mental wellbeing, and overall satisfaction. By addressing the diverse needs and preferences of occupants, thoughtful architectural design can enhance daily experiences and contribute positively to communities and societies at large.

ARCHITECTURE

Historically, the architectural style and use of construction materials have varied for developed and developing countries.

Construction Materials in Developed Countries

The history of construction materials used in buildings in developed countries has evolved over time, reflecting changes in technology, resource availability, cultural preferences, and environmental considerations.

In ancient civilisations, such as Mesopotamia, Egypt, Greece, and Rome, buildings were primarily constructed using locally available materials such as stone, mud bricks, wood, and thatch. Stone was particularly favoured for its durability and structural integrity, leading to the construction of monumental structures like the pyramids and temples.

Then during the Middle Ages and the Renaissance, stone continued to be a prominent building material for castles, cathedrals, and fortifications. However, advancements in technology led to the use of timber framing techniques, particularly in Northern Europe, where forests were abundant. Timber framing allowed for more flexible and intricate designs.

The Industrial Revolution brought significant changes to construction materials and techniques. The mass production of iron and later steel revolutionised building construction, enabling the construction of taller and more elaborate structures. The invention of the Bessemer process in the 19th century made steel more affordable and accessible.

The 20th century saw further innovations in construction materials, including the widespread use of reinforced concrete, which combined the strength of steel with the versatility of concrete. Concrete became a dominant material in both residential and commercial construction due to its durability, fire resistance, and ability to be moulded into various shapes.

After World War II, there was a boom in construction activity, particularly in the US and Western Europe. This period saw the rise of new materials such as glass, aluminium, and plastics, leading to the development of modernist architectural styles characterised by sleek lines and expansive use of glass.

In recent decades, there has been a growing emphasis on sustainability and green building practices. This has led to a resurgence of interest in traditional materials like wood and stone, as well as the development of new environmentally friendly materials such as recycled steel, bamboo, rammed earth, and engineered timber products like cross-laminated timber (CLT).

Throughout history, factors such as cost, availability, aesthetics, structural requirements, and environmental impact have influenced the choice of construction materials. Today, architects, engineers, and builders continue to explore innovative materials and construction techniques to create sustainable, resilient, and visually striking buildings.

Construction Materials in Developing Countries

The history of construction materials used in buildings in developing countries follows a trajectory influenced by indigenous resources, cultural practices, colonisation, technological advancements, and economic constraints.

In many developing regions, local materials such as mud, clay, thatch, bamboo, and palm leaves have been historically used for construction. These materials were abundant, inexpensive, and well-suited to local climates and building practices. Examples include adobe buildings in Latin America, African mudbrick structures, and Southeast Asian bamboo houses.

During the colonial period, European powers introduced new construction materials and techniques to their colonies. This often resulted in the use of imported materials like stone, brick, and timber and the adoption of architectural styles that reflected colonial tastes. However, indigenous materials continued to be used alongside imported ones, especially in rural areas.

Rapid urbanisation and industrialisation in the 20th century brought changes to construction materials in developing countries. Urban centres saw the rise of concrete and steel structures, influenced by modernist architectural trends imported from the West. These materials were often associated with modernity and economic progress.

In many developing countries, resource constraints and informal settlements have led to the continued use of traditional materials such as mud, clay, and bamboo for housing construction. Informal settlements, characterised by spontaneous and incremental growth, often rely on locally available and affordable materials.

With advancements in technology and increased globalisation, developing countries have gained access to a wider range of construction materials and techniques. This includes the use of prefabricated materials, recycled materials, and sustainable building practices aimed at addressing environmental concerns and promoting resilience.

As in developed countries, there is a growing emphasis on sustainability and resilience in construction practices in developing countries. This has led to renewed interest in traditional materials and building techniques, as well as the development of locally sourced, low-cost, and environmentally friendly alternatives.

Overall, the history of construction materials in developing countries is characterised by a dynamic interplay between tradition and innovation, influenced by local contexts, socioeconomic factors, and global trends. The challenge lies in balancing the need for modernisation and economic development with the preservation of cultural heritage and the sustainable use of resources.

New Buildings

Several factors need to be considered when designing a new building to ensure a successful and desired outcome. In all the new building designs I have worked on, there were common attributes. They are interrelated, and a holistic approach is crucial to achieving a harmonious, environmentally sensitive, and optimally functional building. CO_2 emissions have become a dominant consideration in new building designs in recognition of CO_2's contribution to climate change.

Key considerations are:

+ **Purpose and Function:** The purpose and the building's intended use, whether it is a residential, commercial, industrial, or institutional structure, determines the design to align with its function and meet the specific requirements of the intended occupants.
+ **Collaboration and Stakeholder Input:** Engaging with stakeholders, including clients, users, architects, engineers, builders, contractors, and, importantly, facility managers (for commercial applications) to gather input, ensure a comprehensive design solution, and facilitate a sustainable and successful project execution.
+ **Aesthetics and Architectural Style:** Establishing the desired architectural style and aesthetic elements that align with the building's purpose and context. The materials, colours, and overall design composition need to consider the visual and environmental impact, both internally and externally. Experience has taught me that aesthetics and architectural requirements should not override the building functionality and operating systems' energy efficiency goals.
+ **Safety and Security:** Integrating safety features such as fire exits, emergency systems, proper lighting, and security measures to protect occupants and assets.
+ **Accessibility and Universal Design:** To comply with accessibility standards, ensure the building is accessible to all individuals, including those with disabilities, by incorporating features such as ramps, lifts (elevators), wider doorways, and accessible restrooms.
+ **Site Analysis:** Topography, climate, accessibility, and surrounding environment influence the building's orientation, layout, materials, and energy efficiency measures.

- **Building Codes and Regulations:** Compliance with local building codes, zoning regulations, and legal requirements ensures safety, accessibility, and adherence to relevant guidelines.
- **Spatial Planning and Layout:** Optimising the arrangement of rooms, circulation areas, and amenities to enhance functionality, efficiency, and user experience.
- **Structural Integrity** is the assurance that the building's structural system can safely support the intended loads, withstand environmental factors, and meet safety standards. This is vital in locations potentially prone to climate change effects or seismic activities.
- **Construction and Maintenance Costs:** Balancing the design vision with the project budget, considering the costs associated with construction, materials, long-term maintenance, and the crucial life-cycle costing. This now also needs to include implications of the likely GHG emissions and associated costs to achieve net zero requirements.
- **Technology Integration:** Incorporating technology infrastructure and systems that support the building's functionality and future adaptability. This should consider telecommunications, data networks, smart building automation, and artificial intelligence-based energy management systems.
- **Sustainability and Energy Efficiency:** Adopting sustainable design principles and energy-efficient strategies. These include considering the selection of the most efficient electrical and heating and cooling systems together with insulation, water conservation, the use of environmentally friendly materials, renewable energy sources and natural lighting.

EXISTING BUILDINGS

When it comes to energy and GHG minimisation, the emphasis needs to be on existing buildings since they are the source of the operational CO_2 emissions that can potentially be reduced. Usage and operation of a building are the key factors, together with addressing the building envelope, which needs to be made more energy efficient, particularly of the older building stock.

Elements contributing to CO2 emissions.

The building envelope has a direct impact on heating and cooling energies and, therefore, on CO2 emissions through the slab, roof, walls, windows, doors, and thermal bridges.

FIGURE 16 CO2 CONTRIBUTION PERCENTAGES

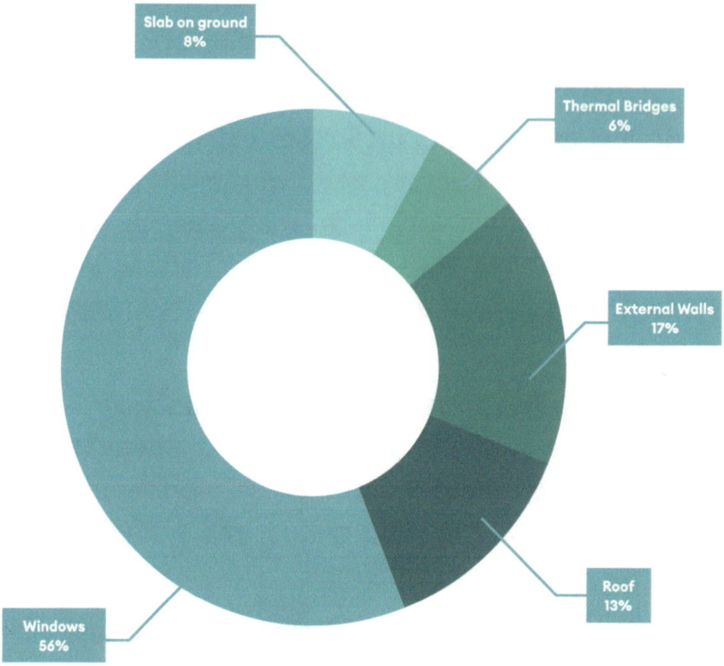

Let us examine each of these contributors, starting with the one that has the largest impact.

Glass and Operational Energy Impact

Walking around a major metropolis, you will probably find yourself surrounded by glass skyscrapers. Are these buildings energy efficient? And why do many houses in colder climates need double (or triple) glazed windows?

The conventional belief is that employing glass in building design provides scenic views and natural illumination. This warrants careful examination. It is imperative to acknowledge that while glass might provide a wonderful scenic landscape view, it is not a very effective barrier against temperature changes. According to research findings by Prashant Kapoor (Kapoor, 2019), floor-to-ceiling glass curtain walls are not appropriate in almost any climate, no matter how much glamour they may add to the perception of a 'five-star' building. He explains that glass allows most of the incidental heat (and light) from the sun to be transmitted indoors. Heat is then trapped inside as it converts from a short wave to a long wave. The long wave heat cannot pass through the glazing, creating a greenhouse effect and accelerating indoor heat build-up. For example, heat entering the east and west façades of an office building in Singapore can admit 750 watts per square metre, which is equivalent to leaving an electric heater running three to four hours daily for each two-square metre section of the façade. This is echoed in the research carried out by Delhi-based researchers Singh and Garg (Singh et al., 2011), who confirmed that energy consumption is proportional to glazed area. For each 10 per cent increase in glazed area, energy consumption for an office in a sub-tropical city like Delhi increases by 15 per cent for clear glass and by 2 to 4 per cent for solar controlled glazing. When the glazed area exceeds 20 percent, the office can get overheated even in winter when daytime external temperatures can go down to 13°C, requiring some cooling for comfort. It is no wonder for new buildings, there are now limitations on glass-to-wall ratios – in simple terms, less glass – especially in walls facing East or West.

The Shard – London - 2023

I was amazed to find full glass façade buildings in Chennai, India, where I spent six months setting up a branch office for our firm in 2008. Regular electricity outages in Chennai meant that cooling systems could not be operated, and hence, occupants were subjected to working in high indoor temperatures – temperatures that could go as high as 35 to 40°C. With the façade being sealed (no openable windows) ventilation was non-existent, once again making the indoor environment extremely uncomfortable, not to mention that it did not comply with the ventilation code as no ventilation system was operating during power outages. Occupants had to continue to work under these unbearable conditions since the labour market was competitive, and workers were reluctant to complain.

Regarding views and natural lighting, it is important to remember that only 20 to 30 per cent of occupants located in the perimeter zones of a commercial building are likely to benefit. On a related point, only a few buildings dim or turn off the artificial lights when natural daylight is suitable. On the other hand, heating and cooling systems continue to cater to the increased cooling or heating of the perimeter zones and incur operating costs and greenhouse gas emissions penalties for the life of the building.

In many countries, I have observed several places of worship that operate only at night (before sunrise and after sunset) having windows. When I questioned one of the architects for having windows in one such high-profile place of worship, there was no logical explanation. I also noticed that in many of these places of worship, congregation members (albeit small in numbers) meet at 4 am for meditation, which means that heating in winter needs to be turned on at 3 am or earlier. With cooling ingress via glass, especially when the outside temperature is well below zero degrees, heating systems are required to work overtime to maintain a comfortable indoor environment.

I personally experienced this in Dushanbe on 13th December 2022. The facility manager of this iconic building confirmed that 'wrong' architectural decisions had resulted in increased operating costs and CO2 emissions. Many buildings audited internationally show that the amount of glass in a building is having a demonstrable impact on building operating costs and GHG emissions.

Energy Exchange Through Glass

Glass encompasses two distinct elements: direct solar heat influx and the transmission of heat or cold between external and internal environments through conduction. The extent of solar heat influx is contingent upon factors such as the building's orientation, the specific type of glass utilised, and the presence or absence of external and internal shading mechanisms. This involves complex calculations of many variables, so the advantage lies in the availability of computer software designed to compute cooling demands accurately. Experts are required to carry out thermal modelling to ascertain the cumulative impact on energy consumption over a year.

Another important aspect of glass is the energy interchange due to thermal conduction. This is termed 'U-value'. The U-value serves as a measure for assessing the efficacy of a material as an insulator. This metric quantifies the pace at which heat travels through a given material. Lower U-values indicate better insulating attributes. The insulating value, or U-value, of glass hinges on its composition. It also changes based on coatings or treatments applied to improve its thermal efficiency. With its higher U-value, double or triple-glazed windows are more thermally efficient.

FIGURE 17 SINGLE, DOUBLE, AND TRIPLE GLAZING

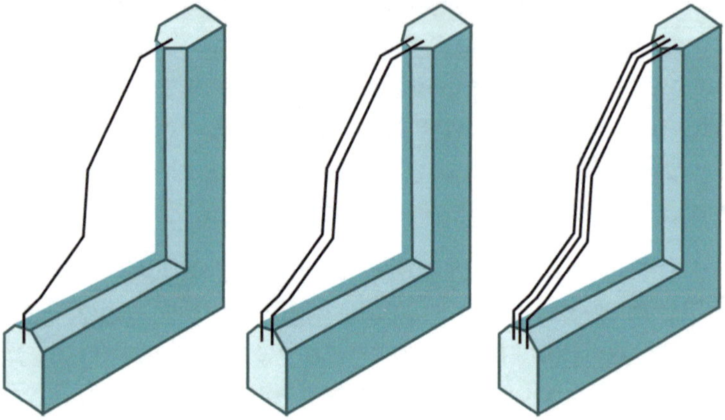

The table shows U-values (measured in W/m²K) for different types of glass commonly used in buildings.

Number of glass panes	Type	U-Value - W/m²K
Single	Clear Float	5.8 to 6.2
Double	Air Filled	2.7 to 3.3
	Low E Coated	1.2 to 1.8
	Argon/Krypton Filled	1.2 to 1.6
Triple	Air Filled	1.0 to 2.0
	Low E coated	0.7 to 1.2
	Argon/Krypton Filled	0.5 to 1.0

Considering that the higher the U-value, the higher the heat /coolth transfer, the above U-values clearly demonstrate why double and triple-glazing windows are widely used to minimise coolth ingress in very cold climates. It is also important to note that these values are approximate and can vary depending on the specific manufacturer, the thickness of the glass, the type of spacer used between the glass panes, and any additional coatings or treatments applied to the glass.

In summary:

- **Heat Gain and Loss:** While energy-efficient glass can mitigate this issue to some extent, standard glass still allows significant heat transfer. In hot climates, excessive heat gain through glass can lead to increased cooling costs, while in colder climates, it can contribute to heat loss and higher heating expenses.
- **Glare and Reflection:** Glass surfaces can cause glare and reflections, which can be uncomfortable for occupants and may interfere with their ability to work or relax. Proper shading and glass treatment strategies are necessary to mitigate these effects.
- **Privacy Concerns:** The transparent nature of glass may raise privacy concerns in certain settings including hotels and motels. Special considerations and solutions such as using frosted or tinted glass, blinds, or curtains, become necessary to address privacy issues.
- **Maintenance:** Glass requires regular cleaning and maintenance to

maintain its transparency and aesthetics. In urban environments, glass surfaces can accumulate dirt, grime, and pollution, necessitating frequent cleaning. We often see window cleaners for high-rise buildings perching on their sometimes-precarious dangling platforms. Technology like drones for cleaning external glass may offer a better solution.

- **Fragility and safety:** Glass is prone to breakage, and shattered glass can pose safety risks to occupants. To ensure safety, building codes often regulate the type and thickness of glass used in certain areas, such as doors and windows.

Let us turn to other building elements that also require looking at the respective U-values.

Internal Shading

Do solar films and internal shades like blinds or curtains reduce energy? Definitely. As we know, glass provides two paths for energy transfer to and from outside to inside environments: direct sunlight ingress warming up the indoors and heat or coolth exchange between inside and outside due to conduction via the glass.

Both curtains and solar film can effectively reduce heat energy ingress through glass windows, but they work in slightly different ways.

- **Curtains:** Curtains provide insulation by creating a barrier between the window and the interior space. When closed, they block direct sunlight, preventing a significant amount of heat from entering the room. Additionally, depending on the material, curtains can also provide insulation against heat loss during colder weather.
- **Solar Film:** Solar film, also known as window tint, is a thin, transparent film applied directly to the glass surface. It works by reflecting and absorbing a portion of the solar radiation that hits the window. This reduces the amount of heat transmitted through the glass into the interior while still allowing natural light to pass through.

The effectiveness of each option varies based on factors such as the quality of the materials used, the colour and thickness of the curtains or film, and the orientation of the windows relative to the sun. In some cases, a combination of both curtains and solar film may provide the best results, offering both insulation and solar radiation control.

Figures 18 and 19 show the impact of using solar films versus having curtains.

FIGURE 18 SOLAR FILM

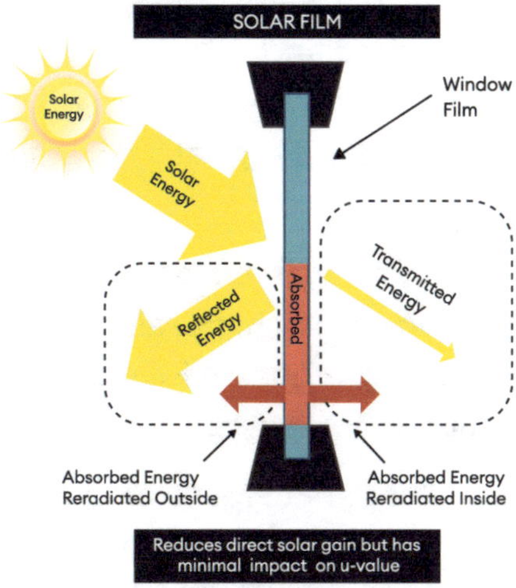

FIGURE 19 CURTAIN

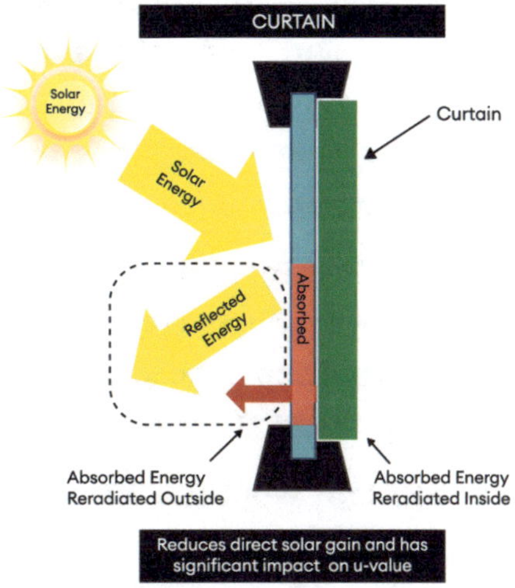

Measurable energy and GHG can be saved by operating the curtains appropriately, Keeping the curtains open during the cold days when sunlight can assist in warming up the indoor environment. At the same time, by keeping the curtains closed at night in cooler climates, the heat remains within the building – I call this the 'blanketing effect'.

Comparisons of the energy savings related to shading are enumerated in the case study in Chapter 16.

Building Insulation

For optimum energy efficiency, a building must be properly insulated from the roof down to its foundation. Each type of insulation has its advantages and drawbacks, and the suitability of a particular insulation type depends on the specific requirements of the building and the local climate. Proper installation, including bridging the thermal gap, is crucial to ensure that the insulation performs optimally and contributes to energy efficiency and occupant comfort.

Below are some common types of building insulation products.

a. **Natural Insulation Materials:** Some eco-friendly insulation options include materials like sheep's wool, cotton, hemp, and straw. These materials are renewable and have low environmental impact.

b. **Fibreglass Insulation:** Made from fine glass fibres, fibreglass insulation is one of the most widely used and affordable types of insulation. It comes in batts or rolls and can be installed in walls, attics, and floors. It is effective for both thermal and acoustic insulation.

c. **Cellulose Insulation:** This type of insulation is made from recycled paper products treated with fire-retardant chemicals. It can be blown or sprayed into walls, attics, and other cavities, providing good thermal performance and sound absorption.

d. **Mineral Wool (Rockwool or Slag Wool):** Mineral wool insulation is made from volcanic rock or blast furnace slag. It comes in batts, rolls, or loose-fill form and offers excellent fire resistance and soundproofing properties.

e. **Spray Foam Insulation:** This insulation type is applied as a liquid that expands and hardens into a foam, creating an airtight seal. It provides superior thermal performance and is commonly used in attics, walls, and crawl spaces.

f. **Polyurethane Foam:** Like spray foam insulation, polyurethane foam is a rigid foam board that offers high thermal resistance. It is often used in commercial buildings and as exterior sheathing.

g. **Expanded Polystyrene (EPS) and Extruded Polystyrene (XPS):** These rigid foam boards are effective in insulating foundations, roofs, walls, and floors. They have good moisture resistance and provide long-term thermal performance.

h. **Reflective Insulation:** This type of insulation uses reflective materials, such as aluminium foils, to reflect heat away from the building. It is often used in attics and in combination with other insulation types.

i. **Aerogel Insulation:** Aerogel is a highly efficient and lightweight insulation material with excellent thermal properties. It is often used in specialised applications where space is limited and maximum insulation is required.

j. **Vacuum Insulation Panels (VIPs):** VIPs consist of a core material enclosed in a vacuum-sealed panel, providing very high thermal resistance. They are used in applications where traditional insulation materials are not feasible due to space constraints.

Adding insulation lowers the U-values of these elements. The U-value recommended for optimum insulation depends on factors such as local climate, building standards and the surface you want to insulate (floor, ceiling, wall, etc.).

Insulation can be made from various materials, as discussed above, and is generally available in a range of shapes, sizes, and formats. Each type of insulation has characteristics that make it suitable for different types of construction and renovation projects.

There are two criteria to consider when evaluating and comparing insulation products.

Firstly, the U-value measures the ability of insulation materials to resist heat flow into or out of a building. The lower the U-value, the more effective the insulation will be. Keep in mind that a material's U-value will be lower if it has a higher density.

Secondly, with most construction projects, the goal is to get the best result possible within the budget. The same is true for insulation. Some types of insulation are more effective than others, but the price per square meter is usually proportional to the performance. This means that if you have a large area to cover, you may want to choose a less expensive option to keep costs down. It is not advisable to just go for the cheapest option without considering other factors because higher-quality insulation will be worth the investment in the long term.

It needs to be pointed out that insulation is not something that needs to be replaced often. Most insulation materials are designed to last around 20-25 years. However, it should be noted that some types of insulation can be affected by phenomena. For example, mineral wool insulation tends to compress over time. Thermal resistance is directly related to the thickness of the insulation, so the more compressed it gets, the more effective it will be. Conversely, other materials, such as polyurethane insulating foam, have mechanical properties that make them more resistant over time.

Walls

Insulating the outside of a wall is best, but it is often necessary to insulate from the inside for economical and practical reasons. Sometimes a combination of approaches is required. It is important to examine the advantages of each approach carefully.

This can involve installing a rigid insulation board and drywall, a wood-frame wall and insulation, or other combinations of insulation. Your choice of method will depend on several factors, including whether there are moisture issues, the need to account for moisture and air/vapour barriers, how you plan to use the space, and, finally, cost. This decision is particularly relevant if you are finishing a basement.

Roof

While your roof shields you from the rain and snow, you may not realise that it can also be a major heat gain or loss source. This makes sense – we all learned in school that heat rises. In fact, the amount of heat loss from the inside to outside during cooler periods can be almost halved by installing insulation. This is worth considering if the roof is not already insulated. The return on investment for installing mineral fibre insulation is generally less than three years.

Heat Losses due to Ventilation and Infiltration

Ventilation is the *intentional* process of replacing air in any space to provide high indoor air quality. Infiltration is the *uncontrolled* entry of fresh air into a dwelling through air leakage paths in the building.

Ventilation and infiltration both bring outside air into the building, forcing out the air that is inside the building. In the winter, the cold outside air replaces the warm inside air. To keep the temperature inside at about 20°C, the heating system must raise the temperature of the outside air to 20°C. This heating of ventilation and infiltration air will add to the heating costs of the building.

With regard to intentional ventilation, the number of air changes per hour is established by the building's designer to comply with building codes. Optimising the number of air changes is necessary to minimise heat loss. However, it needs to be stressed that minimum air changes are recommended in air conditioning design guidelines.

Let us talk about the uncontrolled ingress of air and examine the common sources:

1. **Doors and Windows:** Poorly sealed doors and windows or gaps in their frames can allow air to infiltrate or escape, especially if they are old or not properly maintained.
2. **Chimneys and Flues:** Unused chimneys or flues that are not properly sealed can allow air to infiltrate or escape.
3. **Cracks and Gaps:** Minor openings around windows, doors, electrical outlets, plumbing penetrations, and other building envelope penetrations can allow outdoor air to infiltrate indoors and indoor air to escape outside.
4. **Utility Penetrations:** Openings for utilities such as pipes, conduits, or cables that pass through the building envelope may not be adequately sealed, leading to air leakage.

If not addressed, these infiltration pathways result in increased heating or cooling loads, decreased indoor comfort, and higher energy bills.

5

ESSENTIALS OF ELECTRICAL SERVICES

SHINING TECHNOLOGY

Solar panels harness solar energy and convert it into usable electrical power. In simple language, when the sun shines on the photovoltaic cells, they absorb the solar energy, generating direct current (DC). An inverter collects DC and uses or converts it to alternating current (AC) power, which is the form of electricity commonly used in homes and businesses

FIGURE 20 PHOTOVOLTAIC EFFECT

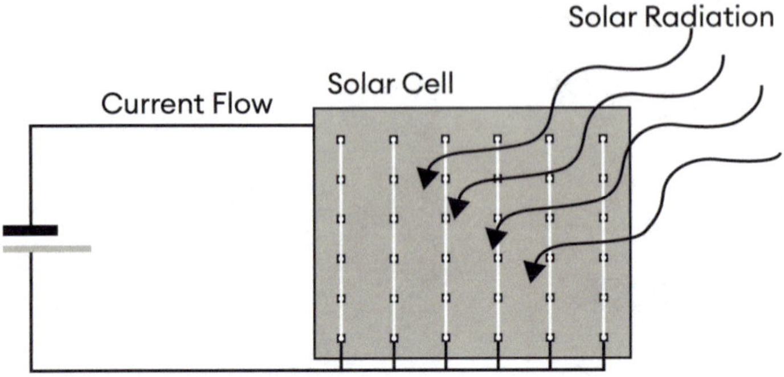

The process is known as the photovoltaic effect. Here is how a solar panel works.

A solar panel consists of numerous smaller units called photovoltaic (PV) cells, typically made from silicon, a semiconductor material. When sunlight strikes a PV cell, the semiconductor material absorbs it. This absorbed light energy loosens electrons from their atoms, generating electron-hole pairs. In silicon, the energy causes electrons to break free from their atoms, leaving behind holes (positive charges). PV cells have an electric field created by doping different silicon layers. The top layer is usually doped with phosphorus, producing an excess of free electrons (n-type silicon), while the bottom layer is doped with boron, resulting in a shortage of electrons (p-type silicon). This n-type and p-type silicon junction forms an electric field at the interface. The electric field at the p-n junction propels the free electrons towards the cell's front surface, generating an electric current.

POWERING BUILDINGS

In this chapter, we explore how buildings and homes are powered. Electrical services in a building refer to the electrical systems and components that provide power for lighting and various electrical functions necessary for the building's operation. Qualified electricians design, install, and maintain these services in compliance with safety standards, electrical codes, and local regulations. Regular inspections and maintenance are essential for safe and efficient operation, preventing electrical hazards.

There are various components that work together to distribute electricity safely and efficiently throughout the structure.

FIGURE 21 ELECTRICAL POWER RETICULATION (COURTESY FARUQ VISHRAM)

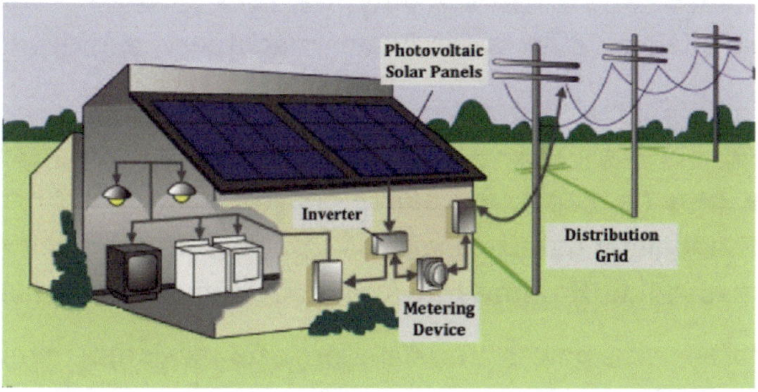

Most buildings receive electricity from a city or town electricity grid, usually at a higher voltage to reduce transmission losses. A transformer adjusts this voltage to a suitable level for building use. If the grid supply is disrupted, such as during a storm, an onsite emergency system like a diesel generator can provide electricity until the grid is restored. A process, known as load shedding, prioritises essential services and is managed by a pre-programmed controller. In some areas, grid electricity is rationed, necessitating frequent use of onsite generators.

Generators may be the sole power source in remote locations without grid access. These generators mostly run on various fossil fuels, though renewable energy systems are increasingly replacing these generators due to their economic and environmental benefits.

The building's incoming electricity connects to the Main Switchboard (MSB), which includes safety circuit breakers. In commercial buildings, the MSB is housed in an electrical switch room. From the MSB, electricity is distributed to distribution boards (DBs) with circuits for lighting and general power outlets (GPOs) for equipment like computers and printers. Each circuit has individual breakers or fuses for control and overload protection. Larger motors, like those for air conditioning, use separate circuits. Critical equipment in hospitals is connected to uninterruptible power supply (UPS) units, which have batteries to maintain power during outages. UPS units require cooling due to heat generation.

Electrical outlets, or receptacles, supply power to various devices and appliances throughout the building. These include standard wall sockets, specialised outlets for heavy machinery, and outdoor-rated outlets.

Electrical services power fire alarm systems, including smoke detectors, heat detectors, fire alarm control panels, and notification devices. Emergency lighting systems also rely on electricity through batteries to provide illumination during power outages or emergencies.

Electrical systems power lifts, elevators, and escalators in multi-story buildings, enabling vertical transportation for occupants.

Electrical services are crucial for security systems, such as CCTV cameras, access control systems, intercoms, and alarms, which protect the building and its occupants from unauthorised access and security threats.

Electrical services support communication systems, including telephone lines, data cabling, and network infrastructure, allowing occupants to connect to the internet and communicate with each other.

Building lighting systems include electrical fixtures, switches, and controls for artificial illumination. General lighting levels range from 300 to 400 lux. Modern buildings use Light-emitting Diode (LED) technology due to its lower energy consumption, longer lifespan, and reduced heat output compared to incandescent and fluorescent lights. Controls like dimmer switches, occupancy sensors, and timers enhance energy optimisation and user comfort

Many homes and buildings incorporate renewable energy sources to reduce grid reliance and promote sustainability.

SOLAR POWER

Solar energy is fast becoming a standard part of electrical services. At the commencement of this chapter, we discussed how solar energy is generated.

Here are a few pertinent points related to associated equipment.

Inverter

As mentioned before, an inverter is a device that converts direct current (DC) into alternating current (AC), enabling the PV system to power devices that require AC, such as those used at home and work. Inverters come in various shapes and designs, but there are two basic types: modified (quasi) square wave and sine wave.

FIGURE 22 – SOLAR POWER - INVERTER

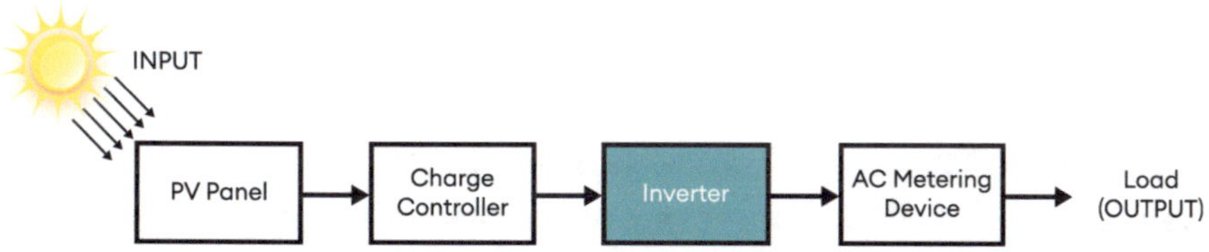

Each type of inverter serves a specific purpose. In systems requiring alternating voltage, it is crucial to ensure that the inverter's input power is never less than the total power of the connected devices. Additionally, the inverter must have the same nominal voltage as the selected batteries. For independent systems, the inverter must be large enough to handle the total power demand simultaneously. The power rating of the inverter needs to be 25 to 30 per cent higher than the combined power of all connected loads. If the load includes an electric motor or motors, the inverter's capacity must be at least three times greater than the motor's capacity due to the high starting current required by motors.

Batteries

Solar panels charge the batteries in systems using batteries by directing electricity into them. When needed, such as at night, a portion of this current can flow back, causing the batteries to discharge slowly. Charge controllers act as one-way valves to prevent over-discharge.

FIGURE 23– SOLAR POWER – INVERTER & BATTERY

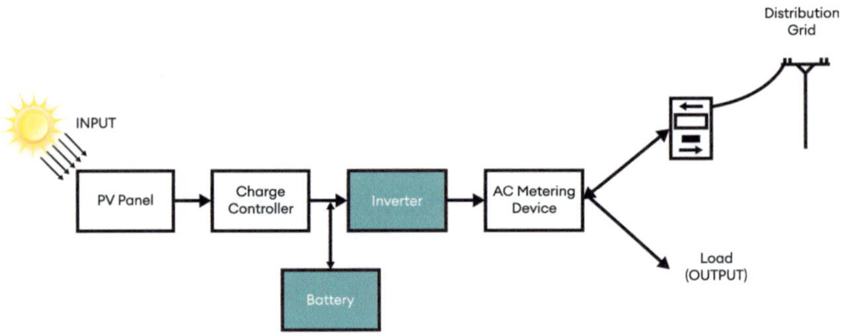

Solar batteries come in various shapes and designs depending on their purpose and manufacturer. When properly used, they can have a long life—on average, 15 years.

The main functions of batteries in a PV system include:

- Storing electricity produced by the solar panels.
- Supplying stable electrical loads.

+ Smoothing out temporary fluctuations in power.
+ Providing overvoltage or high peak currents to electrical loads or devices.

Solar systems typically use deep-cycle batteries, which are different from standard car batteries. Deep-cycle batteries are designed for frequent discharge and slow charging, making them ideal for daily use. These batteries can discharge low-level energy and can be charged and discharged rapidly over many years. The battery must be large enough to store sufficient energy for night-time and cloudy day operations. To determine the battery's capacity, one needs to multiply the total watt-hours per day by the days of autonomy (the number of days the system needs to operate without power from PV panels) to get the required ampere-hour rating of the deep-cycle battery.

In some PV systems, batteries are unnecessary or undesired. Users can store electricity with a local electricity distribution grid via a synchronous converter, which is placed between the PV array and the grid's power meter. These systems, known as cost-effective interactive systems, allow energy storage and distribution through the grid. Many companies offer these services to customers at very affordable rates.

In commercial applications where the electrical load during power disruptions is high, the standby power generator may also be integrated in the arrangement.

FIGURE 24 – SOLAR POWER – INVERTER, BATTERY & STANDBY GENERATOR

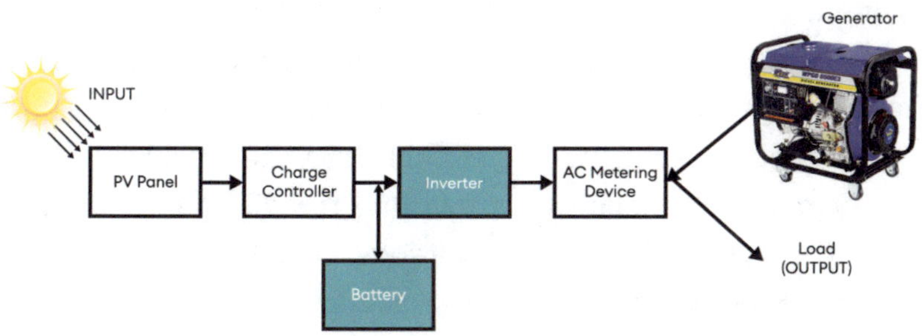

In this arrangement, the consumption of diesel fuel needs to be considered when estimating GHG emissions.

Net Metering

Net metering incentivises the adoption of solar power by making it more financially viable for consumers to generate their own electricity. By using net metering, customers create an opportunity to reduce their electricity bills and get better returns on their solar power system investments. It is to be noted that net metering policies and regulations vary by country and state. There are often limits on the size of the solar power system that qualifies for net metering, caps on the total amount of net metering capacity allowed in each area, and different rules for how credits are calculated and applied.

FIGURE 25– SOLAR POWER – REVERSIBLE METER

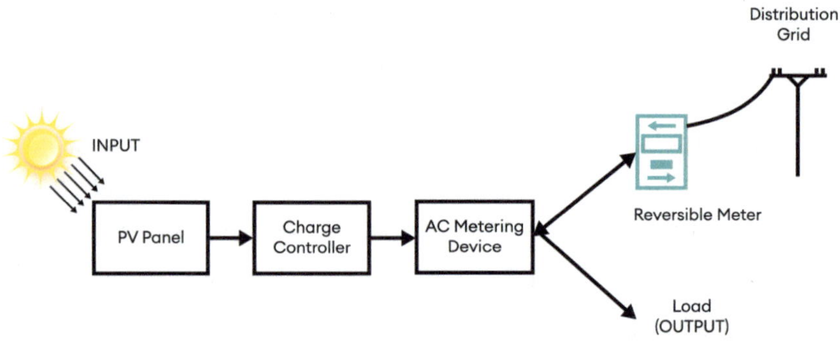

To put it simply, net metering is primarily a billing mechanism applied in many countries that allows residential and commercial customers who generate their own electricity from solar power to feed electricity they do not use back into the grid. During the day, when the sun is shining, these panels might produce more electricity than the customer uses. This excess electricity is fed back into the grid. The customer's electricity meter runs backward, providing a credit against the electricity consumed at night or during other periods when the solar panels are not generating enough power to meet the customer's needs.

In this case, the customer is billed for their "net" energy use. This means they are charged for the difference between the electricity they consume from the grid and the electricity they produce and send back to the grid over a billing period. This essentially means that the grid 'buys' the excess electricity and 'resales' it back to the consumer at the same rate.

The inevitable question is whether the electricity bought back can be classified as renewable and therefore treated as zero GHG emissions. The answer is when electricity is consumed at night in a net metering arrangement, the power drawn from the grid is not necessarily treated as renewable. The primary reason is that the electricity provided by the grid comes from a mix of sources, which can include renewable sources (like wind, solar, and hydroelectric) as well as non-renewable sources (like coal, natural gas, and other fossil fuels). The specific mix depends on the local energy infrastructure and the time of day.

Net metering is, therefore, only an accounting mechanism. It allows customers to balance their energy consumption and production over a billing period, but it doesn't change the physical source of the electricity they consume at any given moment. So even if a customer has a net zero electricity bill due to net metering, the power consumed at night is part of the general grid mix, which includes both renewable and non-renewable sources.

Interestingly, electricity providers in some countries offer 'credits' to customers for providing renewable energy in the form of excess energy when fed into the grid during sunlight hours. In that circumstance, when the customer consumes electricity at night, they are entitled to use these 'credits' to offset their consumption. However, the actual electricity they receive from the grid at night comes from the grid's overall power mix.

We can conclude that while net metering helps promote renewable energy by allowing customers to offset their electricity consumption with solar power generated during the day, the electricity consumed at night is typically part of the broader grid mix and is not exclusively renewable. This has GHG emission implications which need to be evaluated accordingly.

Gross Metering

Where a reversible meter is not incorporated between the customer and the supplier, but excess electricity is still fed back to the grid at an agreed rate per kWh and when needed is bought back by the customer, generally at a higher rate per kWh, the arrangement is termed 'Gross Metering'.

The best way to describe this arrangement is to share our experience.

In July 2023, we installed a 13.5 kW solar power system in our residence. Our feed-in tariff is 15 cents / kWh when we feed our excess energy into the grid whereas charge to us to purchase from the provider is 35 cents / kWh at night and cloudy days.

It was recommended that we use a Solar Edge inverter. That was good advice, and as can be seen below, the dynamic information it provides is well laid out and very informative.

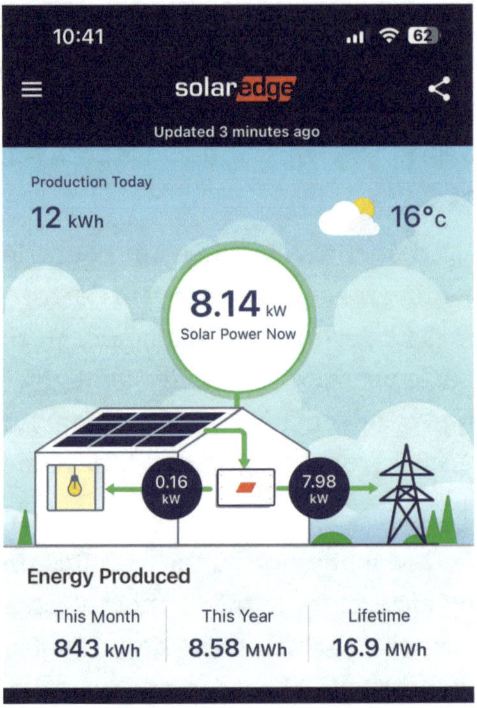

Solar-Edge Inverter – Dynamic Dashboard

Over one year, the total solar energy generated is 16 mWh and CO2 emissions saved is 10939 kg, which equates to around 10.9 metric tons.

Our energy savings are equivalent to planting 212 trees since July 2023. This is according to the Solar Edge inbuilt factor of 51.6 kgCO2e per tree, whereas, as outlined in Chapter 1, the commonly used factor is around 25-30 kgCO2e per tree. If 30 kgCO2e per tree was used, we have 'planted' 364 virtual trees. In some ways, this highlights the discrepancies associated with calculating CO2 absorption by trees.

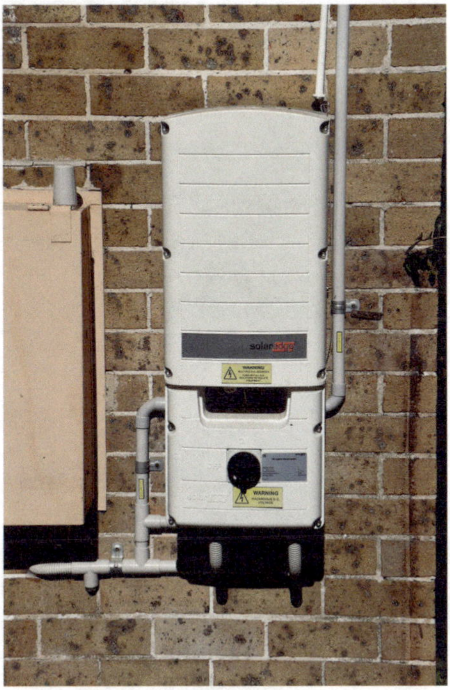

Solar-Edge Inverter

The next chapter introduces the concepts of natural ventilation, air conditioning and the fundamentals of heating, ventilation, and air conditioning (HVAC)

6

COMFORT PROVIDERS

HUMBLE REFRIGERATOR

Here is an exercise you can carry out. Open your refrigerator. Look around the inside walls. You will see the label telling you the type of gas responsible for keeping your food cold. Most likely, that gas is one of the fluorinated gases called a refrigerant. Refrigerants are found in everything from air conditioning systems to grocery store freezers, from industrial warehouses to Slurpee machines. Feel the back of the refrigeration if you can. It will be warm. That is because the warmth from the inside is transferred to the outside by this refrigeration cycle.

Here is a simplified explanation of how heating or cooling energies are transferred from inside space to an outdoor environment using the refrigeration cycle. This energy exchange is a result of the refrigerant's change of phase from liquid to gas and vice versa, with the aid of a compressor and expansion valve. While water boils at 100°C, refrigerants have much lower boiling points. These principles are employed in the humble refrigerator and the air conditioning unit. The technology is known as direct expansion or DX.

FIGURE 26 REFRIGERATOR - HEAT EXCHANGE PRINCIPLE

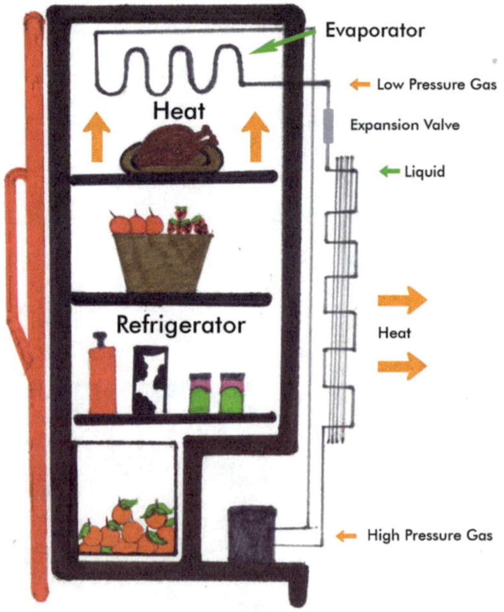

HEATING, VENTILATION & AIR CONDITIONING

Every indoor space needs to comply with the ventilation code as required by the appropriate governing authority. The code stipulates the area of openable fixtures – generally around 10 per cent of floor space for any indoor space to enable provision of fresh air. To put it simply, by providing openable windows and doors that meet the area ratios, the code requirements are deemed to be met.

Openable windows and doors provide a means of natural ventilation, which can have the potential to meet the thermal comfort requirements of an indoor space depending on the prevailing outdoor conditions. A natural breeze at the right temperature, humidity and air velocity can provide comfortable indoor conditions because of the circulating air. Cross-ventilation is obviously the most suitable. This means that windows and doors should be well-placed and open at the same time to allow the breeze to move around. Having attended the Windsor Comfort conferences for several years, I learnt a lot about adaptive comfort and use of natural ventilation. There is a definite correlation, but practical applications are not that common.

This leads us to discuss the limitations of utilising straight natural ventilation. One of the biggest concerns is that the great outdoors is unpredictable and will only become more so as we continue to experience the effects of climate change, including extreme weather events and natural disasters. Secondly, outdoor noise can make building occupants uncomfortable. As the population increases and more infrastructure is developed, people who live in cities are increasingly dealing with more traffic noises, as well as the sounds of planes overhead and trains passing by.

Then there is dust and toxic fumes from vehicles or bushfire smoke blowing into an indoor space.

Whilst straight natural ventilation may not work, many societies all over the world have been using wind catchers and other methods to redirect fresh air down into the indoor space, or cool air up from an underground space.

An example of the principle adopted in Iran which is self-explanatory.

FIGURE 27 WIND CATCHER

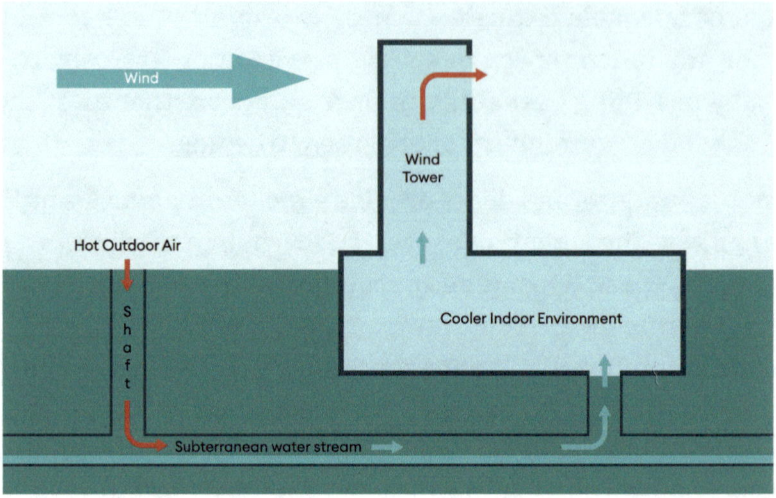

Other cooling methods have been employed for millennia. Records show that in ancient times, the Egyptians hung wet reeds in their windows to cool the incoming air through evaporation. Similarly, history documentaries show that Romans circulated water through the walls of their homes to achieve a cooling effect.

Where natural ventilation could not satisfy comfort requirements, mechanical systems were developed primarily to assist with air movement and cooling. Amongst the most common is the use of ceiling fans. In places like Chennai and Mangalore in India, you certainly require a ceiling fan in your bedroom if you do not have air conditioning to have a good night's sleep. That was our family's experience when we stayed in Mangalore for a few months during the period when our daughter was gaining work experience related to her master's degree in biomedical engineering.

Last year, in my work in Bangladesh, it was interesting to evaluate a school in Dhaka, where adaptative cooling (using natural ventilation and ceiling fans) was creating unacceptable indoor conditions. Classroom temperatures were observed to be 31°C and 85 per cent relative humidity. The system installed on the pretext of adaptive cooling used tempered cooling with the ceiling fans, which at high speeds were so noisy that the students could not hear the teacher. Whilst the students were uncomfortable, it was ironic that all the administration and meeting rooms were fully air-conditioned. To please the parents more so than the students, all classrooms were modified to include air conditioning whilst leaving the ceiling fans for possible use during less humid weather. The upgrade was carried out at great expense and inconvenience to school operations and involved air conditioning of all the classrooms. This enhancement alleviated another problem – that of mosquitoes, which in these places can carry diseases such as malaria and dengue fever into the classroom. This was achieved by pressurising the rooms with higher fresh air quantity in the air conditioning system.

Turning to other areas of such as underground car parks, toilets, and kitchens, for which the code provides the method of establishing the supply and exhaust air quantities for the mechanical systems.

Where occupants desired comfort levels are not achievable with natural or simple mechanical ventilation combined with the fact that most modern buildings are fully sealed, use of artificial means through air conditioning have emerged to provide occupants' thermal comfort.

The History of Air Conditioning

The history of air conditioning started with the need to preserve foods. Foods that are kept at room temperature spoil easily due to the growth of bacteria. At temperature below 4°C (40°F), the growth of bacteria is reduced rapidly. As a result of the development in food refrigeration, other applications followed. American polymath, Benjamin Franklin's pioneering experiments with Dr. John Hadley in the mid-18th century laid the groundwork for advancements in refrigeration technology. Early applications started on the need to cool air for industrial processes rather than for personal comfort. In 1758, Benjamin Franklin conducted experiments with the evaporation of volatile liquids to lower the temperature of an object, giving birth to the principle of evaporative cooling. Dr John Gorrie, another American physician by profession, proposed the idea of using cooling to treat yellow fever patients. He built a machine that compressed air and then allowed it to expand, leading to cooling. While his invention did not gain widespread adoption, it led to future developments.

Another prolific American inventor, Oliver Evans, took the principles developed by Franklin and Hadley and drew up a design for a vapor-compression cycle, or early refrigerator, in 1805, Willis Haviland Carrier, an engineer and inventor born in 1876, was also an American who is widely recognised as the father of modern air conditioning. His ground-breaking work in the field of air conditioning revolutionised comfort cooling, transformed various industries, and fundamentally changed the way people live and work in hot and humid climates. Carrier graduated from Cornell University in 1901 with a degree in electrical engineering. His first job was with the Buffalo Forge Company, where he worked on solving issues related to humidity in industrial settings. The variation in humidity levels in the factory caused changes in paper dimensions, which led to difficulties in the printing process. In 1902, while waiting for a train on a foggy Pittsburgh train platform, Carrier had a crucial breakthrough. He realised that by controlling the temperature and humidity of the air, he could achieve precise control over indoor conditions. He developed the concept of "rational psychrometric formulae", which, in simple terms, is the recognition that air has dry and wet (with moisture) components. As an example, through our physical activities, like going about our normal routine, each of us generate heat which is called 'sensible heat' of around 60 to 70 watts. However, we may sweat and that contributes what is called 'latent heat' – approximately 60 watts. This must be considered when considering artificial cooling using air conditioning systems. This concept, also known as psychrometry, has thus become the foundation for modern air conditioning. In 1906, Carrier designed the first air conditioning system for the Sackett-Wilhelms Lithographing and Publishing Company in Brooklyn, New York. The system involved blowing air over coils containing cold water, controlling both temperature and humidity. This innovation not only improved the quality of printing but also marked the birth of modern air conditioning. In 1915, Carrier, along with a group of engineers, founded the Carrier Engineering Corporation (now known as Carrier Corporation), with the primary goal of manufacturing and selling air conditioning systems. Initially, air conditioning was predominantly used in industrial and commercial applications to enhance productivity and preserve product quality. However, after World War II, the residential air conditioning market began to grow rapidly, and air conditioning became a standard feature in homes, changing the demographics and development patterns internationally, particularly in warmer regions. Carrier continued to work on various air conditioning innovations throughout his life and made significant contributions to the fields of refrigeration and air conditioning. He passed away on October 7, 1950, leaving behind a legacy that transformed the world's comfort and productivity. Air conditioning is now an integral part of modern life, from homes to offices, automobiles, and public spaces, making hot and humid climates much more bearable and facilitating advances in various industries.

Talking about refrigeration, the modern electric refrigerator was invented in 1913 by an American, Fred W. Wolf. It featured a refrigeration unit on top of an icebox. William C. Durant began mass producing domestic refrigerators in 1918, with the first home refrigerator having a self-contained compressor.

Air Conditioning and Refrigeration Fundamentals

In the beginning of this chapter, you were requested to carry out an exercise related to the humble refrigerator. It mentioned the refrigeration cycle. Here is a simplified explanation of how the cycle works.

FIGURE 28 REFRIGERATION CYCLE

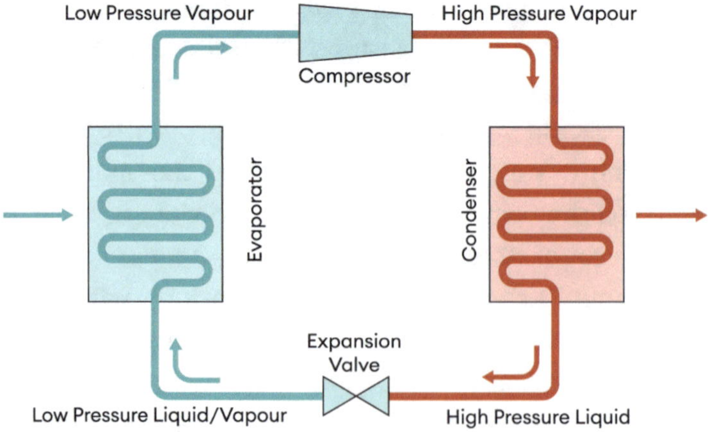

Compression is the first step in the refrigeration cycle, as shown in Figure 24; The compressor increases the pressure of the working gas. Refrigerant enters the compressor as a low-pressure, low-temperature gas and leaves the compressor as a high-pressure, high-temperature gas. This condenses (and thereby releases the heat to the atmosphere) in the condenser, which is generally located outdoors and subsequently changes to a high-pressure liquid. The expansion valve plays an important role in changing the high-pressure liquid to low-pressure liquid/vapour. In the evaporator (cooling coil in the indoor unit) the low-pressure refrigerant liquid evaporates (and thereby creates cooling) into low-pressure vapour. The cycle restarts. It must be reiterated that all these changes of phases are only possible due to the low boiling point of the refrigerant.

This arrangement is also referred to as the air-cooled version since the operation involves energy exchanges using the atmosphere (outdoor condenser). Other versions include water-cooled, which uses equipment such as cooling towers, and geothermal or geo-change, which utilises the ground as a heat source and heat sink. These different versions are covered in more detail later in this section.

Refrigerants

Fluorinated gases are greenhouse gases as explained earlier. They include refrigerants.

Since refrigerants play a vital part in refrigeration and air conditioning. Let us look at the history. Early refrigerants were known to be flammable, and it wasn't until 1928 that non-flammable chlorofluorocarbon (CFC) refrigerants were introduced. CFCs are synthetic chemicals that were effective at keeping things cool but had a treacherous side effect: they caused a depletion of the Earth's ozone layer, exposing humans and all life to harmful ultraviolet radiation.

In 1987, world leaders gathered in Montreal, Canada, to hammer out an agreement to phase out CFCs. This was the birth of the Montreal Protocol on substances that deplete the ozone layer effectively banned CFCs. As CFCs were phased out, they were replaced with hydrofluorocarbons or HFCs. While they work well at keeping things cool, they have a significant drawback: these GHGs can be thousands of times more potent than CO2.

In 2016, recognising the dangers of HFCs, nations once again gathered in Kigali, Rwanda, to craft a new agreement called Kigali Amendment to the Montreal Protocol. Participating countries committed to cut the production and consumption of HFCs by more than 80 per cent over the subsequent 30 years.

Among these was the hydrochlorofluorocarbon (HCFC) R-22, which became the standard refrigerant used in air conditioning systems. R-22 continued to be famous for many decades until scientists discovered that chlorine in CFCs and HCFCs was damaging the ozone layer. R-22, with an ozone-depleting potential (ODP) of 0.055 and a GWP of 1810, has been phased down in Australia (since 2018) and globally under the Montreal Protocol (since 2019), as it has a high GWP. The phase out is supported by bans on new equipment containing R-22. However, when I was in Dhaka in 2023 for a net zero project, I could not only get R-22 but also get new air conditioning units using R-22. One gets suspicious about the 'dumping' of phased-out products from developed to developing countries.

Research and development related to refrigerants has taken a steep rise in recent times and there are increasing number of cooling and air conditioning products on the market with environmentally friendly refrigerants.

Refrigerant Leakage

The refrigerant experiences high and low pressures as part of the refrigeration cycle. Vibrating equipment, such as the compressor, also contributes to this. Over time, this leads to fittings getting loose, resulting in refrigerant leakage.

When refrigerants leak from air conditioning and refrigeration units, the impact on the environment is significant. For example, every 1 kg of R-22 leakage is equivalent to releasing 1,760 kgs of CO2e. This is because the GWP of R-22 is 1,760

American Society of Heating, Refrigeration and Air Conditioning Engineers (ASHRAE) latest Standard 228/2023 is titled 'Standard Method of Evaluating Zero Net Carbon Building Performance'. Note – ASHRAE has termed it Zero Net instead of what the whole world is using - Net Zero. Anyway, the relevance of mentioning this standard is that it deals with refrigerant leakage.

Refrigerant Leakage. The unit leakage from an air conditioning unit can be calculated by taking the manufacturer's specified charge (approximately 1.4 kg per ton) and multiplying it by the typical annual leakage rate for that unit type as shown in ASHRAE Table 9 and by the GWP of the respective refrigerant as shown in ASHRAE Table 10.

It needs to be pointed out that there is no mention or acknowledgement in the standard of the fact that age of the air conditioning or refrigeration unit and condition of the installation are vital considerations that influence the leakage rate. In other words, one could apply 30 per cent leakage on a new refrigeration system in a supermarket. That in my opinion is misleading. Data collected from several buildings that have undergone GHG and Energy audits show higher leakage rate for older and / or unmaintained installations.

Table 9 Typical Annual Refrigerant Leakage Rates by Equipment Type

	Equipment Type	Typical Annual Leakage Rate of Refrigerant Mass Charge Per Year
1	Supermarket refrigeration	30%
3	Commercial condensing units	15%
4	Water chillers	5%
5	Hermetic units with no field installed refrigerant piping	1%
6	Rooftop unit air conditioner	6%
7	Residential heat pump and air conditioner	2%
8	Variable refrigerant flow air conditioner	10%
9	Other refrigeration	2%
10	Other air conditioning	2%

Table 10 Refrigerant Global Warming Potential (GWP)

Refrigerant Type	GWP, kg CO_2e/kg refrigerant
HCFC-22	1760
HCFC-123	79
HFC-134a	1300
HC-290 (propane)	5
R-404A	4970
R-407C	1620

The standard does not cover the point that a procedure for compiling the refrigerant 'top-up' data is a better process to give more accurate refrigerant leakage rate instead of the stipulated fixed leakage rates. Prevention too needs to be encouraged with procedures involving tightening of fittings (bearing in mind that typically refrigerant pipework is connected to vibrating equipment as in compressors). Refrigerant leak tests should also be performed periodically. The standard makes no reference to refrigerant recovery procedures in the event of replacement of compressors and D/X coils, which is mandated in most countries, including Australia.

How can we ascertain the leakage associated with buildings like the one in we have been talking about - the campus building?

Dhaka campus building – Dhaka, Bangladesh 2023

For this campus building in Dhaka with 195 AC units, each with a refrigerant charge of 1.4 kg per ton, applying the leakage rates and GWPs from ASHRAE Standard tables 9 and 10 results in an estimated annual emission of 9.6 tons of CO_2, equivalent to planting of 384 trees per year. This adds around 10 per cent tons of CO_2 to operational GHG tons.

Estimating Cooling and Heating Capacities

Getting back to air conditioning, let us look at how to establish the cooling and heating capacities of the AC unit that will maintain the required indoor comfort conditions.

Estimating the cooling and heating capacities of any non-domestic building involves a much more comprehensive analysis of various factors that influence the space's thermal requirements.

Heating in Buildings

How can we establish heating capacity of a boiler?

Let us examine the basic calculations involved in establishing heating requirements. For glass, walls, and roofs, the respective area is multiplied by the temperature difference between inside and outside multiplied by the U-value for each element.

Taking a room with a window of two-by-two metres with single glazing, the amount of heat lost from the room when the outdoor temperature is at minus 20 degrees Celsius will be 1 kW. If it were double-glazed, it would be about half that – a 50 per cent difference! We can go further to help retain heat by closing the curtains or blinds. As highlighted in the previous chapter, the overall impact could be further energy saving of 5 to 7 per cent. Roof and wall insulation also help keep the heat in. If we had a fifty square metre roof area with no insulation when the outdoor temperature is once again minus 20 degrees Celsius, the heat lost would be 4 kW. With insulation, it will reduce to 1 kW. This is a significant saving in heating energy bills.

The other component of the heating calculation is the fresh air that is supplied to the indoor space to meet code requirements. During the cooler months, this air needs to be heated.

Here is an example. If there are 100 people in a room, the minimum amount of fresh air required to meet the code (5 litres per second per person) will be 500 litres per second. If the outdoor temperature is minus 20 degrees Celsius, then the amount of heating required to heat this air alone would be 24kW. This means a 1kW heater for every five people, equating to a lot of energy required!

With climate change impact the heating demand is continuously increasing. To add to this, the types and forms of heating in many instances have been inefficient, as observed as part of global building energy audit processes.

Summary of Heating Methods

For a domestic application, generally, the term 'ton' of cooling is used. You often hear "For this small room (say 25 m2 with a window) you need a one-ton AC unit". One ton equates to 3.5 kW of cooling capacity. If the unit has a reverse cycle feature, the heating capacity would be around 4.0 kW. How much power will this unit consume at full capacity? Around 1 kW of electrical power. This indicates that the coefficient of performance (COP) of this unit in cooling mode is 3.5, whereas for heating, it is 4.0; that is, for 1 kW of power input, you get 4 kW of heat. This makes a reverse cycle AC unit the most energy-efficient way of heating compared to a standard electric heater.

From an overall comparative perspective, the most efficient method for heating is using ground-source heat pumps (GSHP) due to their high COP of 5 to 6 and stable performance. GSHP will be discussed in detail in the next chapter. This is followed by air-source heat pumps (ASHP), which offer 300-400 per cent efficiency with high COPs, meaning they provide 3 to 4 times more heat energy than the electrical energy they consume. However, their application is limited to moderate climates. The least efficient is electric radiant heating, which should be used with caution as it is energy intensive.

Biomass heating and cooking using wood and pellet stoves are still popular in developing countries. Modern pellet stoves can reach efficiencies of 70-90 per cent. While they are relatively cheaper per kW of heating, they need regular fuel supply and storage and produce CO2 emissions.

The efficiency of active solar heating varies but can be highly efficient with proper design. Renewable energy can significantly reduce heating costs. However, it has a high initial cost, dependent on sunlight availability.

Natural gas furnaces and boilers that have been providing heating in non-domestic buildings for as long as I can remember are being replaced as part of the electrification process. We'll discuss this more when we discuss net zero buildings later in the book.

In summary, heating efficiency is greatly influenced by factors such as building insulation, climate, and the specific technologies used. Combining these heating systems with proper insulation, smart thermostats, and energy management systems can further enhance efficiency.

Air Conditioning Capacity Estimation

On the first day of my 33-year stint as a consulting engineer with Norman Disney Young, I was given the heat-load estimation forms to carry out the assessment for new post-production offices for Channel 7 television station, then located at Mobbs Lane, Epping, NSW, in Australia. There were over fifty forms to be completed – one for each zone and room. Calculations were done for peak heat-load conditions to establish the air quantity required to achieve comfort conditions and for diversified conditions since not all zones will peak at the same time – for example, east and west zones. Those were the days when all calculations were performed manually. However, as discussed later in the book in Chapter 11, there appeared to be time and consulting fees available to carry out heat-load and related calculations, design, and documentation.

FIGURE 29 FACTORS – AC HEAT LOAD ESTIMATION

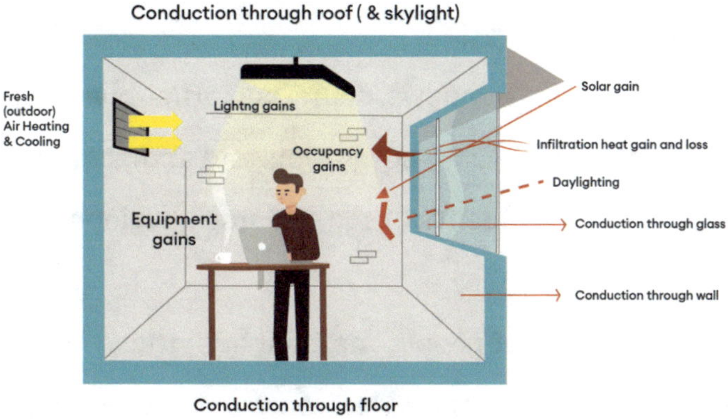

Estimating the heat load to determine a building's required heating and cooling involves considering several factors to ensure accurate calculations.

These factors include:

Building Location and Climate:

- Geographical Location: Latitude, altitude, and proximity to water bodies.
- Climate Conditions: Seasonal temperature ranges and humidity levels

Building Orientation and Layout:

- Orientation: Positioning of the building relative to the sun.
- Layout: Floor plan, number of floors, and room configurations.

Building Envelope:

- Walls, Roof, and Floor Construction: Materials, thickness, and insulation levels.
- Windows and Doors: Size, type, number, placement, and glazing properties.

Insulation:

- Quality of Insulation: In walls, roof, floors, and around windows and doors.

Ventilation and Air Infiltration:

- Natural Ventilation: Windows, doors, and other openings.
- Mechanical Ventilation: HVAC systems and air exchange rates.
- Air Leakage: Sealing quality of the building envelope.

Internal Heat Gains:

- Occupants: Number of people and their activities.
- Equipment and Appliances: Heat output from computers, lights, appliances, etc.
- Lighting: Type (incandescent, fluorescent, LED) and amount.

Solar Gains:

- Solar Radiation: Direct and diffuse solar gains through windows and roofs.
- Shading Devices: Overhangs, blinds, curtains, and external shading.

Thermal Mass:

- Building Materials: Ability to store and release heat (e.g., concrete, brick, stone).

HVAC System Efficiency:

- System Type and Capacity: Efficiency ratings and suitability for the application
- Ductwork: Insulation and leakage.

Usage Patterns:

- Occupancy Schedules: Peak times of use and duration.
- Activity Levels: Type and intensity of activities carried out within the building.

External Factors: Adjacent Buildings and Structures:

- Impact on wind patterns and shading.
- Landscaping: Trees, plants, and water features that can affect microclimates.

Advanced software tools and simulation programs are commonly used to model these factors and calculate the heating and cooling loads more precisely. It is also necessary that the design HVAC engineer has full understanding of psychrometry – as mentioned before is a branch of physics concerned with the measurement and determination of the thermodynamic properties of air and water vapour mixtures.

Air Conditioning Systems

Once the air conditioning capacities are determined the next step is selection of the most suitable type of air conditioning unit or system.

'Air conditioning system' is the term applied to the organised assembly of respective plant and equipment serving a specific application. Key plant and equipment include air filters, fans, cooling and heating coils, refrigeration compressors, condensers, boilers, chillers, cooling towers, humidifiers, volume and smoke / fire dampers, supply and return air diffusers and outside air intake or relief grilles, and automatic controls. These items are selectively assembled in any one of several ways to form a variety of air conditioning system types. The types range from self-contained or unitary units to more complicated larger systems and are detailed in next few chapters.

7

DISTRIBUTED AIR CONDITIONING SYSTEMS

CEILING FAN IN WINTER

The physics principle of hot air rising means that the air at ceiling height, when a reverse cycle air conditioning unit is used for heating, will be at a higher temperature than the air at the level we occupy. Depending on the ceiling height, the amount of heat accumulating in this void space can be considerable before it becomes useful for the intended purpose – to warm up the occupied space. This is where utilising a ceiling fan becomes an energy conserving measure.

Split AC Unit and Ceiling Fan

Ceiling fans can be set on a "winter" or heating mode where it will reverse its direction to push the air down from ceiling space to occupant level. Tests carried out show that this could reduce the energy consumption associated with heating by 5 to 7 per cent depending on the height of the ceiling. This energy-saving technique can only be applied if the fan has the 'summer-winter' selection switch. This facility is generally available in most modern ceiling fans.

UNITARY, SPLIT AND HEAT PUMP UNITS

You will surely recognise this one-piece or unitary air conditioning unit mounted in an external wall or window. It has gained the name of 'window rattler' because, over time, such units tend to become nosier and start to rattle.

A window or wall-mounted unitary air conditioning unit.

SPLIT AIR CONDITIONER

A split air conditioner is like a window unit but split into indoor and outdoor components. An example is one commonly installed for domestic and small commercial applications.

FIGURE 30 SPLIT AC UNIT IN COOLING MODE

FIGURE 31 SPLIT AC UNIT IN HEATING MODE

VARIABLE REFRIGERANT VOLUME

When several indoor D/X units are combined and utilise a common outdoor unit, the refrigerant is varied to meet the demand of each indoor unit. Since the refrigerant is common to all units, this improves the overall system's energy efficiency. Such a system is called variable refrigerant volume, or VRV. Such an arrangement is also referred to as variable refrigerant flow, or VRF.

Generally, applications of VRF are limited to low height buildings because of limitations on the distance of the refrigerant pipework between the indoor and outdoor units – generally limited to around 40 meters.

FIGURE 32 VARIABLE REFRIGERANT VOLUME SYSTEM

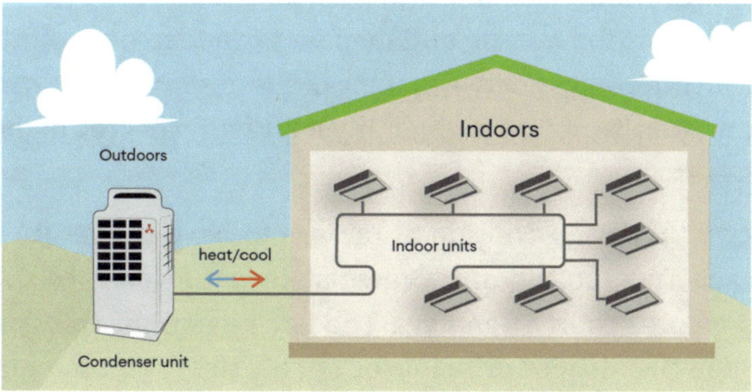

ROOFTOP PACKAGED DX UNIT

For larger spaces, rooftop units are used. As the name suggests, they are mounted on the roof and integrate the cooling and heating components, including the compressor, expansion valves, and coils, with the air handling section. These units incorporate reverse-cycle heating. The air handling arrangement can inject the required amount of fresh air, supply filtered and conditioned air to occupied spaces, and return air to the occupied spaces at the same time. Zone thermostats maintain pre-set conditions.

FIGURE 33 ROOFTOP AC UNIT

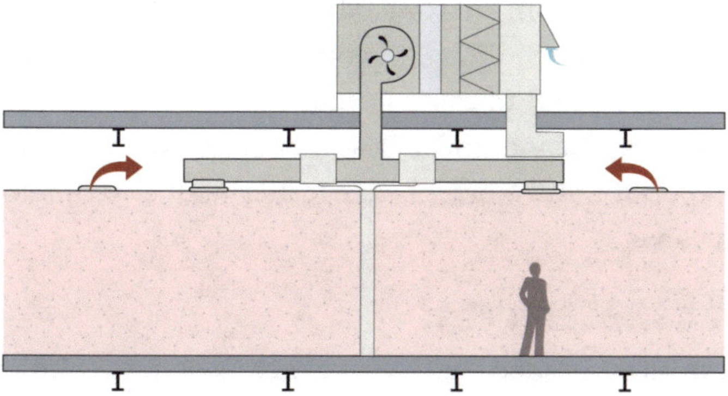

Rooftop units are a good choice for air conditioning places such as warehouses and halls. In 2002, I was involved with converting a warehouse to a place of worship. Two rooftop units were selected, one for where women sit and the other for men's side. The use of two separate systems for women and men was to address the clothing and metabolism differences between men and women. This has meant that the temperature set-point is generally kept half a degree higher in the women's area.

Another vital design consideration was to have the return air back to the respective rooftop unit drawn at carpet level since the ceiling height is greater than 4.5 meters. The key reason for this action was to overcome the physics principle of hot air rising and remaining at a higher level, necessitating the requirement of additional energy for the hot air to reach the occupied level.

Both strategies were adopted for similar projects in Melbourne, Brisbane, Perth, Adelaide, in Australia, and Auckland in New Zealand. These strategies have also been applied for new places of worship worldwide, wherever ceiling heights exceed 4.5 meters.

HEAT PUMP

A heat pumps is a split system that essentially transfers heat from one place to another, using a relatively small amount of electrical energy. They can provide both heating and cooling for buildings and are known for their efficiency and versatility. In heating mode, a heat pump extracts heat from an external source (air, ground, or water) and transfers it inside the building. In cooling mode, it extracts heat from inside the building and releases it outside. Like with the split system, a heat pump has inside and outside energy exchange components namely evaporator and condenser, together with a compressor and an expansion valve.

AIR SOURCE HEAT PUMPS

Air Source Heat Pumps (ASHPs) extract heat from the outside air and are widely used in residential and commercial buildings. They can provide both heating and cooling, making them a year-round solution. They can deliver 3 to 4 times more energy than they consume, making them highly efficient. They are most effective in moderate climates but less efficient in extreme hot or cold conditions. Periodically in winter, a heat pump, like a split system, needs to switch to a 'defrost cycle' that melts any ice that may have formed on the outdoor coil.

LIMITATIONS OF HEAT PUMPS

Heat pumps and split units are rated for certain outdoor temperatures. If there is no cooler outdoor air to exchange, like ambient temperature being above the rated temperature (generally around 480 C), the unit will cease to work. In other words, if the outside temperature goes very high like those experienced during summer in most countries, such air conditioning units will stop working - when they are required the most!

As stated before, reverse-cycle heating is more energy efficient than gas-fired heaters or, indeed, radiant, or oil-filled electric heaters. In the reverse-cycle mode, in cooler conditions, heat from the outside is exchanged with the inside cold conditions. Hence, as in the previous case, if the outdoor temperatures fall below zero, then the unit stops functioning with an annunciation of a low pressure (LP) alarm. This is the reason why air-cooled heat pumps do not work in very cold climates and need additional booster heating with gas-fired furnaces (as observed in installations in colder cities in Canada, the US, the UK, Pakistani and Tajikistani). With the move to electrification, the booster heating for such applications will need to be electric.

WATER COOLED HEAT PUMPS

With the limitations of air-cooled DX units due to very high or very low outdoor temperatures, a water-cooled alternative may be the answer. In the water-cooled version, the energy exchange is with condenser water maintained at a cooler temperature (less than 350C using cooling towers seen at roof level on many buildings).4

FIGURE 34 CONDENSER WATER RETICULATION

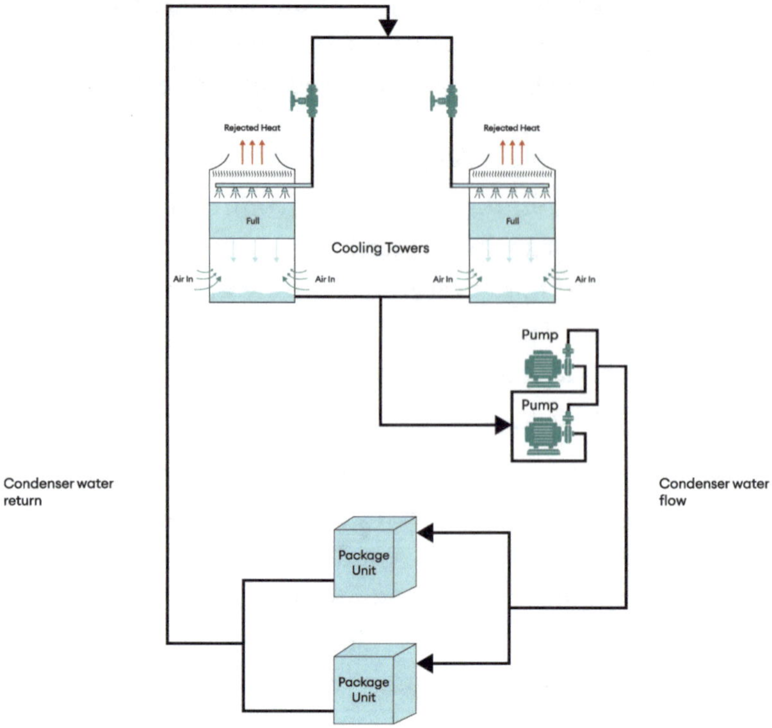

The use of cooling towers primarily addresses the cooling aspects, and hence, most applications are limited to cooling-only types of DX packaged units. In the cooling tower, air is drawn in at a low level and discharged with fan assistance at the top. Water is supplied at the top, and it trickles down. The physics principle involved in cooling the water is evaporation. Several types of cooling towers have varying efficiencies depending on outdoor conditions. If a location has high moisture content, then the evaporation rate decreases, whereas in dry climates, the evaporation rate can be higher, enabling higher heat transfer and hence better efficiencies.

To use reverse cycle heating with water-cooled system would necessitate the condenser water to be heated through a boiler (generally gas-fired, as we will go through when we talk about central air conditioning equipment).

Cooling towers also play a part in water-cooled chillers, as covered in Chapter 9.

LEGIONNAIRES DISEASE

An important point to consider is that a cooling tower is a source of the deadly airborne legionnaires disease.

Legionnaires disease is a type of pneumonia caused by the bacterium Legionella pneumophila. It is contracted by inhaling aerosolized water droplets containing the bacteria, which can be present in various water systems, including cooling towers. The primary cause is the legionella pneumophila bacteria, which thrive in warm water environments. The symptoms include high fever, chills, cough, muscle aches, and headaches. It can also lead to severe pneumonia and respiratory failure. Many deaths of members of the public have been recorded in several countries, and the cause is attributed to this disease. The reason is that legionella pneumonia bacteria can be airborne and transmitted to the public by a building with a contaminated cooling tower. In the most recent case in Melbourne (ABC-NEWS, 1st August 2024), there were 77 people with severe symptoms, most requiring hospitalisation and two deaths of a 90-year-old lady and a 54-year-old man.

It is, therefore, vital a rigorous maintenance regime for the cooling tower, involving the use of chemical treatment of condenser water, be adhered to. In most countries this is covered by a mandatory code.

GEOTHERMAL AIR CONDITIONING

To address the air-cooled limitation, geothermal energy has come back into vogue. It was popular 25 years ago, and I was involved with several applications of geothermal air conditioning systems. Geothermal air conditioning is classified as 'renewable' energy, and there are special grants or tax deductions associated with using this technology in many countries, including Canada.

As a clarification, there are two aspects associated with geothermal and geo-exchange that need to be distinguished.

Ground Energy

Traditional geothermal energy is a form of renewable energy derived from heat deep in the earth's crust. Geothermal energy has been around for as long as the Earth has existed. "Geo" means earth, and "thermal" means heat. So, geothermal means earth-heat. Earth's geothermal gradient is 15° to 30°C/km within the crust. This heat originates from the planet's original formation and minerals' radioactive decay. In many countries, it is harnessed for various applications, including electricity generation.

Let us look at how electricity is generated from these renewable resources.

Types of geothermal plants include using steam directly from a geothermal reservoir to turn turbines or pulling high-pressure hot water from the ground, converting it to steam, and using it to drive turbines. In the binary cycle process, heat from geothermal water vaporises a secondary fluid with a lower boiling point, which then drives a turbine.

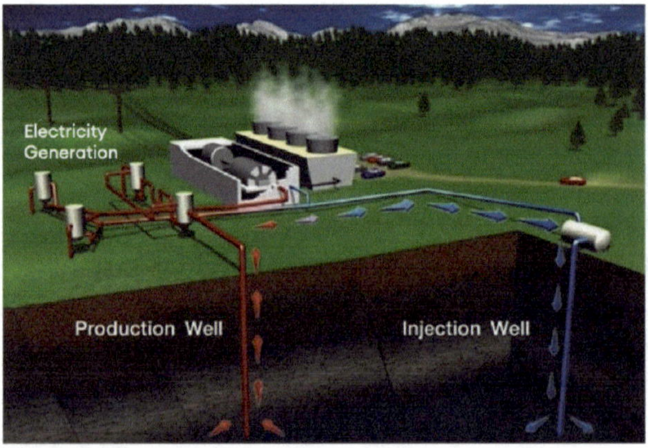

Geothermal energy's reliability and low environmental impact make it a valuable part of the renewable energy mix in these countries:

- **United States:** The U.S. is the largest producer of geothermal electricity in the world, *with plants* located in California, Nevada, Utah, and Hawaii.
- **Iceland:** Iceland is renowned for its extensive use of geothermal

energy, particularly for heating. Geothermal resources meet a large portion of the country's electricity and heating needs.

- **New Zealand:** New Zealand has a well-established geothermal industry with vast geothermal fields in Wairakei, Kawerau, and Ngāwhā.
- **Mexico:** Mexico is another significant producer of geothermal energy, *with major geothermal fields, including* Cerro Prieto and Los Azufres.
- **Italy:** Italy is a pioneer in geothermal energy development, with the world's first geothermal power plant built in Larderello in 1911.
- **Indonesia:** Due to its location on the Pacific Ring of Fire, Indonesia has vast geothermal potential and is one of the fastest-growing producers of geothermal energy.
- **Philippines:** The Philippines is a *major* producer of geothermal energy contributing significantly to the country's electricity supply.
- **Kenya:** Kenya is rapidly expanding its geothermal capacity and is a leading producer in Africa.
- **Turkey:** Turkey has been investing heavily in geothermal energy and has a growing number of geothermal plants.

Besides electricity generation, geothermal energy is also used for direct heating (district heating systems, greenhouse heating, aquaculture ponds) and in various industrial applications.

Geo-exchange (also often referred to as geothermal) Heating and Cooling

It is great to see the resurgence of the geo-exchange (geothermal) technology that has been around for many decades.

Geothermal - more appropriately termed Geo-exchange – technology uses the ground as a heat source in winter or a heat sink during summer conditions. This eliminates the use of cooling towers or boilers. This is because the ground temperature below around 6 metres remains constant throughout the year in most parts of the world (Australia – it is around 15 -170 C).

The geo-exchange principle involves circulating water through a network of polyethylene piping in ground bores around 100 metres deep and utilising heat pump (reverse-cycle) packaged specially designed DX units commonly termed ground source heat pumps (GSHP).

How does it work?

I am excited to share my lecture notes and details of what is involved with this technology which has been acknowledged as a form of renewable energy.

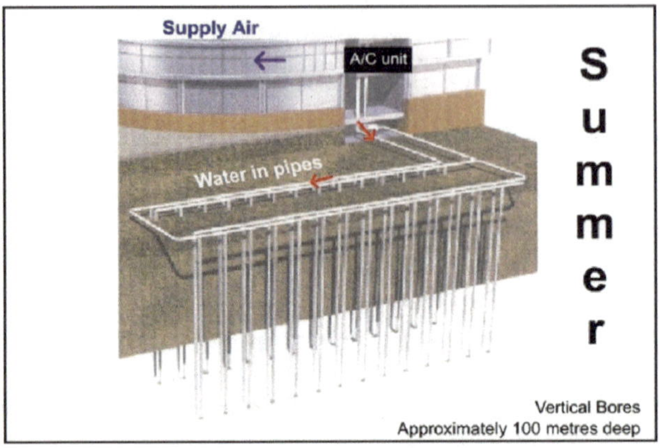

Lecture Notes explaining geo-exchange principle – ground as a heat sink.

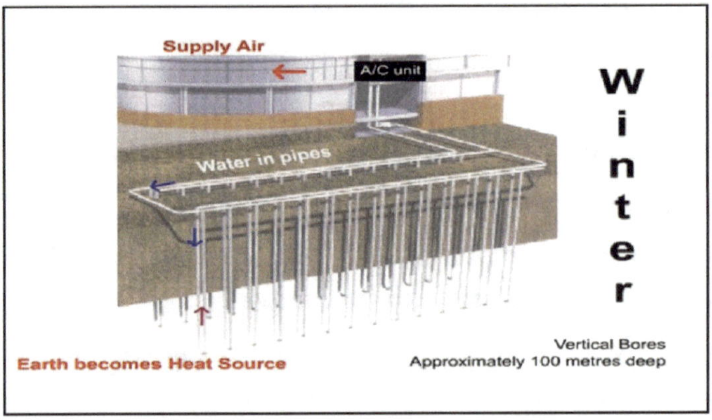

Lecture Notes explaining geo-exchange principle – ground as a heat source.

There are various loop options and each one needs to be evaluated with regards to capacity and cost effectiveness.

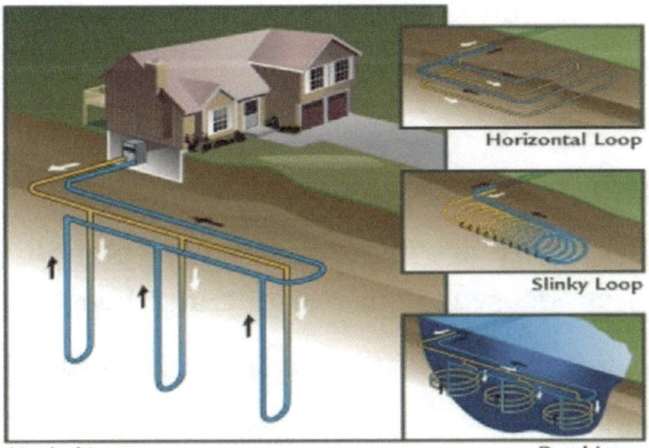

Different types of loops – Geothermal Air Conditioning

Pertinent information

- Capacity – between 4.5 and 6.5 kWr per 100 M bore depending on soil conditions.
- Test bores (suggest 2 off) need to be carried out to ascertain likely bore depth and water table level location.
- Capacity to be total heat rejected and needs to cater for peak loads in respective zones.
- Tests available to verify capacity and spacing.
- Building height limited to 6 levels – due to water pressures in the pipework.
- Extremely important to accurately document bore hole locations.
- Overground pipework may require insulation depending on location.

Advantages:

- Can be set up for extremely efficient operation.
- Can be used to heat and cool.
- Classified as renewable energy.
- Clean operation. No combustion on site.

- No ongoing chemical water treatment involved as otherwise required for cooling towers.
- Long Life (25+ years for a closed loop ground loop).
- Low maintenance of ground source heat pump units.
- The life expectancy of ground source heat pump units is around 20-25 years as opposed to normal split units being around 15 years.
- Minimal maintenance is associated with the ground loop.
- No noisy outdoor units like cooling towers.

Disadvantages:

- Capital cost intensive to install. Pay back vary but in most cases is less than 10 years.
- Not an easy solution for retrofits, due to requirement of land for boreholes.
- Not a cost-effective solution, where land is at a premium – e.g., CBD locations.
- One-third or more of operating energy required from electricity which is typically generated by combustion of fossil fuel.
- Some ground loop types lower water table and often have high maintenance expense.

My Geo-exchange Experience.

I was involved with many installations in Australia some 30 years ago. My experience commenced with Devine Erby Mazlin, an architectural firm inviting me to do a presentation on geo-exchange technology for the proposed Macquarie University's administration building. I showed a video that, unfortunately, did not explain the technology. It was essentially a two-minute-long marketing video prepared by a contractor. I had to prepare in a hurry a detailed presentation on not only how the technology works but a full financial analysis for this proposed Administration Building demonstrating a payback of less than 10 years. The first step, once Macquarie University agreed to proceed, was to carry out test bores to establish the depth and the presence of the water table. The depth confirmed was 96 meters, and 56 bores were required. The project was completed on time and within the allocated budget, as the saying goes. I continued to monitor the performance and was pleased to see that my payback prediction was too conservative – *they achieved payback within 7 years*. That was the beginning of a wave of other projects, including the Western Sydney Record Centre with 75 bores and the Finnish Embassy in Canberra with 26 bores, to name a few. Each one achieved payback well within the predicted timeframes – nominally less than 7 years

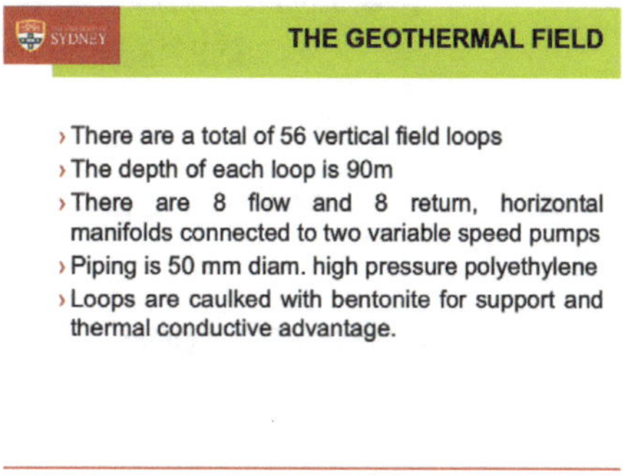

More recently, I have carried out feasibility studies of an application of geothermal air conditioning systems in Canada. The most interesting part of the feasibility study included using solar power to operate the pumps and the DX units associated with the geothermal technology. This would assist in reaching a net zero target.

Details of the geothermal option, with estimated payback of less than 6 years, for a building in Edmonton, Canada, carried out in 2022:

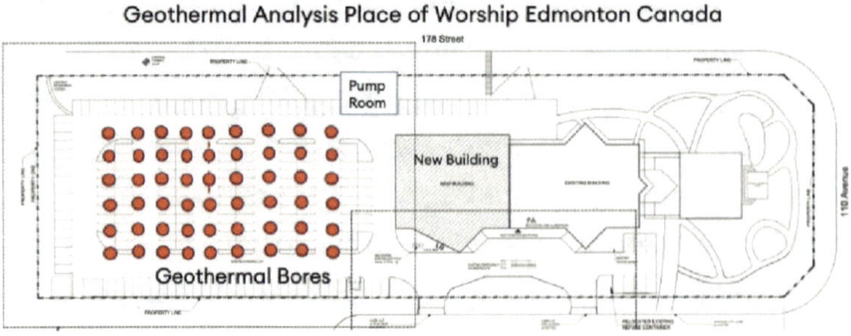

Overview of the site plan showing the proposed location of bores and the building involved.

Financial Analysis

Based on an area of 600 sqm, heat load for the new building = 174kWr = 54 bores

Cost for 54 bores = $315,000

Units + ducting = $367,500

Sub-total = $682,500

Construction incl. Pump Room = $28,500

Total = $711,000

Less government incentive = $125,000 @ $2,500 per ton

Net Investment required = $586,000

Conventional air-cooled system cost = $330,000

Net additional cost = $256,000

Savings= $46,500 per annum

Payback = 5.5 years.

Whilst this was a sustainable solution with the potential to achieve net zero, the geothermal option was not pursued due to reasons related to programming and the need for early handover.

After going through the distributed air conditioning systems, the next chapter concentrates on the various centralised air handling systems.

8

CENTRALISED AIR CONDITIONING SYSTEMS

GREEN STAR EXPERT ROLE

One Bligh Street is a signature office tower in Sydney's CBD that was completed in 2011 and set high standards for sustainability and innovation in high-rise development in Australia. The owners of this building, Dexus and Cbus, had made a commitment at the commencement of the project to achieve 6 Green Stars, as per the rating system developed by the Australian Green Building Council. This is the highest building sustainability rating equivalent to LEED Platinum. The builder was Grocon. The agreement between the owners and the builder was that a sum of $20 million would be paid to the builder once confirmation of achievement of this rating was received from an independent 'green star expert'.

The agreement named three 'green star experts' who they could appoint. I was appointed by the owners and the builder to oversee the progress of the rating during the construction and handover phases. In June 2011, I confirmed that Grocon had fulfilled the 6 Green Star requirements. This was my last major project, as a month later I retired from Norman Disney Young and joined the University of Sydney.

One Bligh Street remains an example of one of the environmentally sustainable buildings that has a combination of air conditioning systems. It has chilled beams in the perimeter zones, which also incorporate ventilated façades whilst the interior zone has variable air volume, primarily to cater for the requirements of the tenant, who had made a pre-commitment to be the anchor tenant prior to the design phase of the building. The building achieved a 6 Star Green Star Office Design V2 certified rating and continues to maintain a 5 Star energy rating as per the National Australian Building Energy Rating System (NABERS). Ten years on, One Bligh Street remains a global exemplar of sustainable tall building design, having been awarded the '10 Year Award of Excellence from the Council on Tall Buildings & Urban Habitat.

FAN COIL UNITS VERSUS AIR HANDLING UNITS

In this section, we will examine the air side of non-domestic buildings. The overall air conditioning systems for such applications fall into different brackets physically, technically, economically, and importantly with respect to their contribution to energy consumption and associated GHG emissions.

A centralised system is one that supports the heating and cooling needs of the entire building. These systems are consolidated units and typically use chilled and hot water as a cooling and heating medium and use extensive ductwork for air distribution. The advantages of the centralised system are that it offers better control and has greater load-management potential. The major disadvantage is that these are expensive to install and require trained and more sophisticated facility managers to operate and maintain.

Further explanation is furnished for each of the major centralised systems to understand better the engineering complexities and contributions of different types of air handling systems. Details are also included in recognition of the fact that some buildings incorporate a combination of multiple air conditioning system types.

Fan Coil Unit

In this arrangement shown below, Fan Coil Units (FCUs) are mounted in the ceiling spaces to serve the perimeter and interior zones of an office building. Each FCU has air filters, chilled water, and hot water coils. A separate fresh air system is required to meet code requirements.

FIGURE 35 FCUS IN CEILING SPACE WITH AN AHU PROVIDING FRESH AIR.

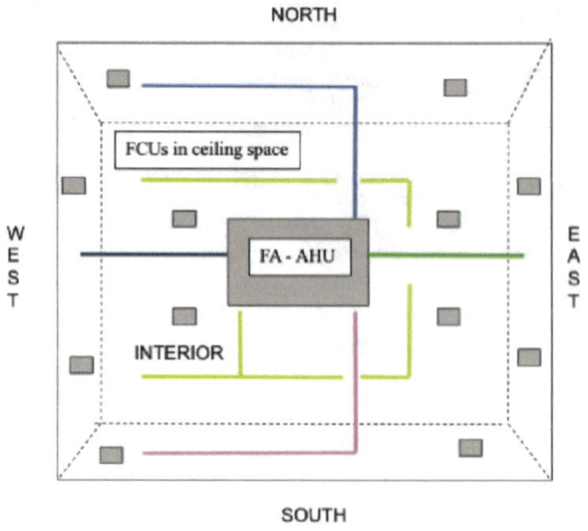

From experience, it appears that such applications continue to be very popular in the UK. This was evident during the review of the mechanical services of the Ismaili Centre Houston (ICH), which is under construction and due to be completed in 2025. The UK-based consultants had proposed 151 4-pipe fan coil units for most of ICH levels 1, 2, 3, 4, and 5 air-conditioning. As a reviewer of the mechanical services, I questioned this design as it would have created a facility manager's nightmare in having to maintain 151 FCUs. I demonstrated through thermal modelling and financial analysis that a fully ducted variable air volume system would be a more energy-efficient and economically sustainable alternative. This was accepted, and the design was changed. This meant a saving of 22 per cent in capital costs associated with the air conditioning budget and an 18 per cent reduction predicted related to operating costs.

CONSTANT AIR VOLUME

A constant air volume (CAV) unit with fresh air, filter and chilled and hot water coils is generally located in a plantroom. Constant volume of air - as calculated to meet the cooling and heating requirements of each zone – is supplied to each perimeter and interior zone. The supply air temperature is such that it will satisfy the zone with the highest cooling demand. The respective reheat coil maintains the required zone conditions for the rest of the zones as determined by its thermostat.

FIGURE 36 CENTRAL AIR HANDLING SYSTEM

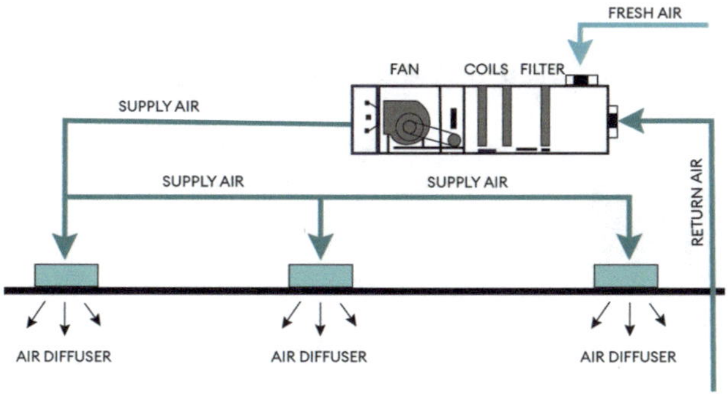

FIGURE 37 CAV WITH AHU AND REHEAT COILS FOR EACH PERIMETER ZONE.

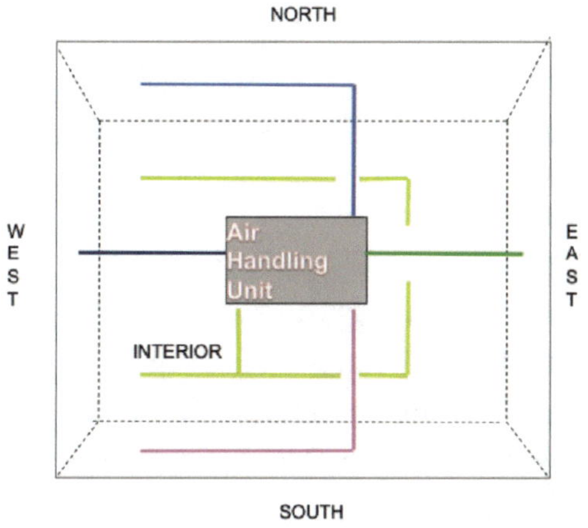

As can be seen in Figure 37, this process demonstrates all the markings of energy wastage. The CAV system's coefficient of performance (COP) is less than 2. Due to increases in oil prices, the energy crisis in the 1970s and 1980s resulted in upgrades and replacements of CAV systems to variable air volume (VAV).

VARIABLE AIR VOLUME

In the conventional or typical VAV arrangement, as shown below, conditioned air is supplied to multiple zones, each zone incorporating a VAV terminal.

FIGURE 38 VARIABLE AIR VOLUME (VAV)

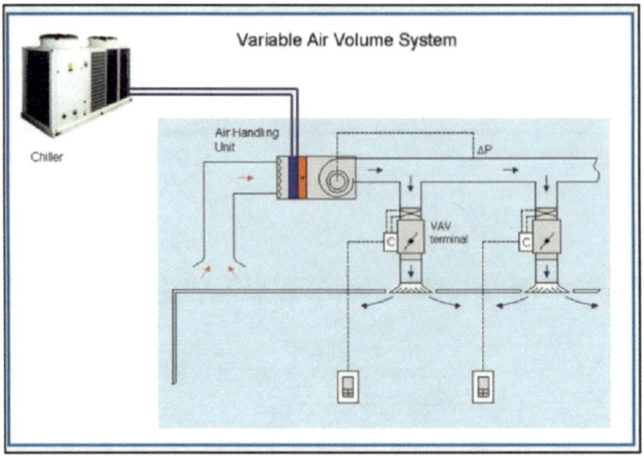

A zone thermostat controls the zone supply air via the respective VAV unit to meet the heating or cooling requirements of the zone, as shown in Figure 38. The VAV unit varies the zone supply air from 100 per cent to a minimum of 30 to 40 per cent depending on the zone requirements with respect to what the designers term air change effectiveness and associated fresh air distribution. The temperature of the supply air is determined via feedback from all the thermostats. Should the supply air temperature be lower than a zone requiring to satisfy the zone conditions, then the supply air is reheated by a VAV reheat coil. As the overall supply air quantity varies depending on zone requirements, a duct-mounted pressure sensor controls the speed of the supply fan. The earlier VAV systems utilised bypass dampers around the supply and return air ducts to divert the supply air into the return air stream when the zone demand decreased. This did not result in any appreciable energy savings. Subsequently, inlet guide vanes were introduced as part of the fan assembly so that as the zone demand decreased, the air drawn in by the supply fan was throttled with the closing of the inlet guide vanes. This would reduce the fan power by 'riding the fan curve'. The actuators for the inlet guide vanes required sufficient torque, which in most cases was provided by compressed air through a 'pneumatic' form of automatic control. It is interesting to note that there are still a few installations in buildings where pneumatics is used even when the overall air conditioning control system is direct digital control. More about this later when we discuss control systems.

Variable-speed drives vary the speed of the supply fan. Thus, at part-load operations, operating energy is substantially saved. The economiser cycle, involving the use of free cooling when outdoor air is favourable, is another popular energy conservation measure in VAV systems.

Enhancements to VAV operation strategies include demand-controlled ventilation (DCV), where the quantity of fresh air is regulated to meet fluctuating demands by using CO_2 sensors to reflect occupancy variations. This strategy, combined with the economiser cycle in a specific application, resulted in an energy reduction of 30 to 45 per cent on average daily energy consumption and 40 per cent on peak demand (Parameshwaran et al., 2010).

The system coefficient of performance (COP) is, on average, around 6.5 with the use of efficient chiller(s) and boiler(s).

Low-Temperature VAV

A more recent development with regards to the VAV system has been the lowering of supply air temperature from 15 to 17°C to around 11 to 13°C. This is referred to as low temperature (LTVAV). Whilst this has resulted in life cycle cost (LCC) savings due to a smaller air handling unit and ducting together with fewer outlets because of reduced air quantity, the downside has been cold drafts and condensing (dew formation) at the outlet because of temperatures being below the dewpoint of air within the occupied zone at times. Careful design and operation strategies via a good control system can overcome these drawbacks in LTVAV.

UNDERFLOOR AIR DISTRIBUTION (UFAD)

Over the past two decades, the underfloor air distribution (UFAD) system has received increasing attention fundamentally due to thermal stratification and energy-saving potential over conventional mixed air conditioning systems, like VAV.

UFAD systems, based on the delivery of conditioned air from under floor level, at temperatures slightly below the mean air temperature within the occupied zone, rely on natural convective processes to transport that air from floor to ceiling, where it returns to the air handling unit. The UFAD system ensures good ventilation effectiveness by delivering conditioned ventilation air directly into the occupied zone.

The UFAD systems have a significant impact on room air stratification and thermal comfort in the occupied zones, and hence, a comprehensive understanding of the airflow patterns, relative humidity, and contaminant particle distribution. (Aghakhani et al., 2012).

FIGURE 39 AIRFLOW PATTERNS IN UFAD

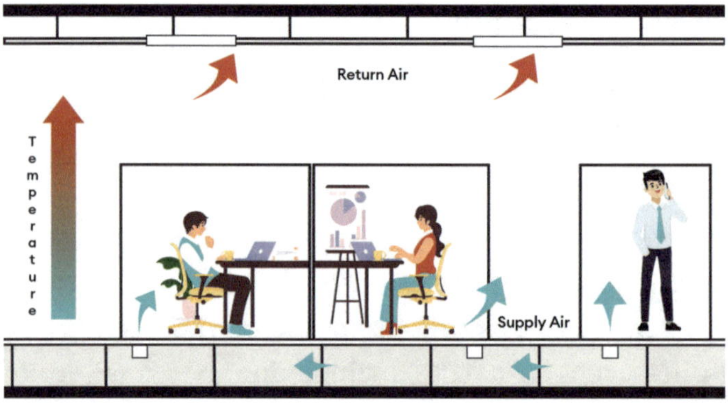

UFAD systems, with a common underfloor plenum for the interior zone, provide ultimate flexibility in terms of locating floor air outlets to suit a layout involving office workers The uniformity of thermal conditions within the interior zone is achieved by having the right air balancing carried out to meet the zone requirements. From experience gained whilst incorporating a UFD arrangement in the IEQ Laboratory at the University of Sydney, I can add that there needs to be an inclusion of individual control within each outlet of floor-mounted diffusers that would enable not only determining the direction of the airflow but also an ability to turn down (marginally) the air quantity.

The main challenge with a UFAD system was the ability to address the varying conditions in the perimeter zones. That often increased the investment costs with use of separate air handling systems for each of the perimeter areas. Apart from being expensive, they were difficult to accommodate architecturally, requiring additional air riser shafts at the perimeter or equipment, such as fan coils installed under the floor, where they could cause noise problems and were difficult to maintain (Taylor, 2016).

Significant contributors to achieving energy efficiency in a UFAD system are power consumption associated with the fans and power consumption associated with a chiller(s) and chilled water pump(s). The energy associated with the fan is constant, and the fact that UFAD requires a higher air quantity means there are no operational energy savings. However, the fact that chilled water temperature is higher due to the supply air being around 18–20°C, there are savings in energy in the provision of chilled water.

Other studies have shown that UFAD significantly saves energy compared to ceiling-based systems in high-ceiling building types and provides satisfactory comfort conditions for the occupants. Therefore, for high-ceiling buildings, such as places of worship, showrooms, hotel lobbies, atriums, and the like, the use of UFAD has significant potential to save energy and increase indoor air quality.

UFAD system has been prevalent in Australia, Germany, Switzerland, Netherlands, Japan, Canada and North America (Lee et al., 2012; Bauman, 2003). It is shown that a well-designed UFAD system improved the ventilation efficiency and IAQ and made it easy to control the local thermal environment, and thereby increasing its popularity. As an additional point, UFAD configuration also enables the incorporation of personalised comfort systems (PCS) through air supply via outlets in workstations, as an example.

Whilst not a strict UFAD, I was involved with the largest displacement ventilation (DV) system in Australia. The air supply and stratification from DV is identical to UFAD. This was a venue for the Sydney 2000 Olympics, comprising an under-seat air conditioning system for 20,000 seats for the main indoor arena. It was proven that limiting air conditioning to occupant head height enabled the venue to save a significant amount of energy, with the payback for the additional cost of the seat air conditioning system being 9.3 years. The venue is presently being used as a premium entertainment facility.

DATA CENTRE

A Data Centre is a facility used to house computer systems and associated components, such as telecommunications and storage systems. It generally includes redundant or backup power supplies, redundant data communications connections, environmental controls (e.g., air conditioning, fire suppression) and security devices.

Large data centres are industrial-scale operations that use as much electricity as a small town and sometimes produce significant amounts of air pollution in the form of diesel exhaust.

Electrical Engineering Infrastructure Design

Electrical Engineering infrastructure design is focused on designing electrical configurations that accommodate various availability and reliability requirements and data centre sizes. Aspects may include utility service planning; distribution, switching and bypass from power sources; uninterruptable power source (UPS) systems; and standby power.

Mechanical Engineering Infrastructure Design

Data Centres use the UFAD principle with conditioned air supplied through raised floors.

Mechanical engineering infrastructure design addresses mechanical systems involved in maintaining the interior environment of a data centre, such as HVAC; humidification and dehumidification equipment; pressurisation; and so on. The design process generally aims at saving space and costs, while ensuring business and reliability objectives are met as well as achieving PUE (equivalent of COP) and environmental requirements.

Computer Room Air Conditioning

Computer Room Air Conditioning (CRAC) units are precision cooling systems and can precisely control the humidity levels in the data centre. Most server vendors allow a relative humidity of 50 per cent, going up to a maximum of 60 per cent RH, and a minimum of 40 per cent RH.

Over-sized CRAC units can cause condensation or static discharges. Too much humidity causes condensation, while humidity lower than 30 per cent RH raises the possibility of static discharges, both of which could be detrimental for server equipment.

Hot/Cold Aisle Containment

Containment of hot/cold aisles and ducting hot air from cabinets are intended to prevent cool/exhaust air mixing within server rooms. Generally, rows of cabinets face each other so that cool air can reach the equipment air intakes at the room's set temperature point.

Containment can also be implemented by physically separating the hot and cold aisles using blanking panels, PVC curtains, or hard panel boards. Containment strategies differ based on various factors, including server tolerance, ambient temperature requirements, and leakage from data centres.

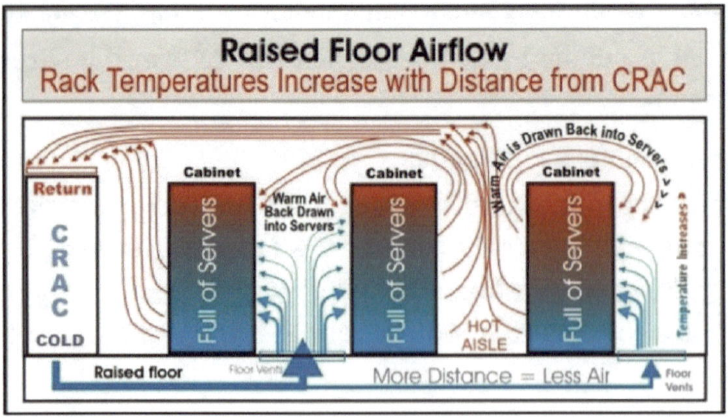

CRAC Unit Arrangement

Case Study

Woolworths, a well-known supermarket chain in Australia, wanted the most efficient data centre with a power usage effectiveness (PUE) of less than 1.6. PUE is total power, including HVAC and IT equipment, divided by IT power. Options evaluated included hot and cold aisle arrangement, chimney cabinets, air curtains, and finally, a custom-built AHU with a ducted system using outside air cooling when the ambient conditions were suitable.

For each option, computational fluid dynamic (CFD) software was used to carry out the simulations.

Over 25 CFD evaluations were carried out in association with Professor John Kent, University of Sydney. Incidently, John had also provided similar service for analysis of the Sydney Aquatic Centre prior to Sydney 2000 Olympics. Sydney Aquatic Centre ended up with three AC systems - one maintaing FINA requirement temperatures around the pool, one for spectators (underseat arrangement) and one for the facade.

The output sample is shown below:

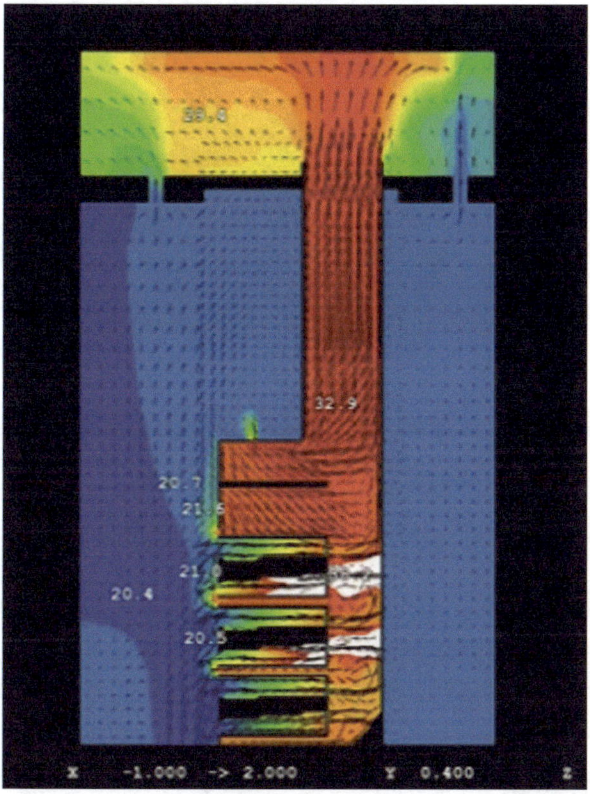

Chimney Cabinet

The final design involved a set of custom-designed interconnected air handling units that could use outside air 'free' cooling when the temperature and humidity levels were within the permissible limits. Being a 24-hour operation, there were many occasions when 'free' cooling could be utilised.

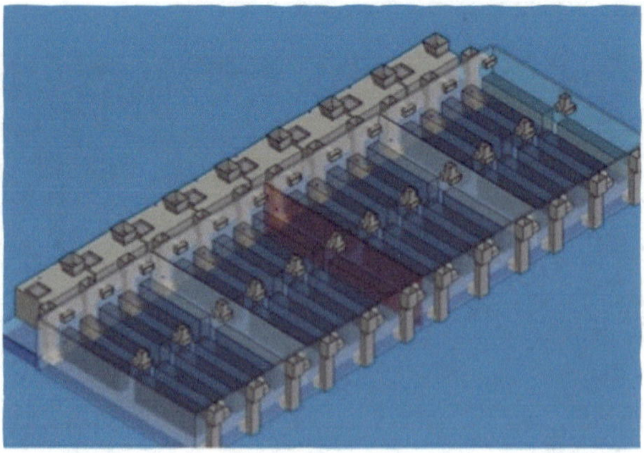

Overhead and underfloor conditioned air supply – Selected Option

The selected system achieved a PUE of 1.53. At last check, it is still one of the better-performing Data Centres in Sydney, Australia.

CHILLED BEAMS

Let us change gear to talk about a system that is unique where unlike the systems we have gone through, a Chilled Beam (CB) does not have fan. It employs radiant and convective cooling principles.

In the Australian commercial buildings sector, chilled beams have been increasing in popularity since the turn of the century largely due to the prevailing market perception of their energy efficiency accruing from not having to transport large volumes of conditioned air around the building, but instead, just small volumes of chilled water. This logic is encapsulated by comparisons of the thermal properties of air and water. The specific heat capacity of water is 4.187 kJ/kg K, and its density is 1000 kg/m3, whereas the specific heat capacity of air is 1.005 kJ/kg K, and its density is 1.29 kg/m3. Therefore, to transport 1.29 kJ of energy requires 1000 litres of air compared to just 0.3 litres of water. The pumping energy for circulating water amounts to 38 per cent of the fan energy required to circulate air for 1.29 kJ. This, combined with space efficiency and quiet operation, is driving the popularity of chilled beam systems in many 'green building' developments.

FIGURE 40 CHILLED BEAM SYSTEMS - PASSIVE AND ACTIVE (TRANE)

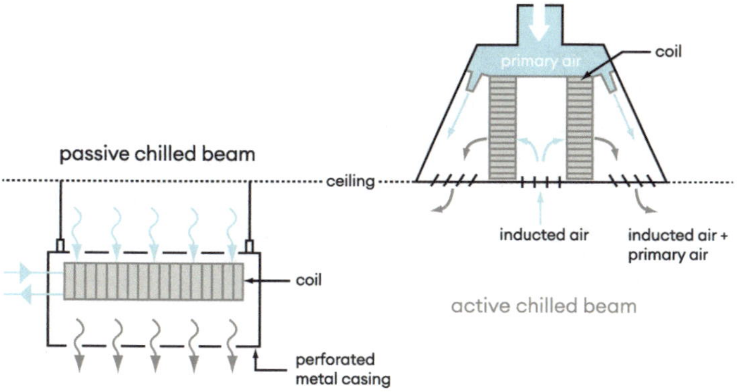

Chilled beams are devices that primarily use convection to cool indoor spaces. This means there are no fans within the unit, unlike traditional chilled water fan coil units. Chilled water is piped to each beam, effectively a heat exchanger, which is either integrated into a standard suspended ceiling system or suspended a short distance from the room's ceiling.

There are two types of chilled beams, as shown in Figure 40:

- Active Chilled Beams (ACB), where fresh air, provided through nozzles, induces room air, thereby increasing the heat exchange capacity. Active chilled beam systems are essentially adaptations of the floor and ceiling-mounted induction units used in the mid-1900s. Like the older induction units, coils were included to further temper-induced air.
- Passive Chilled Beams (PCB) may have radiant exchange around 30 to 40 per cent, and convection around 60 to 70 per cent, depending on the ceiling arrangement. Conditioned (de-humified) fresh air is supplied independently of the unit.

Generally, perimeter zones of a building requiring higher cooling capacities are served by ACBs, whilst the interior (centre) zones employ PCBs. A typical arrangement is shown in Figure 41.

FIGURE 41 A TYPICAL ARRANGEMENT – ACBS IN THE PERIMETER AND PCBS IN THE INTERIOR.

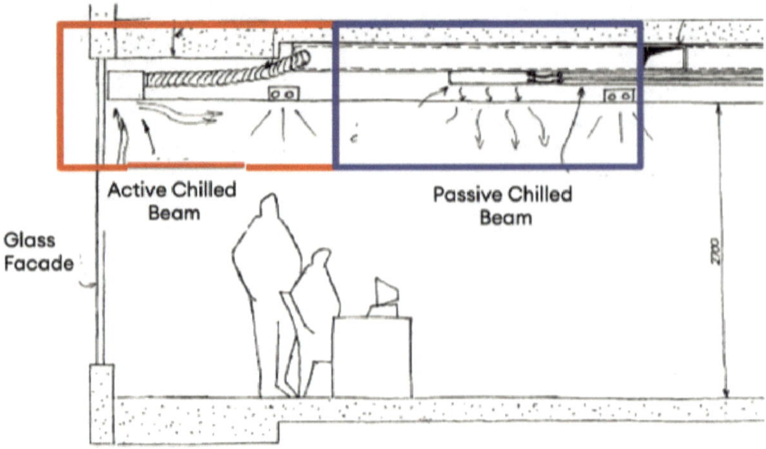

Advantages of chilled beams include less ceiling space taken up, no fan required, and a much quieter operation. I was involved in one of the first CB systems, and the complaint was that it was too quiet. Hence, a background 'white air noise' system was implemented.

However, restrictions and qualifications need to be considered when determining the suitability for specific applications. Chilled beam systems are suitable for use when the following conditions exist:

+ They are not mounted more than 5 m above the floor. This is to maintain the required rate of effective convective airflow,
+ The tightness of the building envelope is adequate to prevent excessive moisture ingress (i.e., avoid condensation on the CB's heat exchanger).
+ Moisture gains due to occupancy and/or processes are moderate to avoid condensation on the CB's heat exchanger.
+ Dew point temperature remains below the temperature of the chilled water supply also to prevent condensation on the CB's heat exchanger.
+ Passive Chilled Beams are not used in areas where considerable or

widely variable air velocities are expected.

The total cooling capacity of an ACB or a PCB is a combination of the airside and waterside cooling capacities. For ACBs, the airside cooling capacity is provided by primary air, and the waterside cooling capacity equals the cooling capacity of the cooling coil.

The waterside cooling capacity, which is the chilled beam coil cooling capacity, can be computed with the water flow energy balance under the steady-state condition in the coil, based on no condensation on the cooling coil surface.

Limitations of Chilled Beam Systems

Active chilled beams (ACB) have been used for more than 30 years, but there appears to be limited data related to these systems' energy savings potential. In various studies carried out, the following have been identified as potential limitations of the chilled beam systems:

- Chilled beams are unable to effectively condition high-occupancy load spaces or other spaces with high latent heat gains due to condensation risks. This limitation includes buildings with high infiltration rates, especially older buildings.
- There are no internationally recognised standard certification programs for rating the capacity and performance of chilled beams or radiant panels.
- The fact that induced secondary air associated with ACB is not filtered and could create long-term unhealthy conditions without proper system maintenance.
- The owner and design team need to work together to assure adequate operating staff training since chilled beam systems are not as common as variable air volume systems.

Chilled beams can save energy in different ways. First, the ventilation load is decoupled from the space sensible load, handling space cooling and outside air requirements without increasing the airflow rate. Second, the use of higher chilled water temperatures (around 17°C) than conventional HVAC systems (around 7°C) leads to higher chiller efficiency.

Comparisons of ACB's energy performance with conventional HVAC systems showed that the impact varied considerably depending on the specific project and the climate zone, but energy savings of 12 to 18 per cent could be achieved (Kurt et al., 2007).

The chilled beam system coefficient of performance (COP) is estimated in overall terms to be around 6.5.

ENERGY SAVING

So how can the energy consumption associated with these types of distributed and central systems be minimised?

There are four ways:

One, it is important to ensure that the cooling or heating equipment is operated in line with the strategy developed by the system designer and detailed in the sequence of operation, generally included in the Building Operating Manual.

Two, by ensuring that the items required to run are brought on only when necessary and only operate for the appropriate period as per the building's occupancy schedules.

Three, the largest source of energy consumption is when heating and cooling are done simultaneously. Systems such as VAV need to be set up correctly with resetting of supply air temperature.

Four, heat reclaim, economiser cycles, and demand-control ventilation facilities must be utilised where incorporated. For buildings with Building Management and Control Systems (BMCS), sophisticated software programs can optimise the energy efficiencies of the HVAC systems. This is discussed in depth in Chapter 10.

Compared to all of the above, significant energy can be saved by adopting best practice. This includes having suitably trained personnel as facility managers combined with ongoing training.

Special Case Study – Ismaili Centre Lisbon Air Conditioning

One of the most challenging yet rewarding projects of my career was designing the air conditioning system for the Ismaili Centre in Lisbon.

When the Centre was completed in 1998, the entire building was air-conditioned except for the Prayer Hall. The architect had decided that natural ventilation, facilitated by operable windows, would provide the necessary comfort. However, this approach proved ineffective, as it couldn't accommodate the cooling needs of the large number of attendees. After a year of operation, four freestanding packaged AC units were installed at the rear of the Prayer Hall as a temporary solution, but the setup was far from ideal. Despite being intended as a stopgap, this arrangement remained in place for 24 years.

Over the years, 11 designs were submitted to meet the permanent air conditioning solution. However, none gained approval due to their failure to meet strict aesthetic and structural criteria. In 2013, I was invited to propose a design. This time, it was accepted. The design adhered to the architectural and structural requirements. Air handling units were installed in adjacent areas of the building, and innovative, long-throw TROX diffusers (capable of reaching distances of up to 25 meters) were camouflaged above the Hall's entry points. Since this configuration had never been used before, I collaborated with Adrianus Hanzal, a researcher at the University of Sydney's Mechanical Engineering School, to carry out detailed computational fluid dynamics modelling. The design was further validated through a mock-up in Lisbon, which confirmed its effectiveness.

It was a privilege to operate the system during the peak gathering of Ismailis in July 2019 for the Diamond Jubilee celebration of His Highness the Aga Khan. The Prayer Hall now provides a comfortable environment for its attendees, many of whom remain unaware that the space is air-conditioned as there is no visible AC equipment.

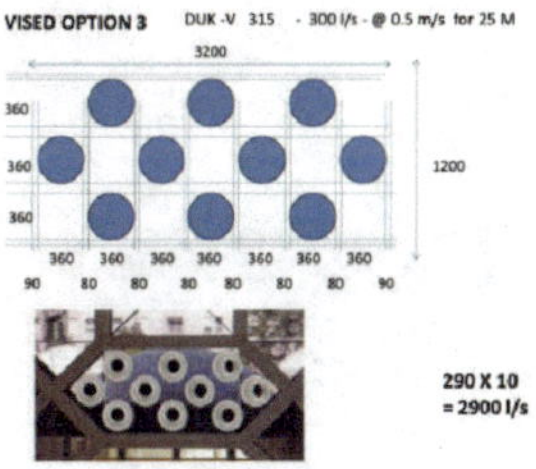

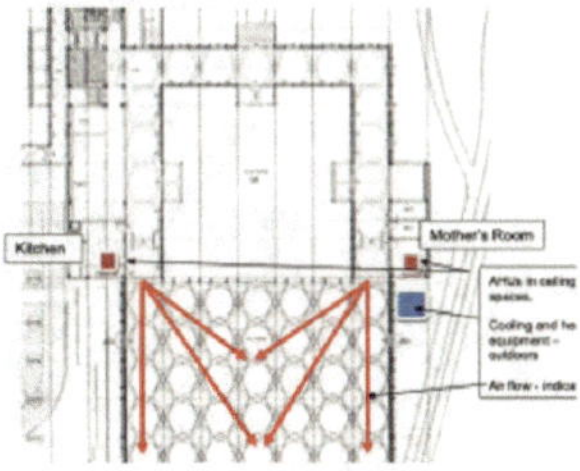

9

COMMERCIAL BUILDING'S CENTRAL PLANT

CHILLER THE ENERGY GUZZLER!

A chiller is essentially a large refrigerator in its simplest form. It produces chilled water using the refrigeration cycle principle, which, as you will recall, uses a refrigerant to transfer energy. That is why a chiller has similar components: a compressor (energy guzzler), an evaporator that cools the water, and a condenser that releases the heat—either to the outside (air-cooled) or via a cooling tower (water-cooled).

During the selection process, there is generally a detailed financial as well as performance-related analysis that is required. It looks at the part-load operation of the machine since the chiller's efficiency drops markedly at low cooling demand situations. In most offices, the cooling demand varies depending on many factors, including the different times of the year or the day and number of occupants in the building. For example, the cooling requirement normally builds up as office workers arrive at their workplace from 7.00 am to 8.30 am. It may be low initially and build up gradually. In most well-designed buildings, there is a low-load or 'swing chiller' (generally half the cooling capacity of the larger chillers) to cater for those circumstances when the cooling load increases from low to high loads and subsequently when it decreases from high to low loads.

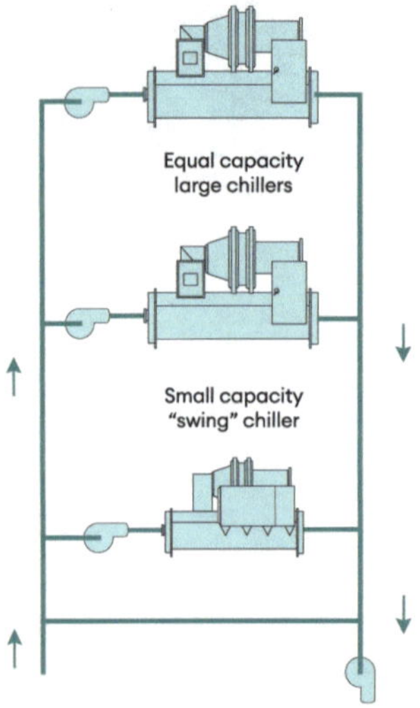

The 'swing chiller' is used in stages to optimise the performance of each chiller. The sequence is shown (for load increasing), with two equal-sized larger chillers and a smaller 'swing chiller'.

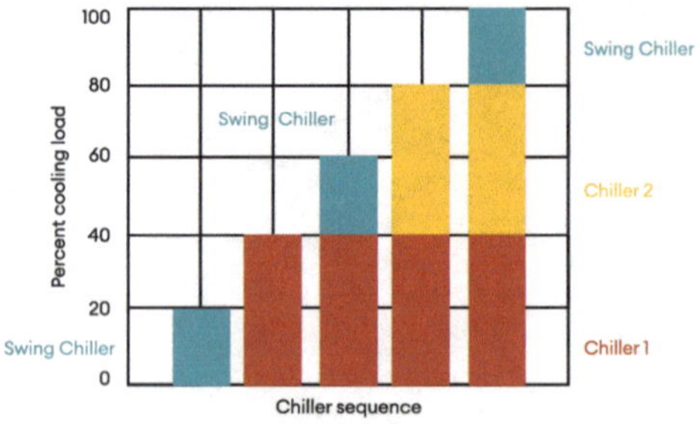

CENTRAL COOLING AND HEATING EQUIPMENT

The air handling systems covered in the previous chapter require heating and cooling from a central location within a building. These are generally housed in a central plantroom. Let us look at key items of equipment utilised in commercial applications that are essential and contribute to energy consumption and GHG emissions.

CHILLERS IN COMMERCIAL BUILDINGS

A chiller is the single item of the air conditioning system in a commercial building that is responsible for a significant proportion of the electrical energy consumption. Cooling equipment in a high-rise building or a hospital, for example, can be responsible for around 10-15 per cent of the electricity consumption.

The choice of chiller type depends on factors like the size of the building, available utilities, cooling load, energy efficiency, and budget constraints. It's essential to select the right type of chiller to meet the specific cooling needs of a building while also considering long-term operating costs and environmental impact.

Chiller configurations:

Types of chillers depend on whether heat rejection is to air or water.

Air-Cooled Chillers: These chillers use air to remove heat from the condenser, and they are often located outdoors. Air-cooled chillers are typically used in smaller to medium-sized buildings with limited or expensive water availability. They are relatively easy to install and maintain.

Water-Cooled Chillers: Water-cooled chillers use a condenser water source, such as a cooling tower or a well, to dissipate heat. The famous

Sydney Opera House uses the Sydney Harbour water for this purpose. Water-cooled chillers are more energy efficient than air-cooled chillers and are commonly used in larger commercial, institutional, and industrial buildings.

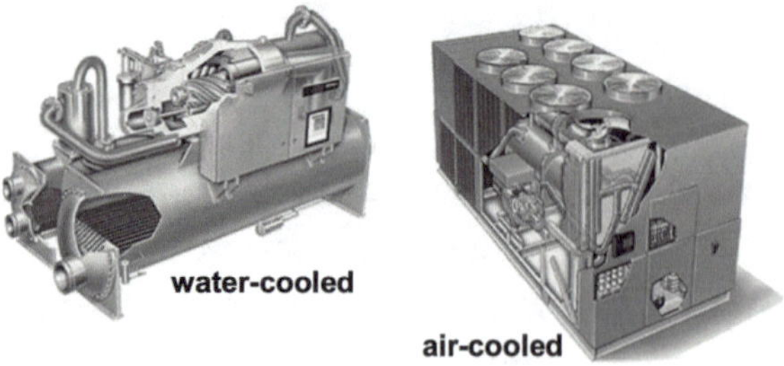

Chiller Plantroom

Air cooled chillers are located on the roof. Water cooled chillers are mainly located in plantroom.

Chillers in Plantroom

Refrigerant Detector in Chiller Plantroom

Chilled & Condenser Water Pumps

Chillers have a life span of around 25 to 30 years. Architects need to design the building to enable associated maintenance of chillers, including tube-cleaning of the evaporator and condenser coils plus eventual replacement of the machine.

Chiller Layout Enabling Tube Cleaning

For a place of worship in Vancouver, there was no provision made for the removal of an aging chiller that incidentally was leaking refrigerant R12 in the plantroom, which also happened to be the return air chamber for the air handling system that served the main prayer hall. The location of the replacement chiller ended up in the loading area with expensive additional chilled water flow and return piping.

Types of chillers

These are dependent on the type of compressor involved.

Absorption Chillers: Absorption chillers use heat energy to drive the cooling process rather than mechanical compression. They were popular in buildings where waste heat is available, such as in co-generation or combined heat and power (CHP) systems. These chillers are less common than vapour compression chillers. The original versions had bromide crystallisation issues and as part of chiller upgrades for pharmaceutical firms like Merck Sharp, Dohme, and Astra Zeneca, NDY, whom I worked for, recommended replacements with standard centrifugal chillers.

Centrifugal Chillers: Centrifugal chillers use a rotating impeller to compress the refrigerant and are known for their high cooling capacity and efficiency. They are often used in large commercial and industrial applications.

absorption
water chiller

centrifugal
water chiller

Screw Chillers: Screw chillers use a screw compressor to compress the refrigerant. They are known for their efficiency and are used in all ranges of building sizes.

Scroll Chillers: Scroll chillers use two spiral-shaped scrolls to compress the refrigerant. They are commonly used in small to medium-sized buildings and are known for their quiet operation and reliability.

Reciprocating Chillers: These chillers use a piston and cylinder arrangement to compress the refrigerant. They are reliable and often used as' swing chillers' as they can operate reasonably efficiently at 20-25 per cent cooling loads. The chiller shown plays the 'swing chiller' role at Angel Place, a 30-story office tower in Sydney.

Refrigerants in Chillers

There have been significant developments in type of suitable refrigerant that needs to be employed which has the least impact on the environment. Chillers that used R404a now use either R407c (55% lower global warming potential - GWP) or R448a (67% lower GWP). Chillers that used R134a now come with R513a, which has a 55% lower GWP. One of the eco-friendly refrigerants I recommended for a chiller replacement project recently was R1234ze (with a GWP of 6) instead of R134a (GWP = 1430).

Chilled Water Reticulation

A typical chilled water reticulation is shown below.

FIGURE 42 CHILLED WATER RETICULATION

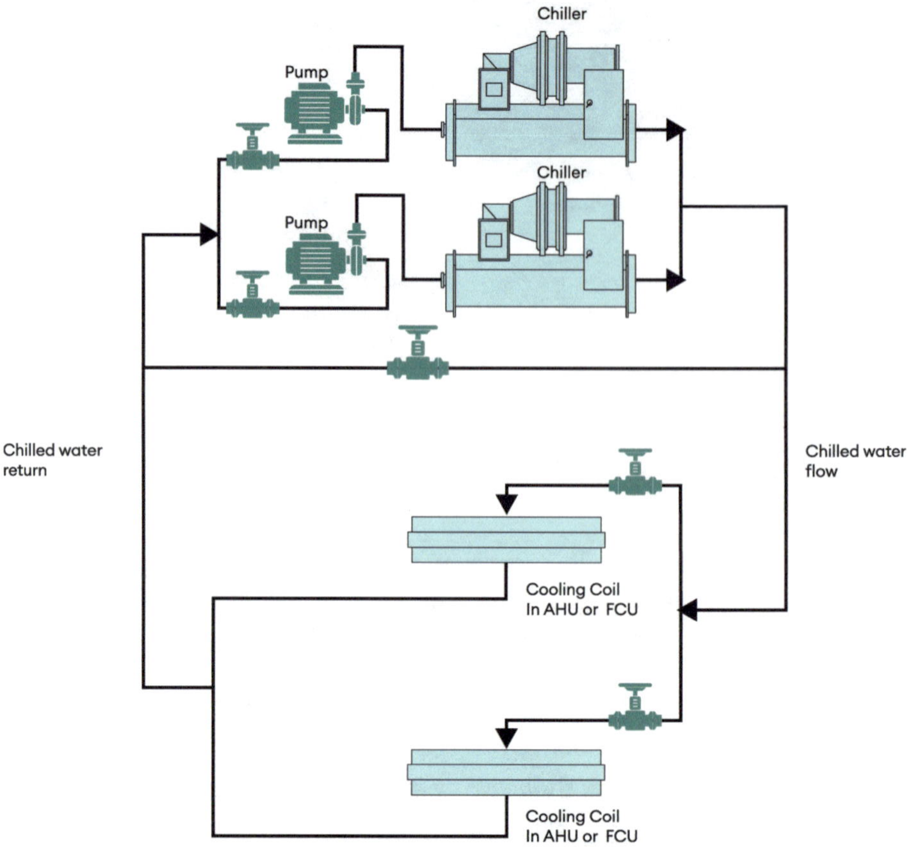

Chilled water pumps often incorporate variable-speed drives to reduce water flow during low-load operations, which contributes to significant energy savings.

BOILERS IN BUILDINGS

Boilers have come a long way!

Each type of boiler has its specific advantages and is chosen based on the building's heating requirements, fuel availability, and energy efficiency goals.

The types of hot water boilers commonly used in buildings include:

i. Fire-Tube Boiler

In this boiler, the hot gases from fuel combustion pass through tubes submerged in water. It is simple, easy to maintain, and relatively low-cost. Due to its compact design, it is used in smaller buildings.

ii. Water-Tube Boiler

In this boiler, water circulates in tubes heated externally by hot gases. The heat transference is efficient, and the boiler is utilised in larger buildings or facilities requiring higher pressures and capacities.

iii. Condensing Boiler

In this case, heat is extracted from exhaust gases that would otherwise be vented. It is increasingly getting popular in residential and commercial buildings due to high efficiency (up to 98%) and lower fuel costs.

iv. Gas-Fired Boiler

As the name suggests, natural gas or propane is employed as a fuel source. It is widely used in residential, commercial, and industrial buildings. The instantons heating residential units are very good – we have one. It is cost-effective and has cleaner combustion compared to oil-fired boilers.

v. Oil-fired boiler

Oil is the fuel source in this instance to heat water. It is common in areas without access to natural gas or reliable electric power.

vi. Electric Boilers

With the move to electrification, electric boilers are becoming more popular. It has the no combustion emissions, quiet operation and is compact in size.

vii. Biomass Boilers

It burns organic materials like wood pellets or chips to heat water.

Still used in buildings in remote places where there is no other energy source.

viii. Solar Boilers (Solar Thermal Systems)

Solar energy heats up the water. It is gaining popularity for used in green buildings or where renewable energy is a priority.

Hot Water Reticulation

Hot water is reticulated from the boiler to free-standing heating units distributed throughout the building. You might know these units as baseboard radiators. The control of heating through these units is often manual, which may also include the ability for different heat settings. Another arrangement is uitilisation of fan coil units with hot and chilled water.

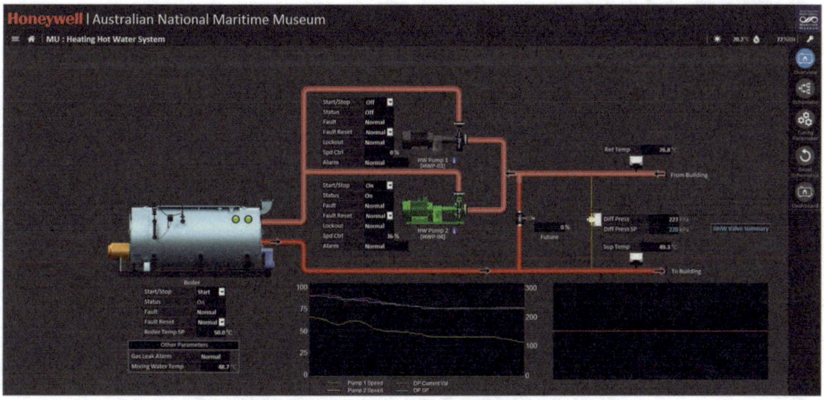

Hot water system at the National Australian Maritime Museum.

Hot water coils in fan coil and air handling units are examples of how heating is incorporated into the air conditioning systems. Heating coils may also be installed in ducts serving different zones. These are called reheat coils because they may reheat the supply air to meet the zone conditions.

We have covered the major hardware aspects of air conditioning systems. The next chapter is all about building management and control system (BMCS) – hardware, firmware, and software!

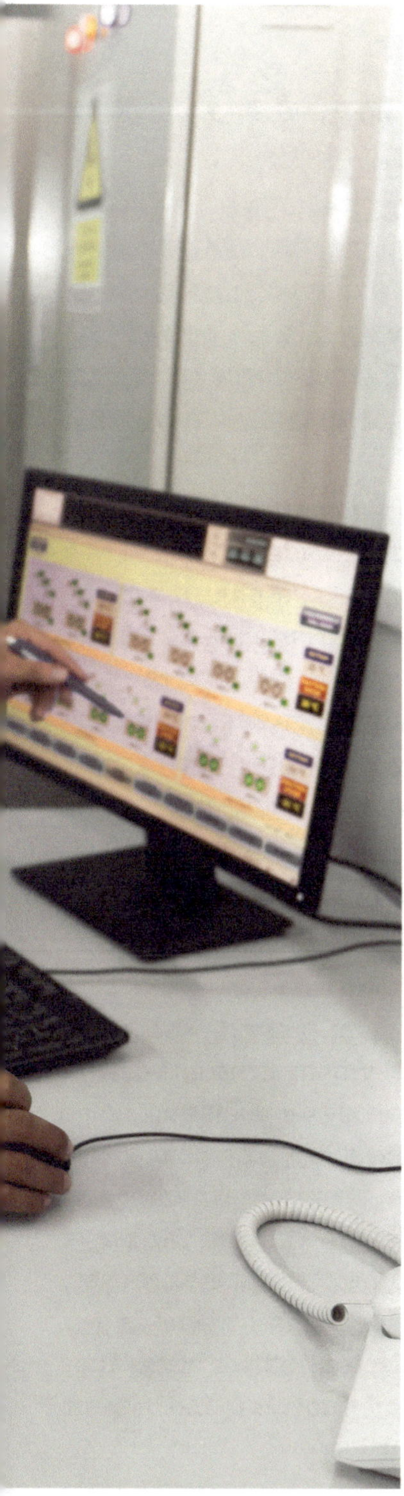

10

BUILDING MANAGEMENT AND CONTROL SYSTEMS

BMCS – MY PASSION

We now arrive at my favourite part of the book, where I will share my 50 years of knowledge and experience with BMCS.

When I came to Australia in 1972, as a fresh graduate, I went to the careers department at the University of Sydney to seek advice on employment opportunities. I got the best guidance from a career advisor whose name you won't believe was Mrs Guidance! She encouraged me to join Honeywell. Hence, I commenced my career in the building industry by securing employment with Honeywell in the building services controls division.

My first project at the firm was designing a control system for a hospital in an Australian outback town called Warialda. Although I was designing the system, when it came to visiting the hospital, it was my manager who went to Warialda instead of me. This was, as he explained, due to the remanent of the White Australia Policy – abolished the year prior in 1971 – still very much alive in the remote regions. I did experience what my manager was trying to tell me two years later when I went to Bourke – another country town – to investigate a control problem. The client who was to receive me at the airport did not turn up. In fact, he refused to meet me once he found out what the colour of my skin was. I am glad to say that those were the only times I experienced such situations in my fifty years.

At Honeywell I learnt all about controls from basics to emerging technologies. Once I was called out to the Seymour Centre, a drama theatre at the University of Sydney, to investigate a hissing noise coming from a thermostat mounted on the stage. The sound was from a compressed air-powered thermostat. To resolve the issue, it was relocated to the return air duct immediately - and off the stage! Those were the early days when Pneumatic Control systems were used. To be honest, I really enjoyed working on pneumatic systems as you could see what was involved instead of the 'electronic black boxes' that BMCS became. BMCS, using artificial intelligence now, is found in most modern and retrofitted buildings.

AN ESSENTIAL OPERATING TOOL - BMCS

A building management & control system (BMCS), also known as a building management system (BMS) or building automation system (BAS), is an electronic system designed to monitor, control, and manage the various mechanical, electrical, and electromechanical services within a building. These services typically include heating, ventilation, air conditioning (HVAC), lighting, power systems, fire systems, security, and other building systems.

Overall, a BMCS plays a crucial role in modern buildings' efficient, safe, and sustainable operation. In the monitoring mode, it displays selected data from various sensors and devices in real-time. It detects faults or abnormal conditions and generates alarms for maintenance or security personnel. It further improves security through integrated surveillance and access control.

As a tool, it controls and adjusts HVAC, lighting, and security operations based on pre-set conditions or user commands. It enhances occupant comfort by maintaining optimal indoor environmental conditions. It implements pre-programmed logic to automate functions like adjusting temperature and turning lights on/off. By performing these functions, the BMCS improves energy efficiency by optimising the operation of systems based on occupancy, time schedules, and external conditions. It can integrate with other building systems, such as fire alarms, elevators, and access control systems, for comprehensive management.

BMCS ARCHITECTURE

BMCS has a single interface for managing and controlling all building systems, often through a computer in the central control room or remotely via a web interface on devices such as mobile phones.

Data gathering (or smart) panels incorporate the input /output facilities and the computing capability to carry out all pre-programmed control and monitoring functions and tasks. They are in themselves able to operate as independent entities should the communication interface between them and the central supervisory console be lost,

BMCS can integrate with third-party software-based systems associated with lighting, chillers, boilers, fire, kitchen equipment, standby power generators, renewable energy systems, and security.

BMCS Selection

To choose the right chiller or a boiler, you need to know its capacity and type. Similarly, for a BMCS you need to obtain an input/output summary to determine the size, in terms of number of points, and hence cost.

Additional items to consider:

Ensure that:

a. the software offered is an open protocol. This means that you are not locked into the same supplier for any further additions to the system.

b. you obtain a 5-year maintenance service contract. In many instances, the supplier may offer a low purchase price but costly ongoing service, especially software upgrades.

c. BMCS operator training occurs in three stages: a two-week initial training period covering the basics, a second training session three months later, and a third at the end of the first year of operation covering how to make future additions to the system if required.

The basic architecture is shown in Figure 43.

FIGURE 43 BMCS

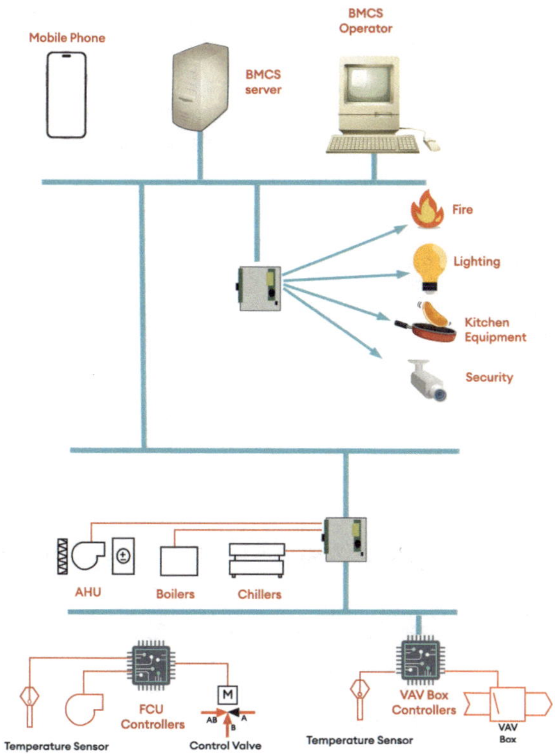

FUNDAMENTALS OF BMCS

Let us start with the basics.

Input / Output

BMCS takes inputs from sensors that measure temperature, humidity, airflow, water flow, energy and water consumption, carbon dioxide levels and other such variables. The system then controls the cooling and heating valves, dampers, and other devices to achieve outcomes in line with the software programming. The technical terms for these are 'analogue inputs' and 'analogue outputs'. The settings and adjustments to set points, range limits, and all interlocks are made through a computer console.

FIGURE 44 – ANALOGUE INPUT & OUTPUT

AI - Analogue Inputs = Process Variable (Sensors)

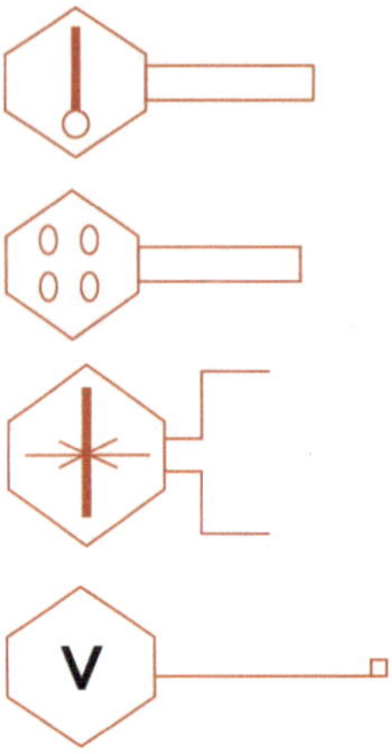

- Temperature - Passive & Loop Powered
  Resistance / 4 - 20ma / 0-10Vda
- Humidity - Loop Powered
  4 - 20ma / 0-10Vdc
- Differential Pressure - Loop Powered
  4 - 20ma / 0-10Vdc
- Velocity - Loop Powered
  4 - 20ma / 0-10Vdc

AI - Analogue Outputs - Modulating Control

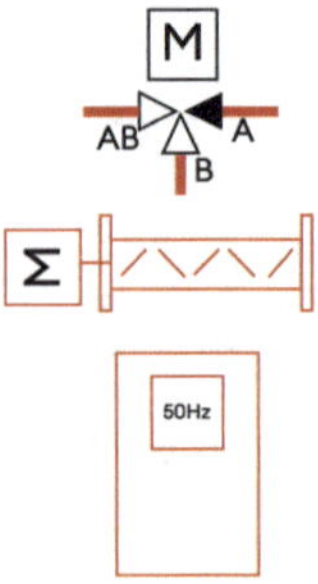

- Control Valve - 0-10Vdc
- Control Dampers - 0-10Vdc
- Variable Speed Drives (Inverters) - 0-10Vdc

FIGURE 45 – DIGITAL INPUT & OUTPUT

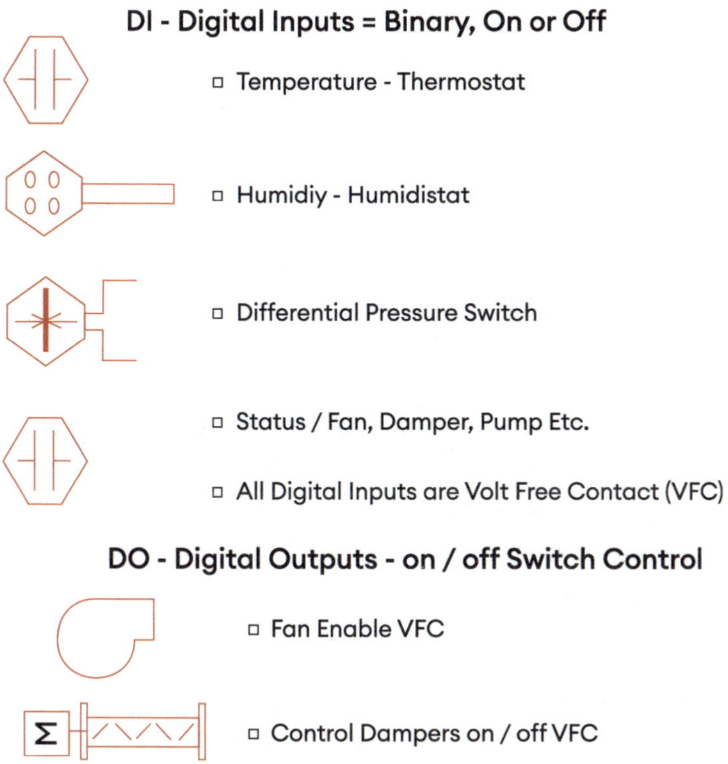

Direct Digital Controls

Inputs and outputs are connected to a control, a computerised module that can be programmed to carry out control loops. Control loops perform mathematical calculations that determine, based on present and past values of the measured or derived variables, how control instructions to other modules will change. The control loop compares the measured value (input from a sensor or combination of sensors) with the nominated set point value, which is the desired value. A control loop can provide three types of control: proportional (P), proportional and integral (PI), and proportional, integral, and derivative (PID).

PID Controls

P = Proportional - output is equal to error

I = Integral output - is equal to error plus the integral term minimising offset (difference between set-point and zone temperature).

D = Derivative - output is equal to error plus integral and derivative terms eliminating offset

For most HVAC applications, the proportional form of control is adequate. However, PI has merits and has become more fashionable. PID was developed for industrial applications and should remain for that. In my opinion, it is unnecessary unless, for example, it is critical to maintain chilled water flow and return temperatures like those requiring close temperature controls. One that comes to mind is the Tidbinbilla Space Centre, near Canberra, where the indoor temperature must be stable to ensure that the electronic clock, which is synchronised with other space centres, maintains its accuracy.

Trend Logs

Lastly, a high-level BMCS has excellent functions, including the ability to record data over selected times, like every 15 minutes, so that an analysis can be carried out. This is called trend logging. This helps to trend temperature and humidity conditions over a set time. Such a facility can investigate occupant complaints related to indoor conditions, where necessary.

BMCS Data Displays

Here are examples of some graphic displays from the Honeywell BMCS at the National Australian Maritime Museum.

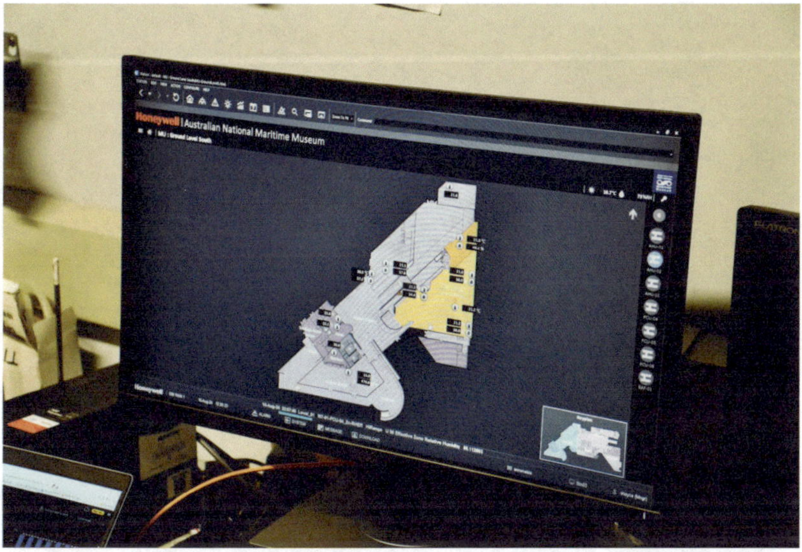

BMCS Console

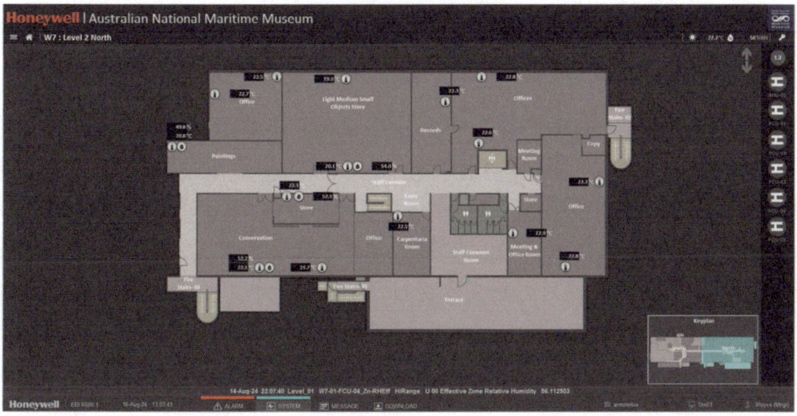

Zone Temperatures and Humidity Levels

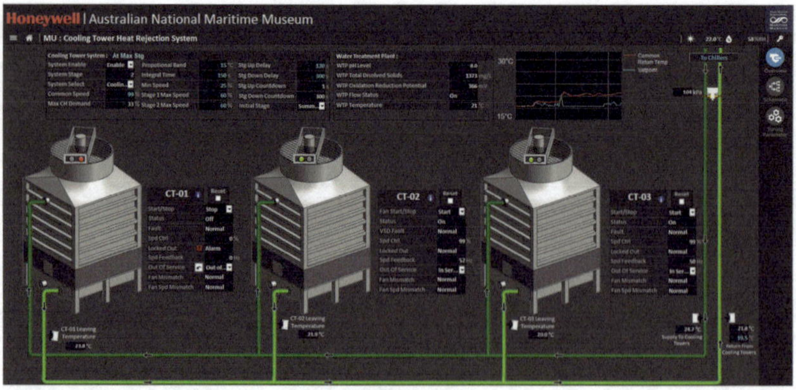

Cooling Towers -Status

BMCS Applications

An on/off manual switch can start or stop a mechanical or electrical system. For most buildings, lighting controls are via a series of manually operated switches in respective areas. Sensor-controlled lighting in toilets, car parks, and other spaces where lighting is required infrequently can make some energy-saving enhancements.

Generally, the temperature setpoint is set manually in a basic unitary and split AC system. With progress in microprocessor technology, most unitary heating or cooling systems now have a better way of controlling the space temperature. Methods include step controls, where the increment of heating or cooling occurs in steps or via proportional control. There is generally no zone humidity control – except in critical operations like operating theatres, data centres and the like.

For smaller buildings with modular heating and cooling systems – like reverse cycle packaged air-conditioning or zone-mounted heaters – manual on/off controls may be sufficient. However, as the number of items to be controlled increases, a mini-BMCS arrangement may need to be implemented. This would ensure that the A/C units or heaters operate only during the times the building is occupied. It would also allow the temperature set points to be adjusted.

For medium-sized buildings, a mini-BMCS can schedule stop/start times. In situations where multiple thermostats are present, the highest or lowest temperatures can be selected to control the amount of cooling and heating. In more modern BMCS systems, mobile phone interfaces allow you to set the scheduling and temperatures remotely.

To meet the requirements of a larger complex, like a high-rise commercial building, a university campus, a hospital, a religious centre, or a multi-purpose facility, BMCS systems are a must and need to incorporate increased capabilities and the right level of sophistication.

BMCS AND ENERGY EFFICIENCY

The BMCS saves energy and maintains comfortable indoor conditions through the following.

Optimised HVAC Control: The BMCS continuously monitors indoor and outdoor temperature, humidity, and occupancy levels. By analysing this data, it can adjust HVAC settings dynamically to maintain comfortable conditions while minimising energy consumption. For example, it can increase or decrease heating and cooling set points based on occupancy patterns and outdoor weather conditions. It can initiate 'free cooling' when the outside air temperature is suitable through what is termed the 'economiser cycle'. It can adjust the quantity of fresh air in line with occupancy levels as determined by CO_2 sensors.

Energy Monitoring and Management: The system can track energy usage in real-time across different building systems. Facility managers can identify areas of high energy consumption and implement strategies to optimise energy usage, such as scheduling equipment operation during off-peak hours or identifying malfunctioning equipment. These evaluations, as well as other well-formatted reports such as monthly and yearly GHG charts, are available with the press of a button on the main BMCS console.

This is an example of solar energy usage and associated environmental data.

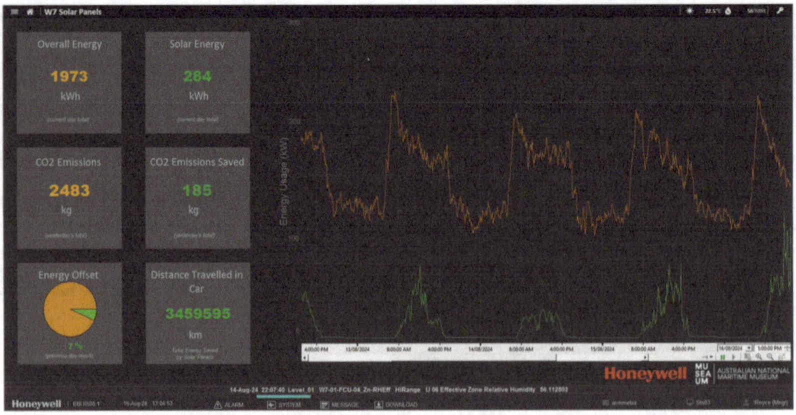

Integrated Lighting Control (optional): Lighting can account for around 20 to 25 per cent of a building's energy usage. A BMCS can control lighting systems based on occupancy, natural light levels, and time of day. It can automatically dim or turn off lights in unoccupied areas adjacent to windows, reducing energy waste.

Fault Detection and Diagnostics: The BMCS can detect abnormal behaviour or malfunctions in building systems, such as HVAC equipment or lighting fixtures. By identifying and addressing these issues promptly, facility managers can prevent energy waste and ensure optimal system performance.

Occupant Comfort Optimisation: Beyond energy efficiency, a BMCS can also enhance occupant comfort. By maintaining stable temperature and humidity levels, adjusting lighting levels, and ensuring proper ventilation, occupants can enjoy a more comfortable indoor.

environment with optimum indoor air quality (IAQ), leading to increased productivity and satisfaction.

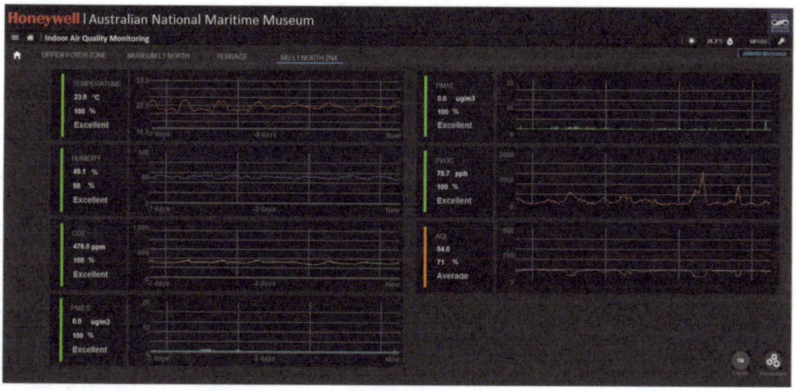

Indoor Air Quality Trends

Remote Monitoring and Control: Most BMCS platforms offer remote monitoring and control capabilities, allowing facility managers to access system data and adjust from anywhere with an internet connection. This feature enables proactive maintenance, rapid response to issues, and optimisation of building performance without the need for on-site presence.

Overall, a well-designed and properly implemented BMCS can significantly reduce energy consumption (estimated to be around 10-12 per cent), lower operating costs, and enhance occupant comfort in commercial, residential, and industrial buildings. It is a tool, and hence, the BMCS operator must develop a thorough understanding and confidence in its usage.

Let us now turn to the other precious commodity we need to conserve, namely water.

11

WATER MATTERS

PRECIOUS RESOURCE – H2O

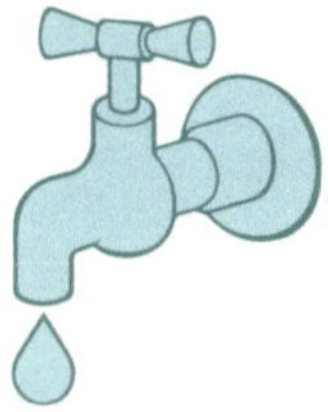

There are several water-saving techniques and ideas that can be adopted in both residential and commercial buildings.

Attending to a leaky tap needs to be the highest priority.

A tap that leaks 10 drips of water a minute may not seem serious. It is! Ten drips of water a minute adds up to 600 drips an hour and 14,400 drips a day, which amounts to the waste of 3 litres of water per day or 90 litres per month.

Following are a few more water-saving ideas:

Low-flow Fixtures: Toilets with reduced flush volumes, such as dual-flush systems, can significantly cut water use.

Low-flow Faucets and Showerheads: These fixtures are designed to reduce water flow without compromising performance, saving water with each use.

Greywater Reuse: Systems that treat and reuse greywater (water from sinks, showers, and washing machines) for non-potable uses such as irrigation and toilet flushing.

Rainwater Collection: Installing systems to capture and store rainwater from roofs for irrigation, flushing toilets, and other non-potable uses.

Dishwashers: Modern dishwashers use significantly less water than washing dishes by hand.

Washing Machines: High efficiency washing machines adjust water levels based on the size of the load, using less water per wash.

Smart Irrigation Systems: These use weather-based controllers to adjust watering schedules based on weather conditions, soil moisture, and plant needs.

Drip Irrigation Systems: Water is directly supplied to the plant roots, minimising evaporation and runoff compared to traditional sprinklers.

MINIMISING WATER CONSUMPTION

An Invaluable Resource

Just as with energy, water is an invaluable resource that needs to be conserved. Water availability and usage fluctuate similarly to energy and are influenced by factors such as climate, location, and building activities. Implementing water-saving strategies within a building is key to fostering sustainability, lowering utility costs, and preserving this invaluable resource. Promoting education is crucial in driving behavioural changes among occupants. Typically, this involves awareness programs that highlight the importance of water conservation and encourage water-saving habits, such as taking shorter showers and turning off taps while brushing teeth.

Water Reticulation

Where potable water is available as part of a town or city water supply system, it is generally connected to a building through a meter that measures usage. This incurs a charge which also covers sewerage and drainage costs.

Depending on the quality of the water supply, a line filter may be necessary before the distribution to the outlet points, including amenities, kitchens, and outdoor areas. Each outlet requires a tap to regulate the amount of water used, and each tap needs to be maintained to ensure it shuts properly.

A major use of water in commercial buildings is as make-up for cooling towers or water-cooled condensers. As you will recall, water-cooled air conditioning systems offer better energy efficiencies and, hence, lower GHG emissions. However, there are water losses involved, mainly due to evaporation from water-based equipment. Hence, there is a need to make up for the water loss, which adds to water consumption totals.

Monitoring systems that display water flow and detect leaks in real-time alert facility managers to issues immediately. Installing sub-meters to monitor water use in different areas of the building helps to identify high-usage areas and promote conservation efforts. Regular maintenance is always necessary. Pipes, fixtures, and appliances also need to be inspected regularly for leaks.

There are water systems that are being adopted in various situations particularly where water availability is limited. Some of these are implemented as district systems.

District Rainwater Harvesting

District rainwater harvesting is necessary in situations where there is scarcity of water. The above-ground rainwater tank is combined with a below-ground rainwater source, which is treated and supplied to homes. This is shown in Figure 46.

Figure 46 District Rainwater Harvesting

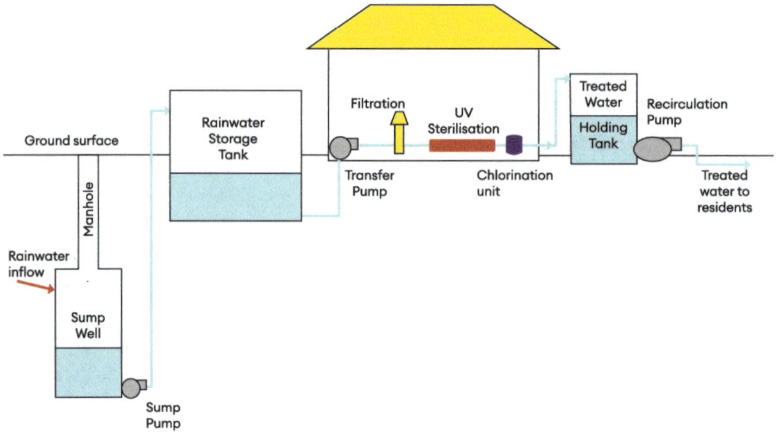

Black & Grey Water Recycling

In this system, drainage water from laundry, bathroom, kitchen, and toilet is treated through a wastewater treatment plant (WWTP) and the recycled water is used for irrigation and toilet flushing system. This is shown schematically in Figure 47.

FIGURE 47 WASTEWATER TREATMENT PLANT

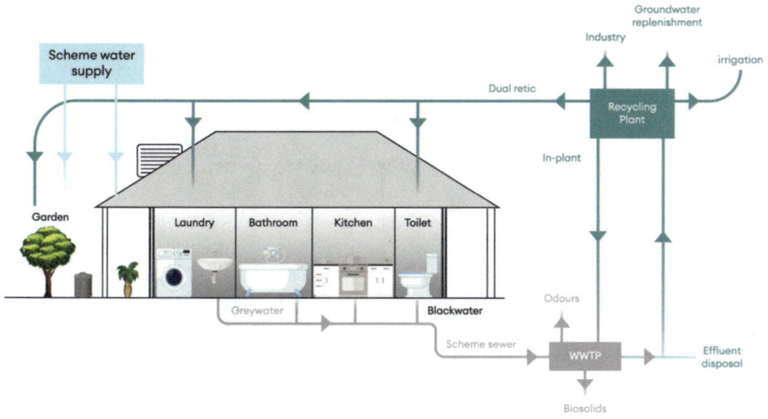

Case Study: Bligh Street in Action

My role as a Green Star expert involved with the verification of the Green Star rating of 1 Bligh Street, Sydney, included assessing the water conservation measures, namely black water harvesting and sewer mining.

Bligh Street combines remarkable architecture with best-practice sustainability. The project boasts a double skin façade along with a naturally ventilated full-height atrium and a complete 'Aquacell' blackwater recycling plant.

It was interesting that when the construction of the building was compete, the blackwater system could not be commissioned since only half of the building was occupied. Which meant that there wasn't enough 'load' to test the very expensive treatment system. It took another year after opening of the building, incidentally by the then Prime Minister of Australia Mrs Julia Gillard, before the building had sufficient occupancy to provide the necessary 'load' for the commissioning of the treatment systems. It is estimated that the blackwater plant saves and recycles 100,000 litres of water a day – that's over 22.7 megalitres per year. This recycled water is then distributed around the building for non-drinking purposes, with 75,000 litres used in the cooling towers and 25,000 litres for toilet and urinal flushing.

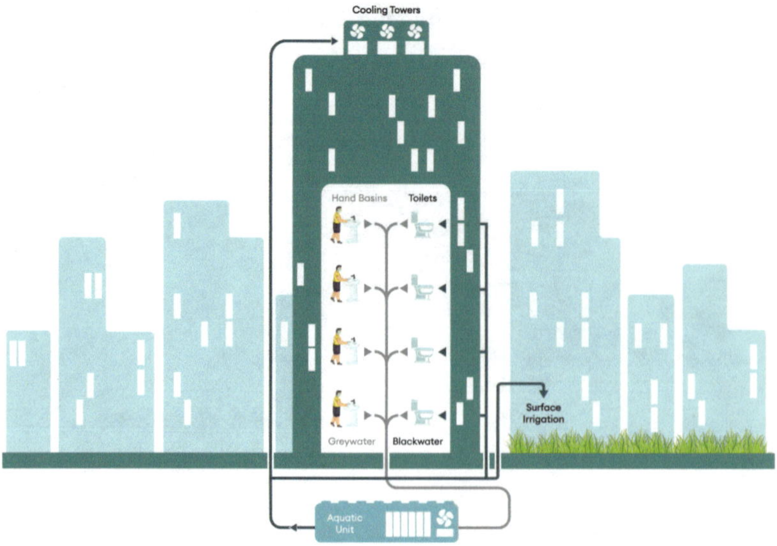

Wastewater is also mined from the nearby sewer piping to supplement the building's blackwater flow. All up, this integrated system easily meets the building's non-potable water demands with amazingly little reliance on existing public infrastructure.

Roof Drainage

Now, to drainage arrangements. A building's rooftop requires proper drainage, with adequately sized down pipes and suitable grates in the indoor and outdoor areas. Allowing water to pool, particularly on the roof, leads to leakage, especially if the building is old. This is especially important as we see an increase in the frequency of storms due to climate change.

You can carry out obvious actions, such as clearing drains that may be blocked and sealing cracks in the roof or replacing the roofing where necessary.

With advent of sustainable designs, more and more roof gardens are becoming evident. Watering and drainage arrangements need to take this into account.

ROOF GARDENS

All building services, including water management, require systems to be commissioned. The next chapter outlines all matters related to the vital topic of building and system commissioning.

12

GETTING READY FOR OCCUPATION

COMMISSIONING ANALOGY

A new electric vehicle (EV) has just come off the assembly line. It needs to have all the physical as well operational checks performed to ensure it complies with the specifications (and associated codes) and that it is safe and ready for the owner to drive.

During the assembly process, quality assurance inspections are carried out progressively to ensure that all the parts fit appropriately and are secured properly. This is an important phase of the process, especially when some of the parts may be covered over and not readily visible once the vehicle is fully assembled. Thus, at completion, the final inspection primarily looks at the finished product.

Operational tests follow a rigorous path on the other hand. Tests are carried out on each operational item, including indicators, wipers, cabin lights, external lights, battery level, temperature, and other indicators, etc. Then come the road tests, where acceleration, steering and brake, suspension and indeed, the entire control system are checked and rechecked. The car is also driven on wet surfaces and snow to ensure safe operation.

Once all the tests are successfully completed, the vehicle is ready for the owner. The owner is provided with full documentation including driving and operational instructions, parts list, maintenance requirements and warranty for a nominated period. During the defect's liability period, the owner is entitled to get defective items attended to and rectified where applicable as part of the warranty.

Earlier commissioning input results in cost savings. The cost versus potential impact ratio of the commissioning can be expressed as the 'X' Factor.

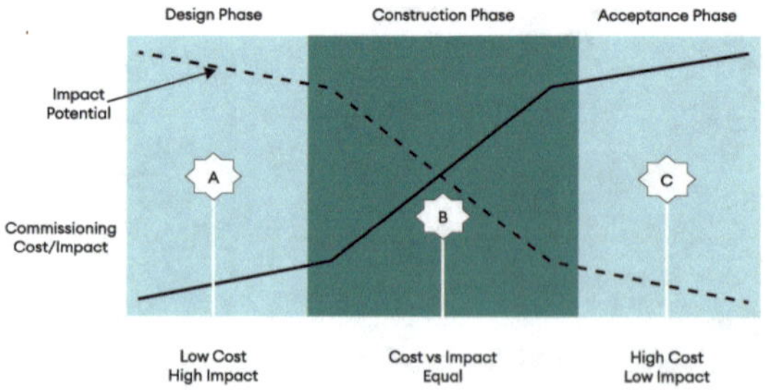

COMMISSIONING AND FINE-TUNING

Like with the EV analogy, commissioning for a building follows a similar process. The commissioning stage of a new building is a comprehensive quality assurance check that ensures all building systems are designed, installed, tested, operated, and maintained according to the owner's project requirements. The goal is to verify that the building performs as intended and meets the needs of the occupants.

'Commissioning', according to the Chartered Institution of Building Services Engineers (CIBSE), is technically defined as the advancement of an installation from the state of static completion to full working order to the specified requirements. This includes setting an installation to work, regulating, and fine-tuning the system.

From experience, I can confidently say that most buildings do not carry out this stage satisfactorily. This is often due to delays in completing the building works combined with the client wanting to move in as soon as possible. There is also the fact that senior design and construction team members must move on to the next project, and it is understandable that project funds are generally low at this stage.

However, if commissioning is not performed adequately, negative effects can persist for years, leading to an increased number of complaints and potential energy waste.

I witnessed this in a place of worship in Bangladesh, where it was obvious that commissioning had not been carried out. This became evident during the building audit process in 2023 when it was discovered that half of the conditioned air supply system serving a section of the front of the prayer hall had been shut off from the outset. The system had been installed in 2012. That meant those sitting in one section had no air supply, resulting in increased complaints related to thermal comfort. To address the situation, the organisation had been relying only on the system that was serving the rear of the hall – resulting in increased energy use. Once the shut-off damper was opened, the building was able to achieve energy savings of around seven per cent. When extrapolated over the 10 years since installation, this one error that could have been discovered at the commissioning stage was responsible for around 24 tons in GHG emissions and cost the organisation an estimated 797,000 BDT (US$6,775).

There are so many such examples that show why it is vital that commissioning is carried out in line with defined procedures.

ESSENTIALS OF COMMISSIONING

Due to the importance of commissioning as a process, building rating schemes like LEED, BREEAM, and Green Star allocate points for commissioning agents' involvement from the commencement of the building project. The commissioning agent oversees the design, documentation, construction, and, finally, the commissioning process.

It is vital that all aspects of commissioning are carried out with diligence. The facility manager (FM) should be involved prior to a new building handover process, especially during the commissioning stage. The FM responsible for the building should also be provided training on all aspects of building operation, including the building management and control system (BMCS).

Commissioning is like an audit of the building process; hence, it is important to understand what is involved. It starts with planning and preparation, where project requirements are defined. Next, Owner's project requirements (OPR): is a detailed document outlining the owner's goals, expectations, and requirements for the building. It is important to establish the basis of design (BOD). BOD is an explanation of how the design will meet the OPR, including descriptions of systems, components, and strategies.

Next is the commissioning plan, which outlines the commissioning process, schedule, roles and responsibilities, and procedures. A team is assembled, including the commissioning agent, owner, designers, contractors, and other stakeholders. The team reviews the design documentation to ensure it meets OPR and BOD.

Subsequently, regular meetings with design teams are held to discuss commissioning requirements and incorporate feedback. These meetings continue during the construction phase.

Functional Performance and Witnessing

The commissioning and witnessing phase in a project schedule includes checking the intended operation of individual components and associated controls under various conditions and modes of operation. The complete sequence of operations is tested, and testing covers all components and systems.

Functional performance testing can only be effectively implemented once all building services are comprehensively completed in the following phases:

a. Whole-building commissioning tests, which cover setting up and testing of each of the building systems, including HVAC, electrical, security, life safety, building envelope, communications, vertical transportation, process equipment, plumbing, hydraulics, and building management and control system (BMCS).

   As discussed in Chapter 10, BMCS plays a vital role in making the building energy efficient and contributing to minimising GHG emissions. Apart from selecting the most appropriate BMCS and ensuring that the operator is suitably trained, an equally important aspect that needs due consideration is setting the system correctly once installed.

b. Appropriate instrumentation is essential in the assessment and checking process. For example, sophisticated instruments should be used to check airflow distribution. To take it a step further, specialist companies may need to be employed to carry out the air balancing, which is extremely important to ensure better comfort conditions.

I need to share a confession where I was involved with water balancing in my role as a contractor. We were checking the water balancing of the air conditioning units at the roof level of Sydney Domestic Airport. It was quite interesting observing planes landing and taking off. I remember commenting on how the landing of a Cessna was delaying take-offs of larger 747s, resulting in significant wastages of fuel. I digress. We were recording chilled water flows using appropriate gauges. When the consultant arrived to witness the tests, the values had changed since it was a dynamic situation and water flows changed as heat load increased. I knew that the consultant would not sign off the test forms unless the values matched the readings on the gauge. I managed to set the required values by adjusting the knob accordingly. The tests were accepted. It was coincidental that later I ended up joining the company where this consultant worked. He accepted my apologies for manipulating the recordings. The message of this anecdote is that the certifier needs to be equally, if not more, proficient in what is involved with commissioning.

c. Dynamic testing and simulating real-world operating conditions to verify system performance under various conditions at different times of the year. This is somewhat akin to testing the vehicle in wet weather and snow conditions.

d. Inter-system testing involving emergency and fire systems under various 'what-if' scenarios. It is quite common to turn off fire alarms during construction, and often, they are not turned back on. Hence, it is important that all systems are checked and thoroughly tested, as this will ensure the safe operation of the building.

As Installed Documentation

Good operation and maintenance documentation of a building and its building services is essential for several reasons, including health and safety, financial accountability, maintenance and operation, and energy and water efficiency.

This documentation needs to include 'as built' drawings and building operation and maintenance instructions. The facility manager receives such documentation at the building's handover. It is important to keep the documentation up to date as changes occur on an ongoing basis.

Warranty Period

Finally, there is the warranty period. During this stage, the following activities are involved.

+ Preparing a short-term monitoring plan.
+ Conducting short-term diagnostic testing.
+ Assisting the resolution of warranty issues.
+ Preparing re-commissioning or continuous commissioning plan.
+ Performing seasonal checks of operations and control strategies.
+ Fine-tuning, like in a motor vehicle, is beneficial for improving efficiency.
+ End-of-warranty walkthrough and listing defects that need to be rectified.

A well-commissioned building is a better-performing building, just as a better-maintained building ensures a high-performing building.

Once the building is commissioned, it is handed over for occupation. The builder officially hands it over to the owner. A prominent building generally has a formal opening. Prior to handover, the maintenance teams are briefed and, where required, trained on how to operate the system. Maintenance regimes and procedures are organised, and the facility management team takes over. The next chapter deals with maintenance management.

FACILITY MANAGEM
DEVICE CHECK
87%
Air ventilation system

13

BUILDING COMPLETED AND OCCUPIED

MAINTENANCE ANALOGY

We will use a similar analogy as we did at the beginning of our discussions on commissioning. Except instead of a new car, let us look at an older car. This can relate better to the vast stock of existing buildings.

As part of a car's ongoing maintenance, it is essential to regularly check tyre pressures, engine oil, and fuel levels. Then there are the periodic visits to the mechanic where brakes and other operational items are attended to. This is part of what is called preventative maintenance. In newer vehicles there is full diagnostic analysis that is carried out to enhance the performance. In buildings, this is like tuning up the BMCS to attain energy savings.

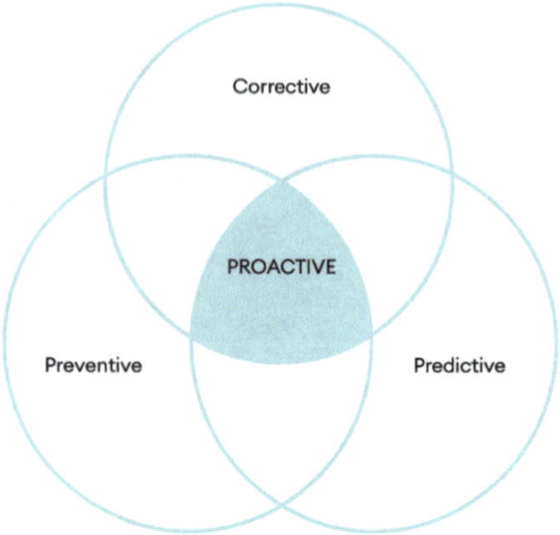

There is also breakdown maintenance when the car stops to perform or just stops. We had this recently and found that the alternator needed replacement in our 12 years old family car. $1438 and two days later, we had our car back on the road. It is inevitable that there are breakdowns. In buildings this applies to all building systems – HVAC, electrical and plumbing.

The major maintenance is either based on time such as 6-months or annual check-ups or on how many kilometres the car has travelled. For buildings this is akin to items like chillers, pumps, and other operating equipment.

For buildings, the computerised maintenance management systems are now interfaced with BMCS. This is the best way to carry out conditioned based maintenance using dynamic data.

BUILDING MAINTENANCE MANAGEMENT

Maintenance management is formally defined as the process of maintaining a building, its assets, and resources while controlling time and costs to ensure maximum efficiency. Effective maintenance enhances operational efficiency thereby creating more opportunities for energy savings within the building.

Regular inspections for deterioration and wear and tear are crucial in a maintenance routine. For instance, routinely inspecting the roof can prevent potential water damage during rain. Drones are increasingly used for roof inspections.

All aspects of building management require some form of maintenance. Simply put, maintenance management involves the care and upkeep of the building, its equipment, and its services.

TYPES OF MAINTENANCE MANAGEMENT

Approaches to building maintenance management vary based on factors such as the building's size, purpose, budget constraints, and the specific needs of its occupants.

Let us look at some of the common approaches.

Reactive maintenance involves addressing maintenance issues as they arise, often in response to complaints or breakdowns. While it can be cost-effective in the short term, reactive maintenance may lead to higher repair costs and disruptions to building occupants.

Preventive maintenance focuses on regularly scheduled inspections, repairs, and replacements to prevent equipment failure and prolong the lifespan of building systems. This approach aims to identify and address potential issues before they escalate, reducing the likelihood of costly repairs and downtime.

Predictive maintenance uses data analysis and monitoring technologies to predict when equipment is likely to fail, allowing for proactive repairs or replacements before breakdowns occur. This approach can help optimise maintenance schedules, reduce downtime, and minimise unnecessary repairs.

Reliability-centred maintenance (RCM) is a systematic approach to maintenance planning that prioritises resources based on the criticality of assets and their impact on business operations. It involves identifying failure modes, analysing their consequences, and implementing maintenance strategies to mitigate risks and optimise asset performance.

Condition-based maintenance involves monitoring the condition of building systems and equipment using sensors and diagnostic tools. Maintenance activities are then scheduled based on the actual condition of assets, rather than on a predetermined schedule. This approach can help prioritise maintenance tasks and optimise resource allocation. As an example, vibration sensors are installed for pumps at the National Australian Maritime Museum (NAMM) for early detection of a pump being out of balance. This measure has translated into cost savings by taking corrective actions in time, avoiding the need to replace the pump.

Total productive maintenance (TPM) is a holistic approach that focuses on maximising the efficiency and reliability of all assets within a building. It involves continuous improvement efforts aimed at eliminating waste, reducing downtime, and optimising maintenance processes. TPM emphasises employee involvement and empowerment to drive continuous improvement initiatives.

Asset management involves strategically managing the lifecycle of building assets to achieve the organisation's goals and objectives. This may include activities such as inventory management, asset tracking, lifecycle costing, and performance optimisation to maximise the value and return on investment of building assets.

These maintenance management approaches can be implemented individually or in combination, depending on the specific requirements and objectives of the building owner or operator.

MANAGEMENT SYSTEM OPTIONS

For a small building, the manual method still works. However, it does require being very organised and having a system that captures all the elements of the building and associated services.

For a more complex building, there is a need to use tools that can not only incorporate maintenance reminders but also keep track of associated costs plus items such as warranties of equipment, maintenance procedures and, in some cases, carry out water, energy and GHG analyses. In these buildings, maintenance management has gone from an old-fashioned, tedious, handwritten process involving spreadsheets and line-by-line maintenance guides to a computerised maintenance management system (CMMS) - a software-based system that plans, tracks, measures and optimises all forms of a maintenance program through one central system.

Operational items like pumps, fans, air conditioning units, heaters, generators, boilers, and chillers must also be documented. Details like model numbers, capacities and operating and maintenance procedures should be noted, as recommended by the respective manufacturers.

MAINTENANCE AND ENERGY MINIMISATION

Good maintenance enhances water and energy efficiency while preventing energy wastage caused by:

- Unnecessary concurrent operation of heating and cooling systems.
- Unscheduled operation of plant, equipment, and systems.
- Incorrect operation because of faulty or uncalibrated sensors.

Let us go through financial aspects especially of the air conditioning systems in the next chapter.

CO_2
CO_2
CO_2
CO_2

14

BUILDING PROJECT COSTING AND DELIVERY

LCC PERSPECTIVE

Life cycle cost (LCC) analysis is defined as "the total discounted dollar (monetary) cost of owning, operating, maintaining, and disposing of a building or a building system (or associated equipment) over a selected period of time". LCC is an economic evaluation technique that determines the total cost of owning and operating a facility or building system (or associated equipment) over its life expectancy period (Fuller, 2016). Building owners apply the principles of LCC analysis in support of decisions regarding construction of new buildings or improvements to an existing facility.

When selecting an HVAC system for a new building or for a major refurbishment of an existing building, LCC becomes a key component in the decision-making process.

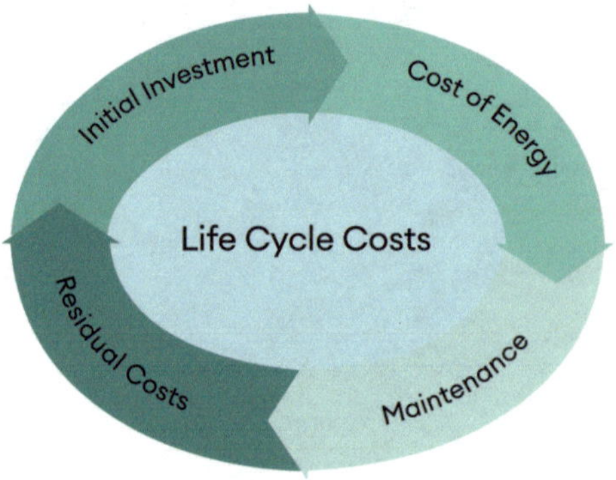

As part of my PhD research, LCC was the central question that was addressed, namely in determining which of the HVAC systems represented the lowest cost option over the life expectancy of each of the systems. In typical commercial office buildings. Variable Air Volume (VAV), Chilled Beams (CB), and Under Floor Air Distribution (UFAD) systems have a life expectancy of around 30 years. After 30 years of operation, some items will need to be replaced due to wear and tear, including chillers, fans, pumps, coils, and dampers. BMCS, generally, is upgraded more frequently over this period as the associated software/firmware becomes obsolete faster than hardware components. Cooling towers may also require upgrading or replacement. Indeed, that was the finding for the Angel Place building, where both the BMCS and cooling towers were upgraded after 18 years.

It is good to see that LCC principles are increasingly used when selecting HVAC and Solar Energy systems for homes.

AIR CONDITIONING SYSTEMS – CAPITAL AND OPERATING COSTS

We have gone through building elements and building services with respect to energy and GHG minimisation. However, we have not talked about the elephant in the room, namely economics. The saying is 'you get what you pay for.' This is very true for buildings overall and building services in particular HVAC.

Literature on this topic is scarce. That is what I discovered when I was researching this topic for my PhD. That is understandable when there are so many variables and dependencies on market values. As part of my thesis, I included a spreadsheet-based tool that enables comparative analyses of various HVAC system types. The tool is essentially based on the LCC principle that calculates capital, operating costs, and savings. I have further enhanced the spreadsheet so that it can provide comparative capital and operating costs for major types of HVAC systems in any country. It requires obtaining the cost of the most common type of air conditioning equipment, namely the Split AC Unit. I have selected a 7 kWr or 2-ton (refrigeration) unit as the base. It can condition a 20 square metre area. The price of the unit is one of the inputs for the spreadsheet – the other one being the building square metres that need to be conditioned. Researched factors have been applied to the various types of air conditioning systems. They include:

+ Split D/X system (as a base).
+ Roof Top D/X system.
+ Variable Refrigerant Volume (VRV).

+ Geothermal (geo-exchange) AC system.
+ AHU/FCU served by air-cooled chiller.
+ AHU/FCU served by water-cooled chiller.
+ Variable Air Volume (VAV)
+ Under Floor Air Distribution (UFAD)
+ Chilled Beams – Active and Passive.

This interactive spreadsheet enables indicative budgets of capital investments and cost savings, indicating simple payback timeframes when comparing with the Split AC system.

The following table demonstrates the capital and operating costs in US dollars for a 250 square metres of an office space in Australia, as an example. Using this table, you can work out the indicative budgets for any country by using the cost of a two-ton (7 kWr) Split AC unit.

INTERACTIVE EXCEL-BASED TOOL TO ESTABLISH COMPARATIVE AIR CONDITIONING SYSTEM CAPITAL AND OPERATING COSTS. BASED ON PURCHASE PRICE OF A SPLIT SYSTEM IN LOCAL CURRENCY

STEP ONE		
Obtain cost of a 2 ton split unit - equipment only		
Country	Energy efficient 2 ton AC - Cost Local Currency	USD - based on conversion rate
Canada	1400	$ 1,000
Pakistan	394999	$ 1,411
India	85200	$ 1,027
Australia	1525	$ 1,068
STEP TWO		
INPUT (Conditioned Area)	250	sq m
2 refrig. ton split unit only	$ 1,068	Australia
Installed Cost (x 2.1) per sq m	$ 112	seves 20 sq m

Type of Air Conditioning System	System Co-efficient of Performance (Average - COP)	HVAC Cost per sq m - from above	Associated bulding cost	Capital Cost USD	Operating Energy - USD	Maintenance USD	Operating Energy & Maint. cost - USD	Operating Cost Saving per annum (wrt to base)	Simple Payback for upgrade from base - years
Split D/X	3	$ 112	$ 11	$ 30,824	$ 17,252	$ 750.0	$ 18,002	Base	Base
Rooftop D/X	3.25	$ 129	$ 26	$ 38,670	$ 15,925	$ 1,125.0	$ 17,050	$ 952	8.2
VRV D/X	3.5	$ 170	$ 34	$ 51,112	$ 14,788	$ 875.0	$ 15,663	$ 2,340	8.7
Geothermal with GSHP	7	$ 179	$ 305	$ 121,055	$ 7,394	$ 937.5	$ 8,331	$ 9,671	9.3
AHUs - air cooled chiller	4.5	$ 299	$ 37	$ 84,171	$ 11,501	$ 1,750	$ 13,251	$ 4,751	11.2
AHUs / FCUs - water cooled chiller	5.5	$ 342	$ 53	$ 98,714	$ 9,410	$ 2,000	$ 11,410	$ 6,592	10.3
Variable Air Volume	6.5	$ 392	$ 43	$ 108,865	$ 7,963	$ 2,250	$ 10,213	$ 7,790	10.0
Underfloor Air Distribution	6	$ 308	$ 123	$ 107,884	$ 8,626	$ 2,000	$ 10,626	$ 7,376	10.4
Chilled Beams - Active & Passive	6.5	$ 549	$ (99)	$ 112,592	$ 7,963	$ 1,125	$ 9,088	$ 8,915	9.2

As can be seen, this tool provides indicative comparisons that would assist in deciding on a suitable type of HVAC at the initial concept stage. This would need to be verified during the design stage since the investment budgets will depend on local market conditions, the number of suppliers, the cost of labour, and the level of competition.

Services Integration

Integrating building services – namely electrical, mechanical, and plumbing (MEP) – within the building architecture has been quite a challenging part of my work. One area that has an impact on services systems selection is the way buildings are developed and delivered for institutions and investors.

In Australia during the 1970s and early 80s, the architect, employed by the developer, was the key player involved in assembling the design team and organising the hard copy documentation of a building. I remember referring to architects as 'The Alimighty'. They appointed all the various building consultants, including quantity surveyors, structural, and building services. Architects played a key role in the nomination of the builder. They were involved from concept to handover of a new building.

Those were the days when there was sufficient time to carry out detailed calculations, concepts, and detailed designs, and coordinate all building services with the architectural and structural layouts of the proposed building complex. The documentation process involved overlaying 'sepias' (transparent copies) of drawings on each other to check if there were any clashes between the structure and the building services, especially large air conditioning ducts and water pipes. A quantity surveyor would provide a fairly accurate cost of the project. Documents went to tender for builders to bid on. Once the building works commenced, the architect and the consultant team supervised the construction, and prior to handing over issued a practical completion certification. A 12-month defects liability period followed. Since the architect was essentially the client for the consultants, architectural requirements often took priority over a more efficient HVAC system. Buildings constructed during that era continue to enjoy good energy ratings and generally have fewer complaints related to indoor comfort levels. This was observed during the field tests carried out for my PhD research where nine buildings were analysed.

In the early 1990s, the role of the architect for many of the large projects was taken over by a project manager (PM). I remember seeing a cartoon that portrayed the PM as an 'elephant squeezing the last dollar' from a project. The PM assembled the design team and produced a coordinated set of documents for builders to bid on. Construction supervision of the building and handover to the client was also managed by the PM team – under whom the architect and the design team provided the service.

PROJECT DELIVERY APPROACHES

The late 90s saw the emergence of public-private partnerships (PPP), and as subsets, there were many build, own, operate, and transfer (BOOT) schemes for public buildings such as hospitals and sporting venues. Key buildings associated with the Sydney 2000 Olympics adopted the BOOT approach. They included the Sydney SuperDome (now the Qudos Bank Arena) – a 20,000-seat indoor venue boasting the largest under-seat air conditioning system in the Southern Hemisphere. I was part of the team in the design of this energy-efficient air conditioning 'displacement type' air-conditioning system. Abi Group, the builder, was awarded the contract based on its innovative approach and a financial package that offered the best outcome for the client, the NSW Government. As a side note, a world tour of indoor arenas was organised, and I was part of this tour (which those not included called a junket). I inspected 12 indoor arenas in the US, Canada, and Europe over two tiring weeks. Certainly not a walk in the park! Whilst there was little to learn from other venues, the tour confirmed that Australia was a leader in adopting new technologies, and that building went on to win awards. In 2024, the arena marked its silver jubilee, and it is good to see Sydney's leading indoor entertainment venue is still enjoying low energy bills.

Sydney Superdome – Qudos Arena - 2023

At the same time as BOOT and sub-variants emerged, another delivery method came into being for larger commercial projects. In the guaranteed maximum price (GMP) path, a development team, generally headed by a builder, provides a GMP based on a concept design usually prepared by a team of architects and consultants. In most cases, once the builder is successful in winning the work, they elect to employ design and construct (D&C) contractors to complete the concept design and deliver the project within the GMP limits. This often means that the consultant's energy-efficient concept could be changed by the D&C contractor to potentially a less efficient design. The focus is on capital cost savings, and not operational costs, which could be higher for the life of the building.

We now enter the part of the book that can assist us in lowering the cost of living by taking simple steps in our everyday routines. There are practical and easily executable tips and strategies on how to save energy.

In the next chapter, we will discuss energy-efficient residential buildings and how to reduce our energy bills.

15

ENERGY SAVING IN HOMES

PRACTISING THE PREACHED

Energy conservation was a top priority when our house was being constructed. All walls facing east and west were insulated, which was uncommon forty years ago. The roof is also insulated. The windows on the upper floor have external roll-up blinds to block direct sunlight. On the ground floor, plants provide effective shading from the sun while still allowing natural light when needed. Additionally, all windows have high-quality curtains drawn every night to 'insulate' the glass. In winter, we ensure the curtains are open during the day to capture the free warmth from the sun.

We use the ceiling fan in winter mode to push warm air down from the high-raked ceiling when heating the lounge and dining areas with our 5-star energy-efficient reverse-cycle air conditioning unit. As noted in Chapter 5, we have a 13.5 kW solar system, and hence, we operate energy-consuming appliances like the dishwasher and washing machine during daylight hours. We also dry our clothes using a Hills Hoist. All our lights, both inside and outside, are LEDs. Additionally, we turn off our TV and computers at the power source when not in use. We are practising what we preach.

COST OF LIVING - SAVINGS

This chapter is about reducing energy bills in the home. There are steps that each one of us can take to reduce our carbon footprint by saving energy-and save money too!

We consume energy for lighting, powering appliances, maintaining comfort, and cooking. Energy can take various forms, such as electricity, gas, diesel, wood, coal, and petrol. Factors influencing energy consumption include lifestyle and affordability of energy-consuming equipment.

Typical energy break-up of energy-consuming items:

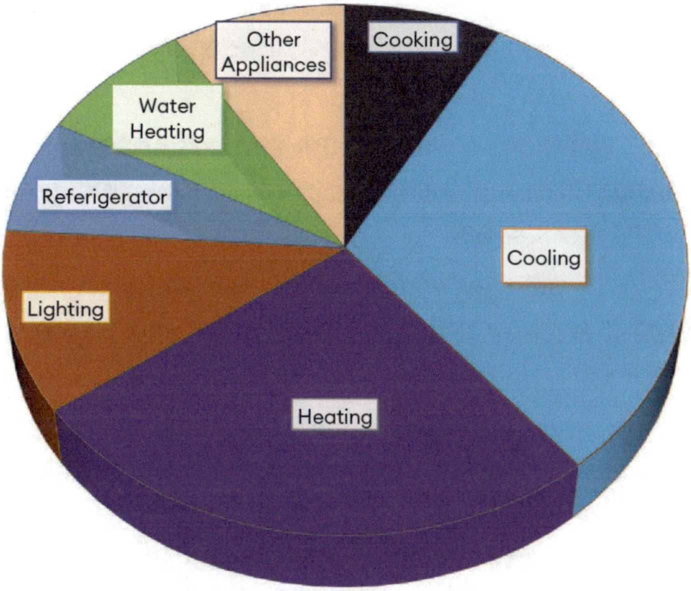

There are great variations in energy consumption of different types of dwellings. The overall design and orientation of the house, such as window placement for natural lighting, can affect energy needs. Larger homes require more energy for heating, cooling, and lighting. Open floor plans may result in higher energy usage, too, due to the need to maintain consistent temperatures across larger spaces. Homes in extreme climates (hot or cold) typically consume more energy for heating or cooling. Seasonal changes also lead to fluctuating energy use. Materials like brick, stone, or energy-efficient windows do help in reducing energy loss.

Reducing Energy in the Home

Regardless, there are a few common approaches when it comes to implementing energy reductions.

+ Select energy-efficient appliances such as refrigerators, washing machines, dishwashers, and televisions, designed to consume less electricity while performing their functions effectively. The Energy Star system can help you understand the energy use and running costs of household appliances. Look at the energy rating label. The higher the rating the more efficient the product.
+ Replace traditional incandescent bulbs with energy-efficient LED lights, which consume significantly less energy and have a longer lifespan.
+ Improve insulation in walls, floors, and ceilings to minimise heat loss during winter and heat gain during summer, reducing the need for heating and cooling.
+ Install energy-efficient windows with low-emissivity coatings and insulated frames to reduce heat transfer and improve thermal performance.
+ Curtains, on average, reduce home energy bills by around seven per cent in warmer months and nine per cent during colder months. During colder months, it is important for the curtains to be open during the day to benefit from the winter sun (based on appropriate orientation) but closed at night. As stated before, this creates a 'blanketing effect' to keep the warmth in and the cold out.
+ Seal gaps and cracks around windows, doors, and other openings to prevent air leaks, which can result in energy loss and increased heating or cooling demands. Draft stoppers at all external doors, on

average, reduce energy bills by five per cent, depending on climatic influences and the extent of infiltration.

- Natural ventilation strategies, such as opening windows and using ceiling fans to circulate air, maintain comfortable indoor temperatures without relying solely on mechanical cooling systems.
- Energy-efficient HVAC systems, including high-efficiency heat pumps and air conditioners, use less energy than conventional systems while maintaining indoor comfort.
- Install programmable or smart thermostats to regulate heating and cooling systems efficiently. These thermostats adjust temperatures based on occupancy and time of day to reduce energy waste.
- Encourage energy-saving habits among household members, such as turning off lights and unplugging electronics when not in use, using appliances efficiently, and setting thermostat temperatures wisely.
- External shading can reduce energy use by up to 50 per cent. Shading devices can be fixed or roll-down awnings. Better still, if land is available, plant appropriate trees that could provide shade. These have the added benefit of absorbing CO_2, thereby reducing GHG emissions even further.

Implementing these energy-saving measures can significantly minimise energy consumption, lower utility bills, and contribute to a more sustainable environment through reduced GHG emissions.

The Electric Kettle

Let's take a kettle, for example. If a kettle heats one cup of water to 100°C four times a day for a year, it will consume 81.7 kWh of energy a year. This equates to 0.06 tons of GHG emissions, equating to two trees worth of CO_2. If only one cup of water is needed, but that kettle is filled up to capacity, it is heating six cups of water every time it is used. In that scenario, the energy consumption yearly is 258.5 kWh – equating to 0.24 tons of GHG emissions. Heating a whole kettle when you only need one cup leads to a whopping 216 per cent increase in energy usage and GHG emissions yearly! However, if the temperature is set to 80°C instead of 100°C, you cut your energy usage by 24 per cent. Consider this the next time you have a cuppa.

I have done the maths to quantify simple ways to save energy to enable individuals to make informed decisions.

Water Capacity	Water Temperature set - Deg C	Measured Electricity kW	Time taken to boil - minutes	Per hour kWh	Daily	Annual kWh	Energy Increase/ Decrease kWh	Increase/ Decresae Energy %	GHG (NSW) - Tons	Equivalent Trees
l cup	100	2.18	1.54	0.06	4	81.7	base			
l cup	80	2.06	1.25	0.04	4	62.7	18.9	-23%	0.04	1.7
6 cups	100	2.42	4.39	0.18	4	258.5	176.8	216%		
6 cups	80	2.29	3.52	0.13	4	196.1	62.4	-24%	0.13	5

Refrigerator

Every time we open the refrigerator door, we are adding heat into the refrigerator. That refrigerator will then work overtime to cool down. This means that the energy-consuming compressor operates for a longer period. If over twelve hours, you open the fridge every hour, compared to three times an hour, you can reduce your energy usage by around 24 per cent a year. The longer the door is open, the higher the energy wastage. The door alarm is a good quasi-energy-saving device but be mindful and do not wait for the door alarm to tell you to save energy by shutting the door.

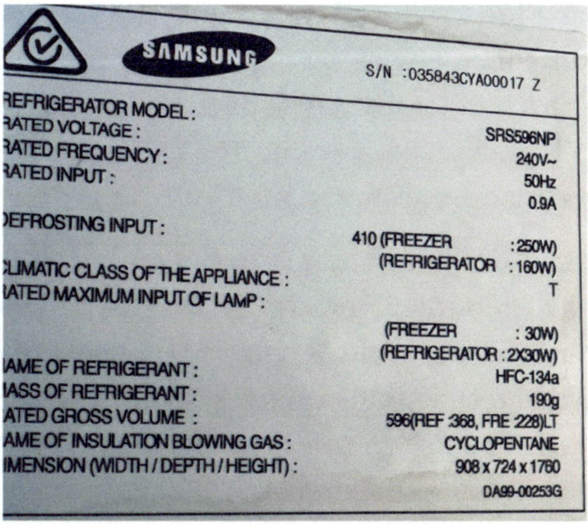

Following is an analysis carried out:

REFRIGERATOR	Measured (average) - kWh	Per day (12 hours)	Annual kWh	Annual Increase in kWh	Change %	GHG (NSW) tons	Equivalent Trees
Opening door once in an hour	0.08	0.96	350.4				
Opening door two times every hour	0.13	1.56	569.4	219	63%	0.39	15

There must always be adequate air space around the refrigerator, especially around the back and the top. This is because, as you will recall, the refrigeration principle is based on energy transference between the inside and the outside. Any heat build-up at the rear side of the refrigerator impacts refrigerator efficiency. Additionally, ensure the door seals are airtight to prevent heat ingress.

Washing Machine and Clothes Drier

Goes without saying that the appropriate loading selection settings of both the washing machine and the clothes drier need to be utilised properly. The power consumption of a clothes washing machine can vary depending on factors like the model, washing cycle, and water temperature. However, the difference between a fully loaded and half-loaded machine primarily depends on how the machine handles the load size. Many modern washing machines have sensors that adjust the water level and cycle duration based on the load size. In these machines, power consumption for a half load is typically less than for a full load because the machine uses less water, and the motor operates for a shorter duration. Since power savings are not proportional, running the machine with a half load often leads to higher energy consumption per kilogram of laundry. For example, if a full load consumes 1 kWh, a half load might consume around 0.7-0.8 kWh, not exactly half.

Older machines that do not adjust based on load size will consume almost the same amount of power regardless of whether they are fully loaded or half-loaded. This is because the machine uses the same amount of water, and the motor runs for the same duration regardless of load size. Hence, the golden rule remains that a full load of washing is generally more energy-efficient per unit of laundry.

How does the operating power compare to the published power rating of the machine?

The power usage varies during different cycles, such as washing and spinning cycles. Evaluation carried out on the washing machine shows the following:

Cycle Time - minutes	2	21	5	18	8	55			
Washing Machine Start	Water Filling	Washing	Water - Empty & Refill	Washing	Spinning	Daily kWh	Annual kWh	GHG (NSW)	Equivalent Trees
Measured kW	0.24	0.35	0.26	0.34	0.52				
kWh	0.01	0.12	0.02	0.10	0.07	0.32	118.08	0.08	3.2

Clothes washing is carried out during sunlight hours to take advantage of the free solar energy. Hence equivalent number of trees shown above are 'virtual trees' planted.

We only use the clothes dryer on rainy days. Like the washing machine, the clothes dryer's power consumption varies depending on the load.

Tests carried out of the clothes drier show the following:

Air Drier Rated Power kW	Measured (average) kW	Time - hours per day	Days (average)	Annual kWh	GHG (NSW) tons	Equivalent Trees
1.5 - 2.0	1.3	1.5	250	487.5	0.3	13

To dry our clothes, we use the famous Australian Hills Hoist—a great example of the combination of solar and wind energies. Amazingly, the

Hills Hoist has not gained international popularity. I have not seen it being used much elsewhere in the world.

Based on the calculations, the use of the Hoist has resulted in a saving of around $249 per annum in our estimate.

Dishwasher

Like with the washing machine, the dishwasher's appropriate loading features need to be utilised properly..

The power consumption of a dishwasher, like the washing machine, depends on the load size, model, cycle type, and the presence of load-sensing technology. Here is how the power consumption typically compares between a fully loaded and a half-loaded dishwasher. Many modern dishwashers have sensors that adjust water usage, heating, and cycle duration based on the load size. In these cases, running a half-load usually consumes less energy than a full load. However, the reduction in power consumption, like the washing machine, for a half load is often not proportional. For example, if a full load uses 1.5 kWh, a half load might use around 1.1-1.3 kWh. The energy savings come from using less water and shorter heating times, but many fixed energy costs (like starting the cycle) remain the same.

Older dishwashers that lack load-sensing technology will often use the same amount of power regardless of the load size. These machines use the same amount of water, heat it to the same temperature, and run the cycle for the same duration, meaning there's little to no energy savings with a half load.

Dishwashers are designed to be most efficient when fully loaded, as the fixed energy costs are spread over more items. Once again, the golden rule remains that a full load of washing is generally more energy-efficient per dish cleaned.

How does the operating power compare to the published power rating of the machine?

The power usage varies during different cycles, such as washing and drying cycles. Tests carried out on our dishwasher show the following:

Cycle Time - minutes	4	27	6	18	15	70			
Dish Washer Start	Water Filling	Washing	Water - Empty & Refill	Washing	Drying	Daily kWh	Annual kWh	GHG (NSW)	Equivalent Trees
Measured kW	0.24	0.35	0.26	0.34	0.42				
kWh	0.02	0.16	0.03	0.10	0.11	0.41	148	0.10	4.0

Dishwashing is carried out during sunlight hours for us to take advantage of the free solar energy. Hence equivalent number of trees shown above are 'virtual trees' planted.

Bathroom Radiant Lights

You notice the spike in the power consumption dashboard as soon as you turn on the radiant lights. The energy usage of radiant lamps in a bathroom can vary based on their power rating, usage frequency, and the number of lamps. Here's how you can estimate the annual energy consumption for radiant lamps in an average one-bathroom home:

We have radiant heat lamps with two bulbs each, each with a power rating of about 325 watts (W) per lamp. Let's assume the lamps are used for 30 minutes per day.

Energy consumption per day: Power (kW) × Time (hours)

For two 325W lamps used for 0.5 hours/day: 0.65 kW × 0.5 hours = 0.325 kWh/day

Annual energy consumption: 0.325 × 365 days = 118.63 kWh @ 35 cents = $41.50

Infiltration

Calculating the infiltration of unconditioned air through a gap under an external door and its impact on energy consumption involves several steps. First, we need to estimate the air infiltration rate and the additional cooling or heating load required, and then we convert that into energy usage.

Here's how this can be approached:

The infiltration rate through a gap can be calculated using the formula: $Q = A \times v$

Where:

Q = airflow rate (cubic meters per second, m^3/s)

A = area of the gap (square meters, m^2)

v = velocity of air through the gap (meters per second, m/s)

Hence, for a gap of 15mm under a door 770mm wide

Q = 0.015 × 0.77 @ 1.0 m/s = 0.01155 m3 /s.

Let us calculate energy consumption based on:

- Temperature difference between inside and outside air (ΔT) = 10 deg. K
- Specific heat capacity of air (approx. 1.005 kJ/kg· K)
- Air density (approx. 1.2 kg/m^3)

- Coefficient of Performance (COP) of AC unit = 3.5
- Timeframe - 8 hours a day and 200 days a year

Energy impact = (0.01155 x 1.005 x 1.2 x 8 x 10 x 200) / (3.5 x 1000)

The annual energy impact due to air infiltration through the gap under the external door is approximately 0.064 kWh. In a colder climate with a higher average temperature difference, the impact would increase.

Heating and Cooling

As stated at the beginning of this chapter, heating and cooling are responsible for 57 per cent of the energy consumption typically. Our experience is similar. For heating, I prefer to use an electric rug to cover my knees and legs. This is on the basis that my research confirmed that warmer feet and a cooler head are signs of good comfort. During very cold nights, we occasionally utilise a 2-kW portable electric heater.

Inverter-type air conditioners (ACs) use a sophisticated mechanism to regulate the speed of the compressor motor, allowing it to operate at variable speeds instead of the fixed speed used in non-inverter units. Unlike non-inverter ACs, which turn the compressor on or off to regulate temperature, inverter ACs adjust the compressor speed to match the cooling demand. This means the compressor runs continuously but at varying speeds, depending on temperature and the desired set point. The inverter technology converts AC (alternating current) to DC (direct current) and then inverts it back to AC at the required frequency. By adjusting the frequency, the inverter controls the speed of the compressor motor. Inverter ACs are particularly more efficient when operating at partial loads (less than maximum capacity), which is the condition for most of the time in typical usage scenarios. Inverter ACs also have a soft start feature, meaning they do not draw a large amount of current when starting up, which reduces energy spikes. Inverter ACs typically save between 30 per cent to 50 per cent of energy compared to non-inverter units, depending on usage patterns, temperature settings, and environmental factors. Reduced energy consumption leads to lower electricity bills.

Evaluation of the 7 kWr (2-ton) inverter AC unit indicates a COP of 3.6 compared to a non-inverter AC of generally 3.0.

Time	T	T +5	T+ 10	T+15	T+ 20	T + 25	Average	COP
Measured kW	0.65	2.6	2.7	1.5	2.69	1.4	1.92	3.6

Case Study – Residential AC & Pool Heating

The following layout shows how zoning provisions within the AC systems, combined with the use of curtains in a fully glazed dining room and the use of a heat pump to warm pool water, have resulted in 32 per cent savings in electricity bills compared to business as usual.

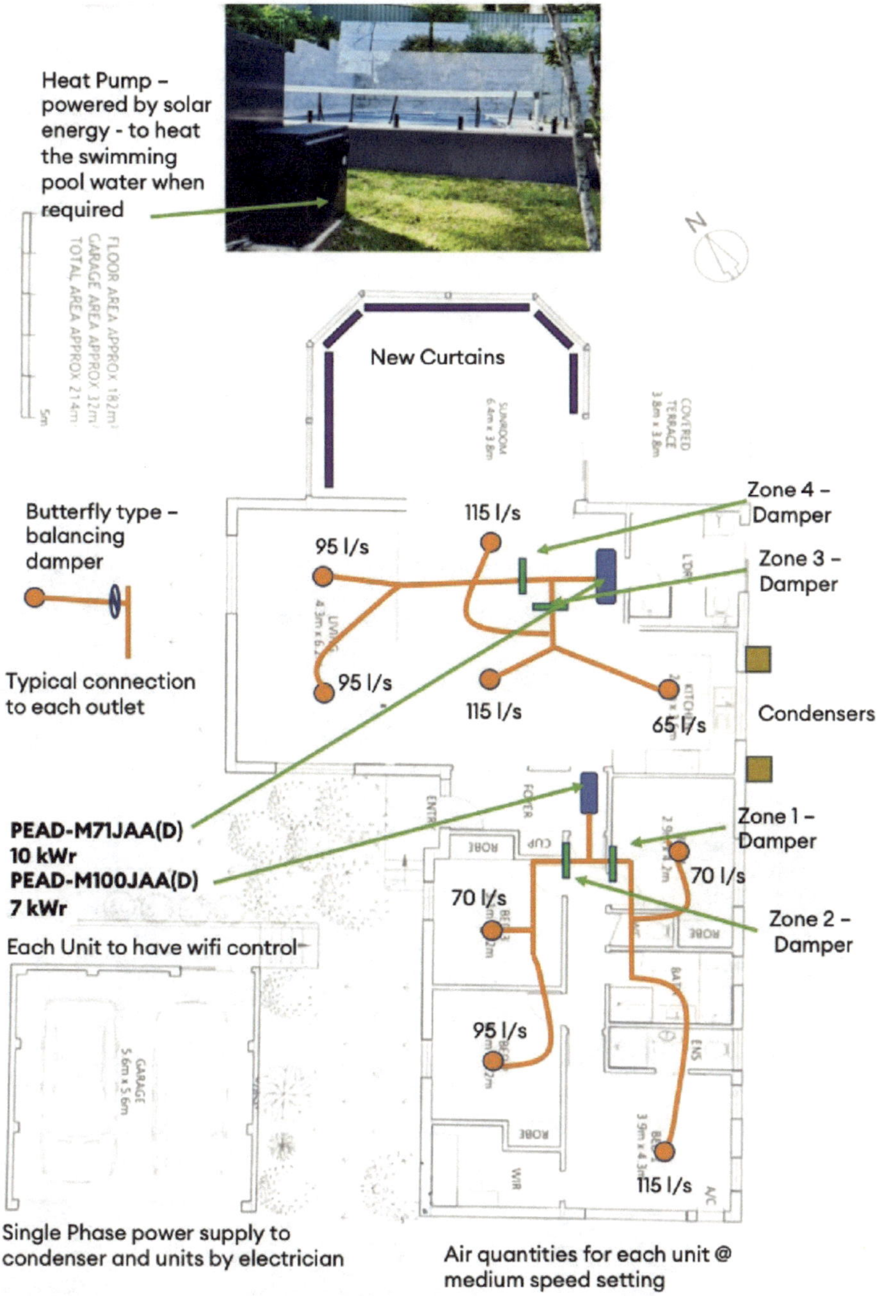

Zahra & Amyn Nathwani Residence - Wahroonga

NET ZERO HOME

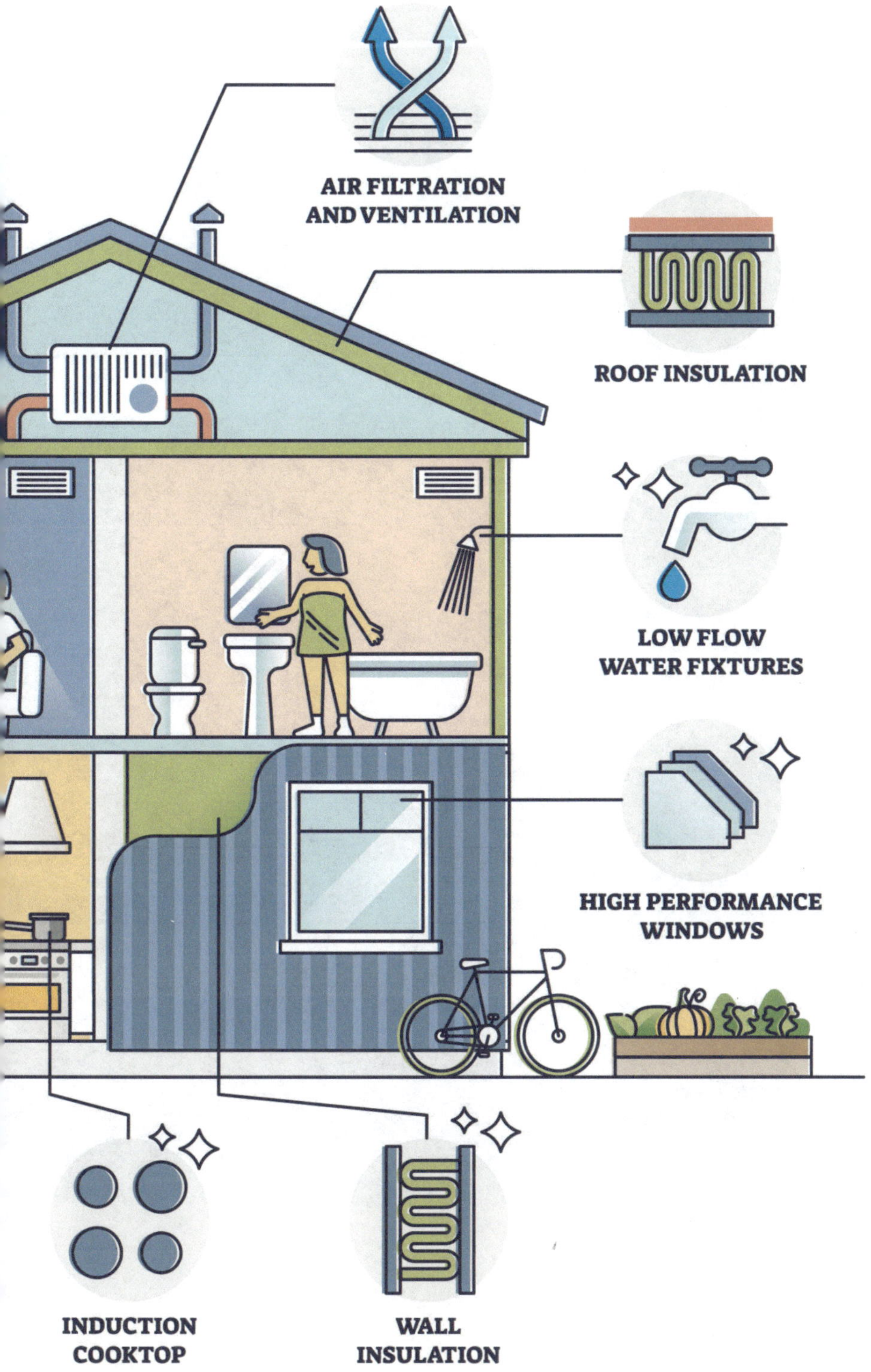
AIR FILTRATION
AND VENTILATION
ROOF INSULATION
LOW FLOW
WATER FIXTURES
HIGH PERFORMANCE
WINDOWS
INDUCTION
COOKTOP
WALL
INSULATION

CO_2

16

ENERGY AND GREENHOUSE GAS MINIMISATION IN BUILDING

AN AUDITOR'S TASK

The purpose of a financial audit is to form a view on whether the information covered in the financial report, taken as a whole, reflects the organisation's financial position at a given date. It looks at the annual losses and evaluates options on how these losses can be minimised. The audit outcome also provides a platform to analyse options for future revenues and how the organisation can maintain its profitability.

When preparing the financial report, auditors must follow auditing standards, which are generally set by a government body. Once auditors have completed their work, they write an audit report explaining what they have done and giving an opinion based on their work. With some exceptions, all organisations must have an audit each year. Other organisations may require or request an audit depending on their structure and ownership or for a special purpose.

What do auditors not do?

- Check every figure in the financial report-audits are based on selective reviews of data provided only. They do not look at every transaction carried out by the organisation by testing the adequacy of all its internal controls.

What auditors cannot do?

- Predict the future. The audit relates to a specific past accounting period. It does not judge what may happen in the future and cannot provide assurance that the organisation will continue in business indefinitely.
- Be there all the time-the audit is carried out within a defined timeframe, and auditors are not always present at the organisation.

Together with similarities in methodology and approach, there are distinct parallels from financial audits that can be applied to building audits-our key topic for this chapter.

AUDITING NON-RESIDENTIAL BUILDINGS

Non-residential buildings are very diverse. They cover all types of buildings ranging from smaller standalone offices and restaurants to larger structures like shopping centres, educational institutions, medical facilities, entertainment venues, hotels, data centres, and high-rise offices, to highlight a few. Each type of building varies in its energy consumption and greenhouse gas (GHG) emissions.

Carbon Emissions and Scopes

As part of the GHG emission minimisation process, we need to understand what the GHG sources are in the first place. Three scopes categorise the different kinds of emissions an organisation creates in its operations and in its wider 'value chain' (its suppliers and customers). It is unclear why they are called 'scopes' rather than 'groups' or 'types', but the name comes from the Greenhouse Gas Protocol, which is the world's most widely used greenhouse gas accounting standard.

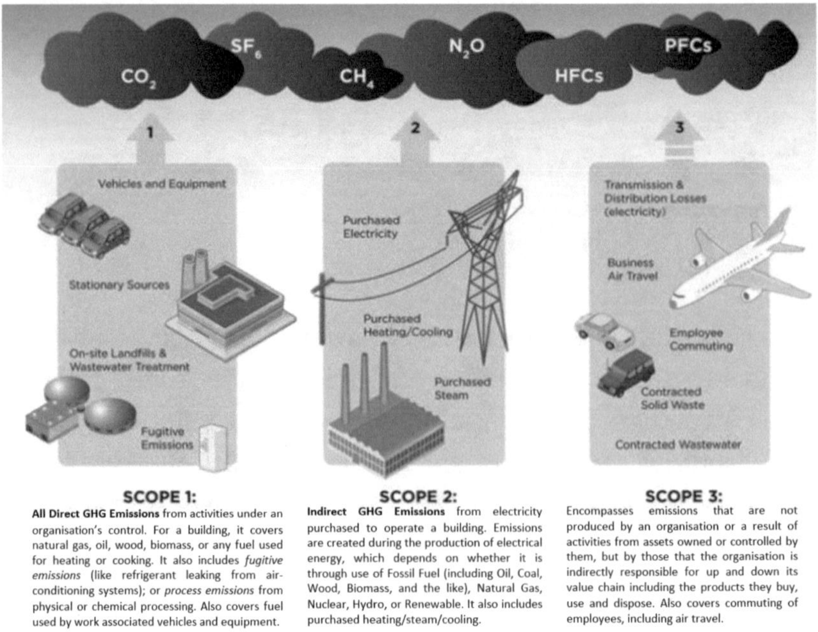

GHG Scopes. Source - IEA

As stated in this protocol: "Developing a full GHG emissions inventory – incorporating Scope 1, Scope 2 and Scope 3 emissions – enables an organisation to understand its full value chain emissions and focus its efforts on the greatest reduction opportunities".

Scope 1 and Scope 2 are the most relevant categories for building audits. Note: Scope 3 refers mainly to indirect emissions arising from value chain.

Scope 1: All direct GHG emissions from the activities of an organisation or activities under its control. A building may use renewables or fossil fuels like gas, oil, wood, or biomass. Scope 1 also covers fugitive emissions from equipment leaks (like refrigerant leaking from air-conditioning equipment) or process emissions from physical or chemical processing. Building audits exclude emissions from vehicles associated with a building.

Scope 2: Indirect emissions from electricity purchased to operate a building. Emissions are created during energy production, produced by either fossil fuels or renewables.

ENERGY & GHG AUDIT

This is where the rubber hits the road. This is where an owner, tenant, facility manager, consultant or interested individual will be able to implement ways to minimise the energy usage and operating costs of a building. To gauge the performance of any operation, it is necessary to start by establishing the baseline. For a business, this would involve carrying out a financial audit for a given year. This would help identify opportunities to improve business performance. Similarly, for a building, it is vital to evaluate energy and GHG minimisation opportunities by carrying out a detailed building audit. The audit helps to achieve better performance with reduced energy (and GHG emissions) and potentially a net zero status.

Net Zero Status

Before delving into energy and GHG audits, let us examine what constitutes a net zero building. Net zero refers to a state in which the amount of GHGs – primarily carbon dioxide (CO_2) and other human-caused emissions – released into the atmosphere is balanced by the amount of GHGs removed from the atmosphere over a specified period. This timeframe provides a clear target for action. It is a crucial concept in the context of addressing climate change because it aims to achieve a balance between the emissions we produce and the emissions we offset or remove, ultimately resulting in no net increase in atmospheric GHG concentrations. In other words, for every ton of GHGs emitted, an equivalent amount must be removed or offset.

The term 'net zero' has become part of everyday conversation. We hear it on the news and in talk shows, where there are regular discussions and debates on how a country or an organisation is going to, or not going to meet the net zero commitments announced by organisations and governments at forums such as climate change conferences.

Ideally, a net zero building is "an energy-efficient building where, on a source energy basis, the actual annual consumed energy by the building is less than or equal to the on-site (or appropriate off-site) renewable-source-generated energy" (Chanchpara, 2019).

What is a Net Zero carbon building?

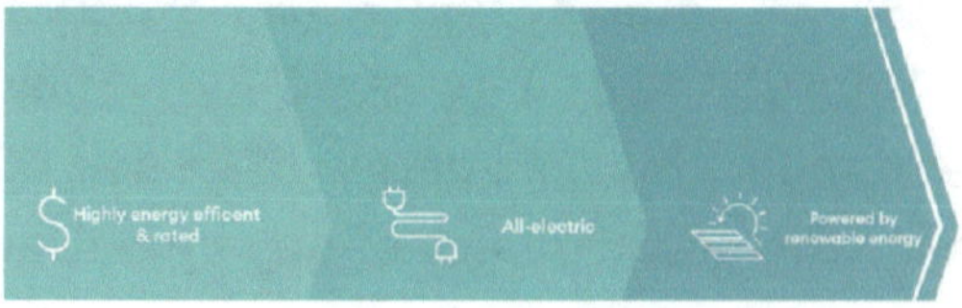

This resonates with the principle that I advocate for attaining net zero for existing buildings. We need to focus on reducing energy consumption and transitioning to renewable energy sources. This could be by retrofitting older buildings with new technologies, improving insulation, encouraging occupant behavioural change, and installing renewable energy systems like solar panels to provide clean energy.

Science Based Targets Initiative (SBTi)

There are various strategies available to help an organisation reach its net zero goal. For example, the science-based targets initiative (SBTi) provides a framework for companies to set GHG emission reduction targets that are in line with the latest climate science. They have detailed strategies and approaches related to various sectors including industrial, agriculture, and the like.

However, with regards to buildings, according to the advice published on 26th July 2024, SBTi has just commenced its work to establish what approach needs to be taken. This is evident in the following excerpt:

"We're developing science-based target-setting methodologies, tools, and guidance for companies in the **building** sector and other stakeholders. We aim to help companies to understand and implement the level of climate ambition required to meet the 1.5°C goal of the Paris Agreement". It is unbelievable that they have left it up to the present to look at the 'building sector', which is responsible for around 40% of GHG emissions.

SBTi quotes the following:

"The buildings sector is a major contributor of emissions worldwide, accounting for over one-third of global energy consumption and emissions.

Of this, around 3 Gt CO2e are direct emissions (https://www.iea.org/reports/energy-technology- perspectives-2020), a further 9.8 Gt CO2e are indirect emissions from electricity and heat consumption, and 3.5 Gt CO2e from materials. (https://www.iea.org/reports/energy-technol%20ogy-perspectives-2020)

Floor area (of the built environment) is set to grow approximately 75% over 2020-2050 (https://www.iea.org/reports/net-zero-by-2050), meaning CO2 emissions will rise dramatically if no decarbonization efforts are made in the sector."

The approach for the decarbonisation work that I am associated with involves carrying out energy and GHG audits primarily of existing buildings.

Energy and GHG Audits

There are multiple reasons to conduct an energy and GHG emissions audit. By studying and evaluating the building's current energy profile (usage pattern and consumption), a target for net zero GHG emissions can be set. This requires establishing a benchmark year based on energy consumption data from the previous two years. An energy use intensity EUI (annual energy consumption divided by area) is then established. The next step is to identify energy inefficiencies and wastage. This is followed by prioritising opportunities to improve energy efficiency. To achieve net zero, alternatives for renewable energy and achieving energy security are explored.

My auditing experience.

The first energy audit report I ever saw was in my first job as a project engineer at Honeywell in 1972. It was a comparative analysis between two buildings. I was also frequently required to attend training courses on energy management, where audits formed part of the content.

After Honeywell, I took a position as an HVAC contractor with T O'Connor and Sons, where I often questioned the HVAC design intending to enhance it and make it more energy efficient. One such questioning of a design-led to my next career move from contracting to consulting, joining Norman Disney Young (NDY). I still recall the life-changing meeting with Allan Disney – the 'D' in NDY, who became my mentor and, indeed, my role model. I followed in his footsteps and became the environment and marketing director at NDY. When I retired in 2011, I became an adjunct professor at the University of Sydney, like Allan had done when he retired.

It was at NDY where I spent 33 years and was not only involved with designing energy-efficient buildings but through NDY's M-Plus division, which I managed, I carried out several energy audits. Like Allan, I was also active in sharing, via industry presentations, the lessons learnt from the energy minimisation exercises and audits. I recall Allan making an industry presentation on an energy efficient VAV air conditioning system at a 30-stories Office Tower, 400 George Street, Sydney. I was assisting him by manually changing the presentation slides since, during those days, we did not have computers that could be connected to the projector. Serendipitously, 400 George Street also became a key building as part of my PhD research – exactly 30 years later! Its energy efficient VAV system continues to provide lower energy bills.

I continue to share knowledge and experience as I provide training internationally as a time and knowledge (TKN) volunteer for the Aga Khan Agency for Habitat (AKAH), as the energy and GHG minimisation strategist. While a lot has changed since those early days, the fundamentals related to energy audits remain the same.

Since air conditioning is a major contributor to energy consumption in buildings, the American Society of Heating, Refrigeration, and Air Conditioning Engineers (ASHRAE) has published various guides covering topics such as how to design energy-efficient air conditioning systems and the formulation and implementation of energy audits.

ASHRAE Level 1 Audit

ASHRAE Level 1 audit is also called a 'simple audit', a 'preliminary audit', or a 'walk-through audit'. It is the basic starting point for energy optimisation. It involves brief interviews with site operating personnel, a review of the facility's utility bills and other operating data, and an abbreviated walk-through of the building. The audit is geared toward the identification of the potential for energy improvements, understanding the general building configuration, and defining the type and nature of energy systems. The audit nominally results in a preliminary, high-level energy-use analysis for the entire facility and a short report detailing the findings, which may include identifying a variety of recognisable efficiency opportunities. Usually, the report does not provide detailed recommendations except for very obvious system or operational faults.

This audit is intended to help the energy team understand where the building performs relative to its peers, establish a baseline for measuring improvements, and decide whether further evaluation is warranted and, if so, where and how to focus that effort. It also outlines a range of financial incentives available from federal, state, local, and utility sources.

Level 1 Audit - Limitations

The Level 1 audit does have limitations. They are primarily walk-through assessments, which means they do not probe deeply into the building's systems or operations. As a result, they may overlook more complex issues that require detailed analysis to identify.

The recommendations in a Level 1 audit are often general and may not be sufficient to implement significant energy savings. These audits typically suggest easy and quick fixes rather than comprehensive solutions.

Energy savings estimates in Level 1 audits are often based on preliminary calculations and assumptions rather than detailed measurements and analysis. This can lead to less accurate predictions of the potential savings from recommended measures.

Due to the brief nature of the audit, data collection is limited to visual inspections and basic information gathering. This means that important factors influencing energy consumption, such as detailed equipment performance or occupant behaviour, might not be fully accounted for.

Level 1 audits typically do not include a detailed cost-benefit analysis of the recommended energy efficiency measures. Without this, building owners may find it difficult to prioritise and justify investments in energy-saving improvements.

Because of its high-level approach, interactions between different building systems may not be thoroughly assessed. This can lead to missed opportunities for integrated energy-saving solutions.

Level 2 Audits

The next step for most facilities is the ASHRAE Level 2 audit. The audit starts with the findings of the Level 1 work and evaluates the building's energy systems in detail to define a variety of potential energy-efficiency improvements. These include the building envelope, lighting, HVAC, domestic hot water (DHW), and plug loads, such as computers and other office equipment. This study starts with a detailed analysis of energy consumption to quantify base loads, seasonal variation, and effective energy costs. From there, the audit includes an evaluation of lighting, air quality, temperature, ventilation, humidity, and other conditions that may affect energy performance and occupant comfort. The process also includes detailed discussions with the building ownership, management, and occupants to explore potential problem areas, as well as clarify the program's financial and non-financial goals.

The Level 2 audit results in a clear and concise report and briefing with the owner and management team describing a variety of energy conservation measures (ECMs), including no cost and low-cost measures, modifications to system controls and building automation, operational changes, and potential capital upgrades. The findings include general costs and performance metrics, as well as a means for the owner to evaluate the ECMs and make informed decisions on their adoption.

Many of the ECMs revealed during the audit can be implemented quickly with rapid or immediate financial payback for the owner. Other ECMs may require a more detailed analysis of benefits and costs, and the other goals that are important to the owner. The audit needs to define subsequent steps to accomplish this analysis and decision-making.

Level 2 Audit - Limitations

While an ASHRAE Level 2 energy audit provides a more detailed analysis than a Level 1 audit, including a comprehensive building survey and energy analysis, it still has certain limitations.

While Level 2 audits offer more depth than Level 1, they may still not be as thorough as necessary to identify all potential energy savings, especially in very large or complex buildings. For a comprehensive understanding, a Level 3 audit might be required.

Level 2 audits are more time-consuming and resource-intensive than Level 1 audits. They require more extensive data collection, analysis, and on-site inspections, which can be costly and may disrupt building operations. Despite being more detailed, Level 2 audits might still miss certain data points or nuances, especially if there are access limitations or if certain systems are not easily observable during the site visits. Although Level 2 audits include a cost-benefit analysis of recommended energy-saving measures, this analysis might still rely on standard assumptions and might not fully capture the specific context or operational nuances of the building. Level 2 audits typically evaluate individual energy-saving measures rather than a holistic approach that considers the interaction between different systems within the building. This can result in missed opportunities for integrated energy-saving solutions.

The quality of a Level 2 audit can vary significantly depending on the expertise and thoroughness of the auditors. Inexperienced auditors might overlook certain energy-saving opportunities or fail to provide actionable recommendations. The recommendations from a Level 2 audit, while more detailed, may still lack specific guidance on how to implement the measures. Building owners and managers might need additional support to turn the audit findings into concrete actions. Level 2 audits might focus more on cost-effective measures with relatively short payback periods, potentially overlooking more substantial, long-term investments that could yield greater energy savings and sustainability benefits over time.

While Level 2 audits include financial analysis of energy-saving measures, they may not provide a comprehensive financial plan or explore all available financing options, incentives, and rebates that could support implementation. The audit represents a snapshot in time and might not account for future changes in building usage, occupancy, or technological advancements that could affect energy consumption and savings potential. For some energy consevation measures (ECMs) involving complex interaction among building systems and potentially large financial investments, digging deeper into the building operation and the human factors influencing performance may be necessary. This is where the ASHRAE Level 3 audit becomes essential.

Level 3 Audit

Before making significant investments in capital, personnel, and other resources, the owner will want to have a much more thorough and detailed understanding of the benefits, costs, and performance expectations. This is the purpose of the 'investment-grade' Level 3 audit. Investment levels can range from medium to very high. In most cases, since this cannot be clearly determined or accurately estimated in advance, the recommendation and scope definition for a Level 3 audit is usually an outcome of the Level 2 process.

This audit focuses on a 'whole-building computer simulation', where a computer program is used to model how the building would respond to changes in the energy systems, whether those are major HVAC retrofits or architectural modifications to walls, windows, and roofs. The ASHRAE Level 3 audit involves much more detailed data collection over weeks or months. Data loggers, such as I-Buttons, may need to be placed over a defined period, such as a week or two, to monitor the operation of pumps and motors, temperatures of affected spaces, lighting levels, switching behaviour, and other factors. The resulting data is then used to calibrate the digital replication of the facility so the model responds to inputs and changes the same way the building would be expected to respond. This calibration is validated by simulating a year or more of minute-by-minute climate conditions to see if power and energy usage in the model mirrors the actual energy power and energy usage.

Once the three-dimensional computer model responds like the real building, 'what-if' exercises can be carried out. This could include replacing single-glazed windows with double-glazed windows. Combining these processes with construction-grade cost estimating enables informed decisions.

Level 3 Audit - Limitations

The main drawback of a Level 3 Audit involving full modelling is the cost, together with the capability (and experience) of the modeller and the limitations of the modelling software. Unless the building was built using building information modelling (BIM), where software is used to model the building at concept and design stages, accurately modelling an existing complex building can be very costly and time-consuming. Here, the expertise and experience of the modeller also play a major role.

One example of a Level 3 audit I completed in 2018 at a place of worship in Calgary, Canada, comes to mind. The building was modelled as accurately as possible over the course of more than three weeks. Using 2019 weather data, energy consumption was established and compared with the actual energy consumption for that year. They could not be reconciled. After spending a significant amount of time trying to resolve the issue, we discovered that the version of the modelling software we were using did not incorporate how to address radiant heating. In the end, a detailed physical audit of the building was carried out, and it did become a candidate to achieve net zero status, once all the ECMs were implemented.

RECOMMENDED ENERGY AUDIT METHODOLOGY

Given the various limitations of the ASHRAE Levels 1, 2, and 3 audits, a more pragmatic and practical methodology has been developed. This incorporates both a walk-through audit (as per Level 1 ASHRAE standard 211, 2018) and an investment grade audit (IGA), equivalent to ASHRAE Levels 2 and 3, but without requiring detailed modelling, except in special cases.

It needs to be reiterated that the operation and management of electrical items, including heating and cooling systems, significantly affect energy consumption and associated GHG emissions. Hence, the auditor's understanding of these building services is vital.

Applying the fundamental principle of 'what can be measured can be managed', data acquisition becomes the key first step of the assessment and evaluation process. After all, the quality and accuracy of data determine the value and benefits of outcomes.

Key steps:

a. Organise building and energy systems data acquisition.

b. Carry out a walk-through inspection and observe physical and operational items. It is essential to compile photographic evidence with traceable identifiers, including the building number, the number of floors, specific windows, and even details such as faulty blinds.

c. Utilities consumption data needs to be obtained and checked for accuracy by reviewing at least three utility invoices. Establish energy use intensity (EUI) - annual energy consumption per unit area.

d. Confirm prevailing factors for conversion from energy utilisation to GHG emission.

e. Establish a baseline for yearly energy consumption (kWh) and GHG emissions (tons).

f. Evaluate building and building services to determine annual operational energy (kWh) to match the annual energy of the baseline year.

g. Identify and cost each energy conservation measure (ECM).

h. Tally all potential GHG savings resulting from ECMs and subtract from total GHG in the baseline established to work out the 'gap' for which renewable energy would be required to achieve net zero status.

Data Acquisition and Evaluation

The facilities management (FM) team is the best source of reliable and accurate data necessary for an audit. Utmost diligence needs to be applied in capturing each relevant detail, like each transaction record associated with a finance audit.

Data gathering starts with basic information about the building, including envelope, electrical, and HVAC details, and how the building is operated and managed. To assist with data acquisition, a suite of input forms has been developed. These can be completed using the good old paper method or, to make it environmentally friendly, via a spreadsheet, entering the information using appropriate technology.

Basic Building Information

<table>
<tr><th colspan="5">INPUT DATA</th></tr>
<tr><td>Building Name</td><td colspan="2"></td><td>Date:</td><td></td></tr>
<tr><td>City</td><td colspan="2"></td><td>Year Built</td><td></td></tr>
<tr><td>Country</td><td></td><td colspan="2">Building (s) - Built Area - sq m</td><td></td></tr>
<tr><td>Street Address:</td><td colspan="4"></td></tr>
<tr><td>Owned / Leased</td><td></td><td>Outdoor Temperature (Deg C) - Maximum & Minimum</td><td></td><td></td></tr>
<tr><td>If Leased, remaining lease period - years</td><td></td><td>Outdoor Humidity (% RH) - Maximum & Minimum</td><td></td><td></td></tr>
<tr><td colspan="5">Brief History of the complex- including any major modifications since built, proximity to Ocean (if applicable) & any other pertinent or relevant information.</td></tr>
<tr><td colspan="5"></td></tr>
</table>

This form is used to obtain basic information about the building, including location, local weather, and whether the property is owned or leased. The latter is an important consideration to ensure that the building will still be part of the portfolio to meet an owner's net zero target. If the building is already leased, the audit would only consider tenant-related items. Otherwise, the whole building would be audited.

One case study I can share to illustrate this point was a building in Dushanbe, Tajikistan, where the tenant only occupied one floor of a building. They wanted to achieve net zero by 2030. The lease agreement was reviewed every year and generally renewed. Hence, decisions had to be made concerning longer-term energy savings, such as upgrading to an energy-efficient air-conditioning system and installing solar power on the roof. The outcome was that the tenant and the owner agreed to share the capital costs involved. The owner saw the enhancements as a beneficial investment.

Baseline Year and GHG Emissions

A baseline year that reflects the building's 'normal' operation is essential to achieving net zero GHG by a target date.

A building's energy consumption is continuously changing—there is no static model of energy use. Better energy management, then, relies on having the right data at the right time, which would allow building managers to gain knowledge to make smart operational decisions to reduce energy usage.

The beginning of an audit is marked by gathering energy consumption data for the period of one year from all forms of utilities. All energy and GHG savings are measured against this baseline.

For buildings whose energy consumption is influenced significantly by local climate, data is also obtained for at least the previous six months of the benchmark year. Special techniques involving various software can 'normalise' the data concerning the weather. The same technique must be adopted for the target year.

The energy usage values must be accurate for the respective

consecutive months. Like financial audits, verifying the values by spot-checking a selection of the utility's invoices is required.

This spreadsheet is used to acquire energy consumption data from all utilities for a selected year.

Year	ENERGY CONSUMPTION									
2023	Electricity (kWh)	Cost - USD	Diesel (Litres)	Cost - USD	Gas (M3)	Cost - USD	Wood Kg	Cost - USD	Any Other Fossil Fuel	Cost - USD
Jan										
Feb										
Mar										
Apr										
May										
Jun										
Jul										
Aug										
Sep										
Oct										
Nov										
Dec										

Once energy data is compiled and verified, GHG emissions can be ascertained by multiplying each utility with the respective conversion factors. The electricity conversion factors vary as they are dependent on how the electricity is generated (renewables or non-renewables). Electricity conversion factors for several contries have fluctuated over recent years. Following are some examples:

Country	CF - kgCO2e/kWh			
	2012 CF	2019 CF	2021 CF	2023 CF
Afghanistan	0.315	0.302	0.206	0.127
India	0.926	0.878	0.726	0.717
Pakistan	0.418	0.594	0.351	0.370
Syria	0.58	0.609	0.662	0.666
Tajikistan	0.001	0.057	0.086	0.080

The baseline year can be established once the GHG emissions have been calculated.

Case Study: Dushanbe

A recent audit in Dushanbe, Tajikistan, included GHG emissions from refrigerant leaks.

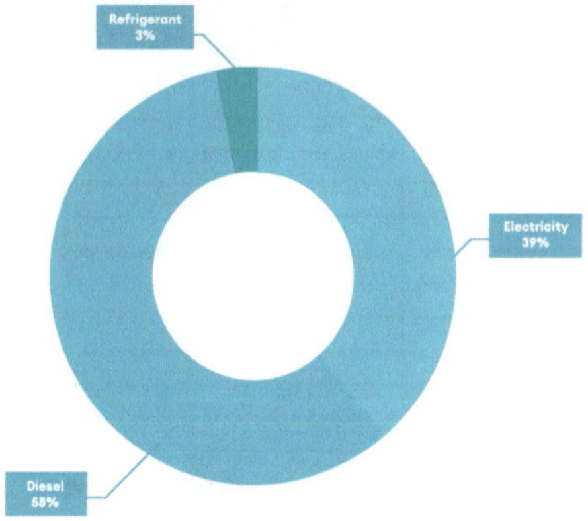

Baseline 2019 – GHG Contributors (Heating using diesel fuel)

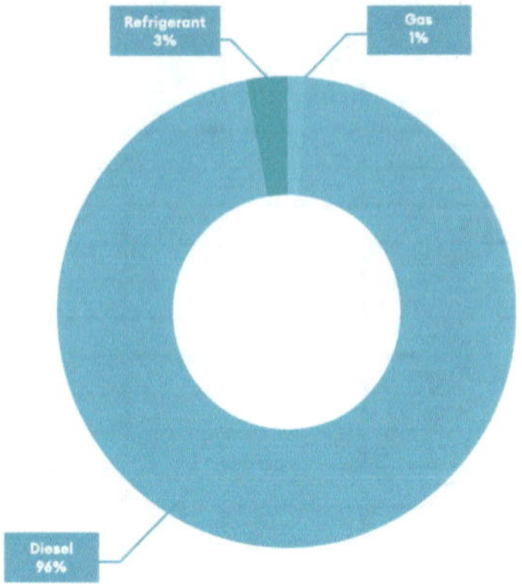

Baseline 2019 – GHG Contributors (electricity using diesel fuel)

Case Study 2: Kabul

In a compound in Kabul, Afghanistan, diesel generators are the main source of power due to the unreliability of grid power. Heating and cooling are via reverse-cycle AC heat pumps, and gas is used for cooking.

The Building Envelope: Walls and Roof

As covered earlier, the building envelope needs to be energy efficient to reduce heating and cooling energy consumption. This means ensuring minimum heat/coolth ingress.

The following input details need to be obtained to carry out the proper analysis.

WALL & FLOORS										
Building Component	Floor Area - m2	Floor carpeted (Y/N)	Floor to Ceiling Height - m	Wall Area m2 - North	Wall Area m2 - South	Wall Area m2 - East	Wall Area m2 - West	Wall Condition - G (good) / N (require attention)	Is wall insulated (Y/N)	Insulation above ceilling if under roof (Y / N)
Building A, F-1										
Building A, F-2										
Building B, Fl										
etc										

Heat transmission through an uninsulated roof is more than two times that of an insulated roof. This is based on conductivity efficiency, as governed by the u-value. Uninsulated, the u-value is around 2.2. For a well-insulated roof with a vapour barrier, the u-value reduces to around 0.8. This demonstrates a massive reduction in heating and cooling systems.

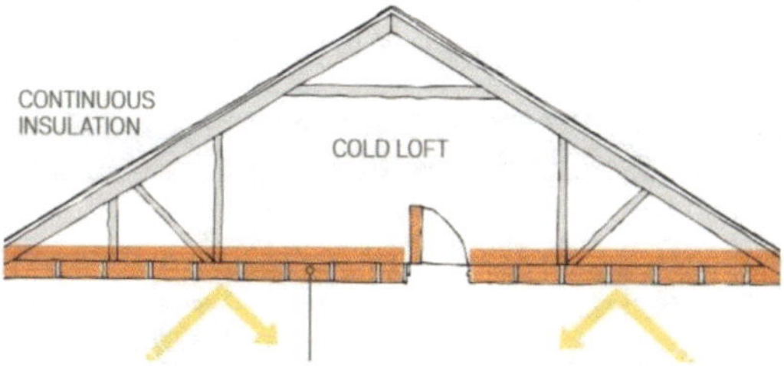

This means that the heating and cooling units serving at the level below the roof would have reduced cooling load, resulting in lower energy consumption and GHG emissions. An important point to note is that depending on the construction material, both walls and roof store the energy and release it over time during warmer days. Insulation, in effect, delays the heat ingress during such circumstances. Therefore, to calculate the heat gain from walls or roofs the equation is as follows.

Heat flow = area x equivalent temperature difference x u-value.

The example below shows the effect of roof insulation on an office building in Tajikistan.

ECM - 8 Roof	Equivalent Diesel Saved (Litres)	GHG Reduction (Tons)	Equivalent Trees Planted	Investment USD	Savings USD	Simple Payback	Return On Investment
Insulation	4,529	12.2	487	$ 76,400	4,801	15.9	6.3%

The savings in kWh with roof insulation range from 0.3 per cent (roof to total area of around 0.8 per cent) to 1.6 per cent with higher roof area compared to overall conditioned space (roof to total area of around 7 per cent). For more complicated buildings, it would be advisable to carry out thermal modelling.

From my experience conducting energy audits and insulating walls for existing buildings, the payback return can be around 20 years. Therefore, it is not recommended for most instances.

Building Envelope: Windows and Doors

Below is a data-gathering form for windows and doors.

WINDOWS & DOORS										
Building Component	Glass Area - m2 - North	Glass Area - m2 - South	Glass Area - m2 - East	Glass Area - m2 West	Glass Type - S = Single. D = Double, T = Triple	Blinds / Curtains (Y/N)	Glass Condition - G (good) / N (require attention)	External Door(s) size	Door Condition - G (good) / N (require	Evidence of air leakage into the room? (Y / N)
Building A, F-1										
Building A, F-2										
Building B, Fl										
etc										

Seals around doors and windows minimise air leaking in or out of a building. From various research findings, the average energy impact is around 0.5 per cent to 1.2 per cent of the overall energy consumption, depending on the age and condition of the building.

As discussed in Chapter 4, the windows and type of glazing have the largest impact on heating and cooling.

The two elements—direct solar heat gain and conduction heat gain and loss, depending on the glass's u-value—contribute to the energy required to heat or cool to maintain the required indoor comfort levels. Unlike with the walls and the roof, the impact is instantaneous. Glass is an excellent conductor with relatively higher u-values compared to other building materials. Chapter 4 also covers impact of glass in buildings

There are various ways to reduce heat gain and loss through glass.

Reducing Heat Transfer Through Glass

External shading – either fixed or retractable, is a perfect heat shield. To estimate the savings, energy modelling may be a better option as there are too many variables to carry out mathematical calculations.

If the glass is not already an efficient glass with low transmissibility factors, solar films (tinting) can be applied. Depending on the orientation of the building and glass-to-wall ratio, energy savings are shown to be around three to four per cent of the energy consumption attributed to electricity.

Blinds save on the direct solar heat gain when closed. Savings are around two to three per cent – depending on type and window orientation. These savings are less than those estimated for the use of solar films.

Research on the use of curtains indicates savings of approximately seven to nine per cent, depending on the orientation of the windows and the glass-to-wall ratio. Higher energy savings are largely due to the curtains' insulating aspect, especially when kept closed overnight in colder climates. During winter months, curtains need to be opened to obtain heat benefits during sunny days.

Modelling confirms these estimates of energy savings and indicates that wool curtains used on a single-glazed window amount to an equivalent u-value of that of a double-glazed window. Curtains save energy, especially when the outside temperatures are well below zero. I observed this in building audits carried out in Tajikistan, Afghanistan, and Canada, where the outside temperatures, in peak winter, are often around -40°C.

Case Study: Kabul

1. Use of Curtains

ECM - 5 Glass	Equivalent Diesel Saved (Litres)	GHG Reduction (Tons)	Equivalent Trees Planted	Investment USD	Savings USD	Simple Payback	Return On Investment
Curtains	4,495	12.0	480	$ 45,723	4,765	9.6	10.4%

2. Application of Solar Film

ECM - 6 Glass	Equivalent Diesel Saved (Litres)	GHG Reduction (Tons)	Equivalent Trees Planted	Investment USD	Savings USD	Simple Payback	Return On Investmen t
Solar Film	3,143	8.5	340	$ 68,584	3,332	20.6	4.9%

3. Shade and Solar Technology

ECM - 7 Glass	Equivalent Diesel Saved (Litres)	GHG Reduction (Tons)	Equivalen t Trees Planted	Investment USD	Savings USD	Simple Payback	Return On Investmen t
Shade & solar	4,495	50.8	2032	$ 371,500	20,200	18.4	5.4%

'Shade and Solar' is a new technology that provides appropriate external shading (with suitably spaced panels to meet indoor daylight requirements) and, at the same time, each shading panel has photovoltaics able to generate around 80 watts (peak) of electricity. They can be retrofitted in existing buildings. The panels rotate following sun angles (using AI-based pneumatic controls) to achieve maximum shade and solar energy. The provider is Solskin – a firm based in Zurich, Switzerland. I visited the factory in April 2024 and carried out further evaluations concerning available maintenance and support in developing countries. The firm is in the process of arranging support in various countries.

Electrical Items

Electrical items in this context cover lighting and IT equipment. Data gathering includes obtaining the rated electrical information from equipment nameplates together with details of all indoor and external lights. It is important to obtain the operating times as per the data acquisition form.

LIGHTING							
Building Component	Indoor Light Fittings Mounting. C= Ceiling, W = Wall, F = Floor	Outdoor Light Fittings Mounting L= Landscape, W = Wall, F = Floor	Number of Light Fittings	Watts per fitting - W	Is it LED? (Y/N)	Operating hours per day - h	Total - kWh
Building A, F-1							
Building A, F-2							
Building B, Fl							
etc							

Energy reduction measures include upgrading all lighting to LED. The benefits include less energy usage and heat output, which can also result in savings in cooling loads. Another common energy-saving measure is using occupancy sensors to ensure lights are only on when the room is occupied.

To establish the operating energy in kWh, hours of operation need to be ascertained by requesting the information outlined in these forms and observing operations (and asking appropriate questions) during the walk-through.

Other electrical data required is related to office equipment, including all IT-related items.

ELECTRICAL EQUIPMENT - IT RELATED						
Building Component	Elec. Equipment. C = Computer, M = Monitor, S = Server, R = Router, P = Printer, Sc = Scanner, Sh = Shredder, U = UPS, Pr = Projector, O = Other	Model number on nameplate	Number of same model items	Nameplate Power - Watts	Average Operating Hours per day - h	Total - kWh
Building A, F-1						
Building A, F-2						
Building B, Fl						
etc						

It should be noted that most IT equipment continues to use energy (plug-load) when in 'sleep' and 'hibernate' modes. On average, a desktop computer in sleep mode typically consumes around one to five watts of power. Laptops generally have lower power consumption in sleep mode, often ranging from .5 to three watts. The power consumption of a printer in sleep mode can range from less than one watts to around five watts, as does the power consumption of a monitor in sleep mode and a TV.

Thus, one energy-saving consideration would be to switch off the IT equipment at the source.

Occupants often have heaters, personal fans, or even portable air conditioning units to provide comfort. These items contribute to energy consumption and hence are required to be accounted for together with other items such as vacuum cleaners. It can be challenging to determine operating hours, but every effort needs to be made to establish the total operating energy - kWh - for each item.

ELECTRICAL EQUIPMENT - GENERAL						
Building Component	Equipment - H = Heater, V= Vacuum Cleaner , PA = Portable AC unit, Misc = any other item not listed	Model number on nameplate	Number of same model items	Namepl ate Power - Watts	Average Operating Hours per day - h	Total - kWh
Building A, F-1						
Building A, F-2						
Building B, Fl						
etc						

Cooking-associated Data

Gas is the most common utility used for cooking. Wood is still used as fuel in developing countries. For a building to attain net-zero carbon, all fossil-fuel-based cooking items, hot water and standby power generation equipment need to be upgraded to be electric. This aspect of the electrification process is being encouraged universally.

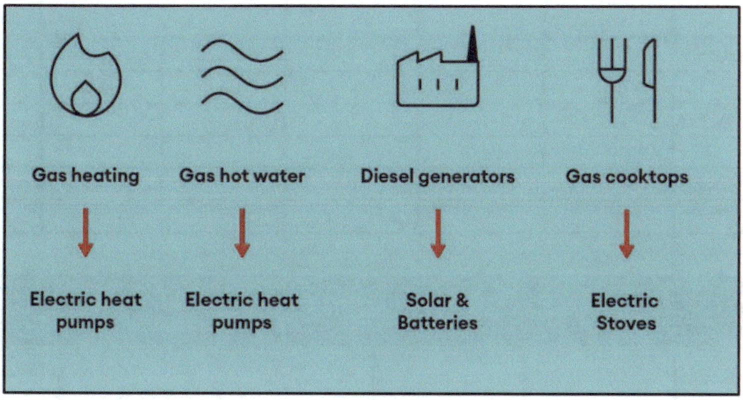

Electrification

The data for the tables on the next page needs to be gathered with the best estimates of operating hours.

COOKING STOVE						
Building Component	Cooking Stove - Model no.	Gas (G) / Electric (E) / Wood (W)	Unit Capacity kW - as per nameplate	Number of same model items	Average Operating Hours per day - h	Total kWH
Building A, F-1						
Building A, F-2						
Building B, Fl						
etc						

OVEN						
Building Component	Oven	Gas (G) / Electric (E)	Nameplat e Power - W	Number of same model items	Operatin g Hours per day	Total kWH
Building A, F-1						
Building A, F-2						
Building B, Fl						
etc						

ELECTRIC KETTLE / URN					
Building Component	Water Urn / Kettle	Nameplate Power - W	Number of same model items	Operating Hours per day - h	Total kWh
Building A, F-1					
Building A, F-2					
Building B, Fl					
etc					

As covered in the previous chapter, it is important that correct amount of water is boiled, as this will result in potential energy savings.

REFRIGERATOR						
Building Component	Refrigerator / Refrigerated Cabinets - model	Refrigerant	Nameplate Power - W	Number of same model items	Operating Hours per day - h	Total kWh
Building A, F-1						
Building A, F-2						
Building B, Fl						
etc						

It is important that the frequency of opening the refrigerator door be minimised and that the door is not left open longer than necessary, as this will result in potential energy savings. The door seals too need to be checked regularly to ensure they are airtight.

Air-conditioning Systems

Air conditioning systems, responsible for providing indoor comfort, are also a major contributor to a building's energy consumption. Data acquisition forms for air conditioners cover various types of systems. It is vital that the age of the equipment be noted, as that may determine whether the equipment has reached end-of-life and may need to be replaced with a more energy-efficient unit. There are also GHG emissions related to refrigerant leakages.

Below is an example of a refrigerant leakage calculation.

Refrigerant Leak		
HVAC Units	198	Refrig Tons
R22 at 1.5 kgs per ton	297	kgs
Leakage @ 2%	5.94	kgs
R22 GWP	1810	per kg
Total GHG	10.8	Tons

There are various types of packaged D/X air conditioning systems. The data to be gathered in each case is essentially very similar.

Packaged DX Systems									
Building Component	AC Unit Type: S = Split D/X, R = Roof Top D/X, W = Water Cooled D/X Fan Coil, V = VRV, G= GSHP	D/X AC Unit model as per nameplate	Number of same model items	Unit Capacity - Refrig. Tons . 3.52 kWr = 1 ton	Rated / Estimated COP	Electrical Power - kW	Operating hours per day - h	AC Unit - Refrigerant	Date Installed
Building A, F-1									
Building A, F-2									
Building B, Fl									
etc									

Ground source heat pumps (GSHP), as part of geothermal, or more appropriately geo-exchange systems, are becoming popular again. Whilst they may be few and far between presently, it is likely that over time these systems will serve more buildings.

Geothermal systems are often part of a district heating and cooling system, whereby the building purchases chilled water and hot water. I have come across two such arrangements, and in both instances, the calculations for GHG emissions were largely dependent on the type and accuracy of the instrumentation used to measure energy. For such a circumstance, data gathering needs to be a special case and expert assistance may need to be sourced.

The other major type of HVAC system is air handling and/or fan coil units using chilled water and hot water.

The following spreadsheet covers various types.

Chilled Water System									
Building Component	AC Unit Type: F= Fan Coil Unit, A = Air Handling Unit, C = Chilled Beams, U = UFAD, V = VAV	A C Unit / Chilled Beams Model	Number of same model items	Unit Capacity - Refrig. Tons . 3.52 kWr = 1 ton	Rated / Estimated COP	Electrical Power - kW	Operating hours per day - h	Chiller - Refrigerant	Date Installed
Building A, F-1									
Building A, F-2									
Building B, Fl									
etc									

As outlined in Chapters 7, 8, and 9, each type of air conditioning has different coefficient of performance (COP) values. For each type, the connected power can be calculated by knowing the total cooling and heating capacities and dividing by the respective COP. The higher the COP, the lower the associated electrical power.

Depending on the type of system, the associated items may include equipment that uses fossil fuels, such as a natural gas boiler. In that case, the boiler would need to be replaced with an electric one as part of the electrification process.

Fans

Various types of fans need to be evaluated for how much energy they use. This is done by checking the model and the rated power as per the nameplate, together with hours of operation.

The following is the form for compiling the relevant data on fans.

Fans						
Building Component	Fans Application: C= Ceiling Fans, T = Toilet Exhaust, PS = Car Park Supply, PE = Car Park Exhaust, K = Kitchen Exhaust	Fan Model	Number of same model items	Nameplate Power - W	Average Operating Hours per day	Date Installed
Building A, F-1						
Building A, F-2						
Building B, Fl						
etc						

The two main categories of fans are axial, such as ceiling fans, and centrifugal, typically used in applications like kitchen exhaust systems. Like with pumps, the energy used is directly related to the resistance it must overcome. The resistance is subject to whether ducting, or air filters are involved. The other factor to consider is the speed of the fan. The higher the speed selected, the higher the power consumption. Ceiling fans generally have multiple speeds, so a 'load factor' of around .65 is applied. In most instances, they run at medium or low speeds.

Electrical Connected versus Operational Loads

The total connected load is calculated by adding together all the nameplate values or calculated power. This applied to all electrical loads associated with lighting, IT-related equipment, miscellaneous items, HVAC systems, and fans. However, until the item is in operation, it uses no energy. For example, if there are ten light fixtures and only five are switched on, calculating the power consumption is simple. Multiply the power of each fitting when switched on by the time it is switched on. If the power is from a fossil fuel power generator, the power can be converted to the amount of GHG emissions.

The following are comparisons between connected (kW) and operating (kWh) electrical loads. You will notice that the lighting operating load reflects the fact that lighting generally is switched on for longer periods – especially the external lighting, often for security and safety reasons.

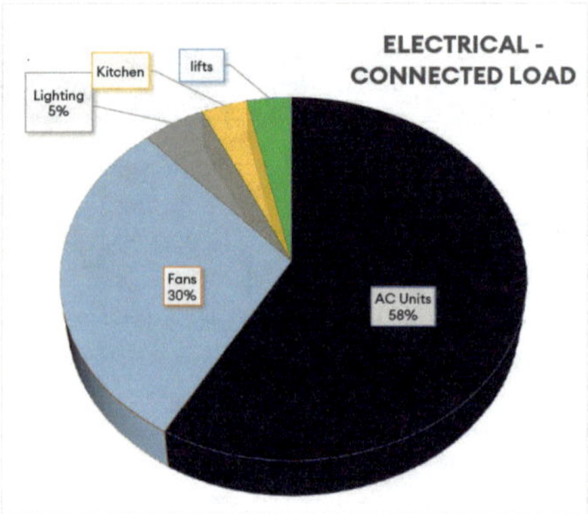

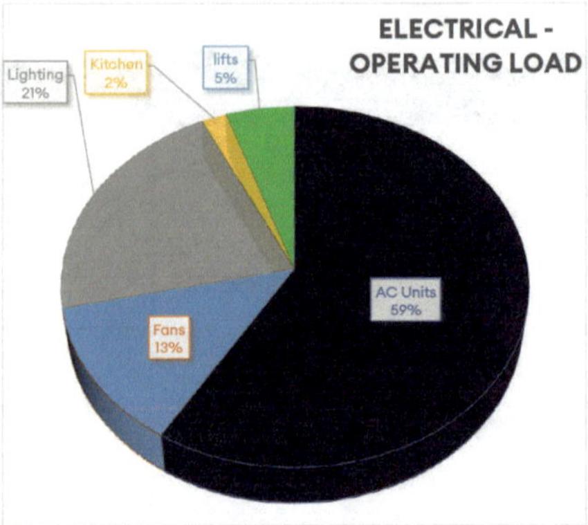

To ascertain the power consumed, it is important to understand the respective systems and apply the appropriate 'load factor'. These generally range from .9 for systems with high 'resistance' (or compressor utilisation), to .65 for less resistance, such as free-standing and ceiling fans or for the AC unit. It needs to be highlighted that an air-conditioning unit will use maximum power only when the compressor is active and in cooling/heating mode.

As shown in the previous chapter, the approximate 'load factor' for an HVAC split system is also around 65 per cent. This is because once the set-point temperature is reached, the AC unit only uses power to circulate conditioned air, and the compressor cycles on and off.

Once compiled, the total electrical operating energy must match the baseline year's annual electrical consumption. Annual energy bill reviews can be used to monitor GHG emissions on an ongoing basis. This would enable tracking GHG emission reductions as ECMs are implemented progressively.

Case study: Kabul,

This example highlights the application of rated power, 'load factor', and hours of operation to arrive at the operational power usage.

Office Kabul, toilet/bathroom											
Building No:	Number of lights	Watts per fitting	Sub Total Watts	Number of exhaust fans	Watts per fan	Sub-total Watts	Total load	Load factor	daily hours	days	Energy kWh
1	3	12	36	3	20	60	96	0.65	8	365	182
2	12	12	144	12	18	216	360	0.65	8	365	683
3	4	12	48	4	20	80	128	0.65	8	365	243
4	36	12	432	36	25	900	1332	0.65	12	365	3792
5	4	12	48	4	25	100	148	0.65	8	365	281
6	5	12	60	5	20	100	160	0.65	8	365	304
7	7	12	84	7	20	140	224	0.65	8	365	425
8	3	12	36	3	18	54	90	0.65	8	365	171

For these eight buildings within the same compound, the grid power was unrealisable and hence solar panels were installed prior to completion of the audit. It was therefore necessary to estimate the components in operation during sun and non-sun hours. This enabled realistic evaluations of ECMs since some of the energy would be at zero charge through solar panels.

The break-up of sun and non-sun hours in this instance is shown below.

Operational Electricity		
432364	Overall electricity consumed matches diesel generated electricity (kWh) in 2022	
205867	48%	SUN Hours
226497	52%	NON-SUN hours

Building Management and Control System (BMCS)

BMCS, when used strategically, has the potential to reduce the operational energy of a building significantly. It is acknowledged that not all buildings will have a BMCS. However, where there is a BMCS, information should be gathered in line with the following.

Building Management & Control System						
Make & Mode	Provide brief description of the set-up -	Overall Number of operating I/O Points	Standard (S) or With Airtificial Intelligence (AI)	Any Enery Management Strategies? (Y/N)	Does it serve other Buildings? (Y/N)	Number of Operators Trained
Are there any occupancy sensors?		Number of sensors		Areas served		
e there any CO2 sensors for fresh air contr		Number of sensors		Areas served		

To reiterate what was discussed in Chapter 10, a BMCS can reduce energy and GHG emissions. On average, the savings range from 12 to 16 per cent, depending on the BMCS selected plus the experience of the BMCS operator. I am aware of instances where facility managers are reluctant to use the BMCS, and there is more reliance on the supplier of BMCS to be involved. A BMCS has a user-friendly interface, and with AI incorporated in the software, it is becoming easier to operate. It is important to ensure that at least two operators are trained to use it.

During the audit, the facility management team needs to discuss items related to occupant comfort and related topics. The following prompts may be used as part of the survey.

Survey	
Is this issue prevelent?	If yes, provide details
1. Occupants complain of being uncomfortable consistently: too cold / too hot, feeling stuffy (not enough fresh air), etc. if yes, provide details	
2. Occupant's clothing in general is not appropriate for the season	
3. Occupants have their own equipment such as fans, portable AC units, heaters, etc or they open windows (where possible) to be more comfortable.	
4. are there any fresh air supply units in any of the buildings?	
5. Is there rain water tank?	
6. Have any water conservation measures been implemented?	
8. Is Domestic Hot Water system using boilers utilizing fossil fuel like Gas, Wood, Diesel, Biomass, etc ?	
9. Are there any electrically operated air curtains over the entry / exit doors?	

In the case study of a place of worship, discussions with the facility management team generally result in energy conservation measures (ECMs) like selecting an alternative venue when there are lower number of attendees – such as for early morning prayers.

Next page contains a summary of the ECMs for a place of worship used as an example to demonstrate the net zero process.

Item	Energy Conservation Measure (ECM)	Suggested Implementation Program	Energy Saving kWh	GHG Savings Tons	Investment - PkR	Cost Saving PkR	Simple Payback Years	ROI	Equivalent trees planted
ECM-1 (NO COST)	Best Practice	2024	2,440	0.9	Nil	124,438	N/A	N/A	36
ECM-2 (NO COST)	Electricity Conversion Rate	Automatic	29,658	11.0	Nil		N/A	N/A	
ECM-3 (HIGH COST)	Gas to Electric Cooking Stoves	2026	16,640	6.2	7,234,240	330,245	9	12%	246
ECM-4 (MEDIUM COST)	Use of Curtains	2025	4,463	1.7	569,328	227,592	2.5	40%	66
ECM-5 (LOW COST)	Jali	2025	1,512	0.6	280,000	77,112	3.6	28%	22
ECM-6 (HIGH COST)	Roof Insulation	2025	18,988	7.03	12,725,400	968,375	13.1	8%	281
ECM- 7 (HIGH COST)	Roof Surface Treatment	2025	9,599	3.6	4,241,800	489,528	8.7	12%	142
ECM - 8 (LOW COST)	Occupancy & Lights Sensors	2024	450	0.17	230,000	22,950	10.0	10%	7
ECM - 9 (LOW COST)	Non-LED to LED	2024	1,902	0.7	546,000	97,007	5.6	18%	28
ECM- 10 (NO COST)	Refrigerant Leak Reduction	2024	1,835	0.7	Nil	93,587	N/A	N/A	27
ECM- 11 (HiGH COST)	BMCS	2026	13,834	5.1	9,809,100	705,541	13.9	7.2%	205
ECM-12 (NO COST)	Heat Purge	2024	6,475	2.4	nil	330,245	Immediate	Immediate	96
ECM-13 (NO COST)	Alternative Venue for Morning Prayers	2024	9,066	3.4	nil	462,343	Immediate	Immediate	134
A- Sub-total (Saving) - Metric Tons			**116,861**	**43.3**					
B- Building Specific - Scope 1 & 2 GHG - Metric Tons				**95.0**					
C- GAP (A-B) - Scope 1 & 2 GHG - Metric Tons				**51.7**					
ECM 14 (HIGH COST)	**Renewable/Solar System**	**2026**	**139,209**	**-51.7**	**55,683,429**	**7,497,217**	**7.4**	**13%**	**2064**
NET ZERO	**After All ECMs and Renewable Energy implemented**	**Total**	**372,930**	**0.0**	**91,319,297**	**11,426,180**	**8.0**	**13%**	**3,355**

In this case study,, 13 ECMs save 133.5 tons of GHG emissions. The baseline total is 255.8, as per energy consumption in 2022. Therefore, the 'gap' is 92.4 tons, which is provided by installing solar panels, for which the simple payback is 7.4 years.

The above also includes an implementation plan where low and no-cost ECMS are actioned in the first year after the audit. This is so that savings realised can go towards the subsequent year's budget to implement medium-cost ECMs a year later and high-cost items in the third year after the audit. Thus, the building would be net zero by 2030.

This completes the discussion on building audits.

Case Study - AKU - Kampala

It is befitting that I conclude this chapter with a case study of a new hospital planned for Kampala, Uganda – my birthplace. My role has been to evaluate the engineering services and provide an estimate of the anticipated energy consumption per annum. Faruq Vishram, the expert on renewable energy, has based the selection of solar panels on these estimates. The outcome is that the hospital has the potential to be net zero.

The next chapter is all about 'what if' scenarios, where we look at the number of homes and buildings in the world and pose the vital question of how many of the suggested energy-saving measures can be cost-effectively implemented.

AMP

17

WHAT IF?

THE BUILT ENVIRONMENT

Estimating the total number of homes and buildings globally is complex due to variations in data collection and differing definitions of what constitutes a "home" or "building". For example, some sources include structures such as bridges and monuments in their count of buildings. In contrast, others may only consider structures that are used for human habitation or commercial purposes.

The high levels of regional-to-urban migration in most cities promote the constant change from low-density to high-density housing. This, in turn, is leading to increased non-domestic developments. The urban landscape is constantly increasing the demand for services, including mainly electrical power for comfort and general living, considering that using natural and bottled gas is being discouraged in the quest for net zero.

The world is estimated to have around 2 billion to 2.5 billion residential homes, including single-family homes, apartments, and other types of dwellings. These homes house the global population of approximately 8 billion people, with an average household size that varies widely by region (e.g., 2-5 people per household).

If we include commercial buildings (offices, retail spaces), industrial buildings (factories, warehouses), and public buildings (schools, hospitals, institutional, entertainment), the total number of buildings worldwide is estimated to be around 3 billion to 4 billion.

Asia has the highest number of residential buildings, particularly in countries like China, Indonesia, and India.

UK, Europe, and North America have a significant number of both residential and non-residential buildings.

Africa, Pacific, and Latin America are rapidly urbanising, leading to a growing number of both homes and buildings.

CONCLUDING THOUGHT

As we have seen, numerous factors affect the rate of CO_2 emissions from homes and buildings. By all accounts, the floor area of the built environment is set to grow approximately 75% over the next thirty years, meaning CO_2 emissions will rise dramatically if no decarbonisation efforts are made in the sector.

The various case studies show that a common approach governs the decarbonisation of buildings in developing and developed nations.

What if 10% of the estimated 2.5 billion residences were to make a concerted effort and realise savings of a nominal 2 tons of CO_2 emissions annually, this could mean a saving of 500 million tons of CO_2 – equivalent to 20 billion trees!

Similarly, if only 10% of non-residential buildings were to adopt some of the energy-saving measures outlined in Chapter 16 and achieve 10 tons per building, this would result in an annual saving of 10.5 billion tons of CO_2. – equivalent to 600 billion trees!

Additionally, what if governments were to provide incentives for saving energy? These could be tax deductions for purchasing energy-efficient heating, cooling, and general domestic items (over 4-star energy rated). There could be subsidies to buy items that can reduce energy costs, such as Hills Hoist for naturally drying clothes.

I sincerely believe that promoting knowledge and awareness about the opportunities to save energy and CO_2 emissions in homes and buildings will have the largest impact on minimising climate change. Let us all work together to defeat Mr. CO_2.

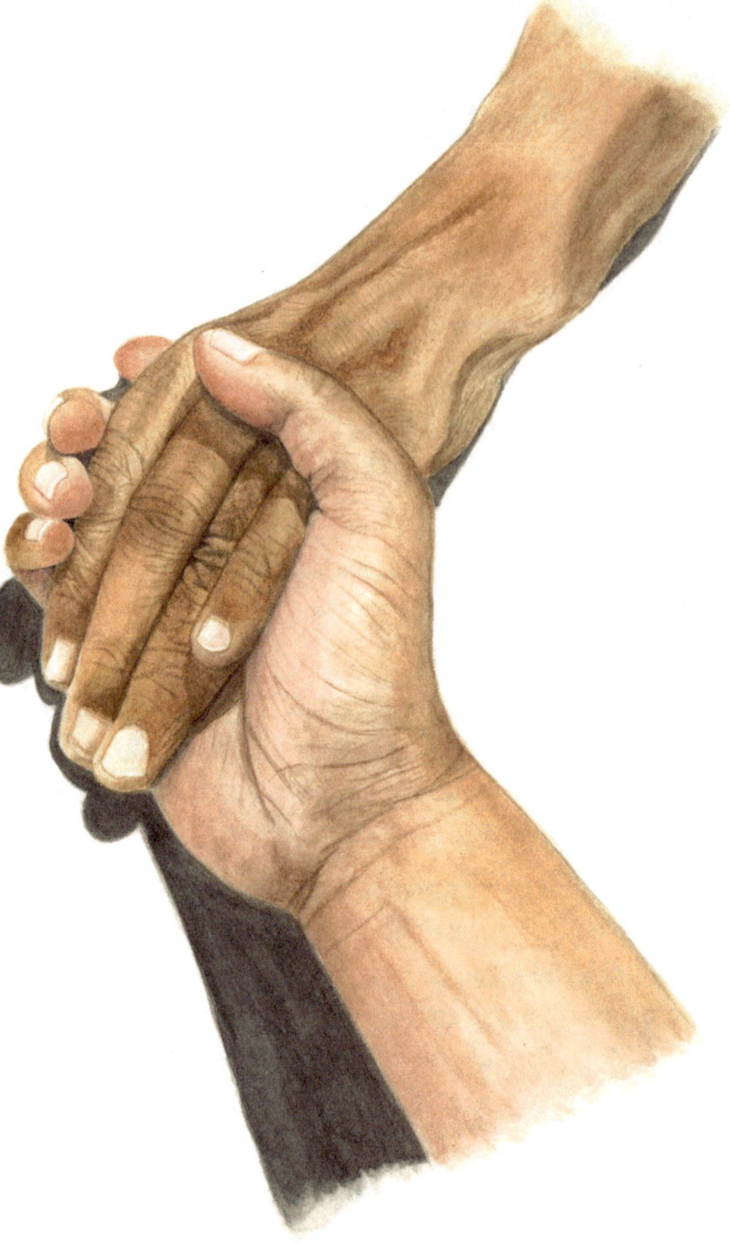

'Grief' - Artist - Rehana Nathwani

This book is dedicated to:

SAMIM NATHWANI

1949 - 2019

Taken away too soon by motor neuron disease

INSIDIOUS MND

Ashak Nathwani
2nd November 2019

Called ALS or MND
Can strike you or me,
It is insidious.

MND creates doubt, panic and utter fear,
Clouding life visions that once were clear
Such a diagnosis is absolutely terrifying,
Since the disease is totally horrifying.

You hang between incredulity and devastation,
With waves of anger and deep frustration
Creating a drowning sensation of despair,
Necessitating twenty-four hours of care.
It is insidious.

Takes away the ability to walk,
Takes away the ability to talk,
It is insidious.

Affects the swallowing capability,
And impacts on the victims' dignity,
It is insidious.

Your mind still remains active,
As every other part starts to give,
Muscle by muscle, limb by limb,
Reversibility chances are slim.
Your body starts to betray you,
And there is little you can do.
In your own body, you become a prisoner,
For your own life, you become a spectator.

Called ALS or MND
Can strike you or me,
It is insidious.

Tragedy has hit home, changing life,
With MND taking way Samim, my wife,
MND is Motor Neurone Disease
Offer a prayer for her soul please.

NEED TO KNOW: MOTOR NEURONE DISEASE

Each day, on average, two Australians die from motor neurone disease (MND) and two more are diagnosed, according to the MND Association of NSW.

Around ten per cent of MND cases are "familial". That is, there is or has been at least one other person affected by MND in the family. The remaining 90 per cent are said to have "sporadic" MND. And the average lifespan for anyone with this disease is three to five years after diagnosis. In Samim Nathwani's case it was three years.

It is an insidious disease. Nerve cells (neurones) that control the muscles that enable us to move, speak, breathe and swallow gradually weaken and waste. You can physically notice the difference and the sufferer loses weight. They also become more sensitive to environmental temperature changes, meaning they will feel colder during winter months and warmer in summer.

MND takes several forms. For some people, the symptoms are widespread from the onset. However, it usually begins by affecting a single limb or aspect of motor function, becoming more generalised as the disease progresses.

There is usually evidence of wasting and weakness in some muscles and fasciculation (twitching) of parts of the muscle, which may be visible under the skin. Sufferers may have only lower or upper motor neurone signs early in the illness but typically develop a combination of the two as the disease progresses. Diagnosis can take up to six months or more. Most people with MND remain mentally alert.

"Samim was watching videos of her grandchildren 15 minutes before she passed away peacefully on November 2, 2019," says Samim's husband Ashak Nathwani AM. Discovered some 150 years ago, MND still has no cure. The only treatment currently available is Reluzole, taken in tablet form twice a day, which can extend the life of an MND patient by up to two months. "Increased research needs to concentrate on the cause and elimination," Nathwani says.

"If combined global effort could address COVID-19 and come up with vaccines in record time, so can a global effort make a difference to MND."

Ashakali Nathwani AM is the Ambassador for the NSW Motor Neurone Disease Association and the designer of the submarine air conditioning system. His wife, Samim, died from MND in November 2019. Her family donated the cost of the air conditioning system as a tribute to her, to allow ongoing early childhood experiences by visiting the HMAS Onslow.

For more information visit: mndnsw.org.au

A portion of the proceeds from this book will be donated to relevant organisations supporting MND research

DEEP DIVE

The following is reproduced with permission from the AIRAH Magazine.

An innovative cooling system has allowed young and old to experience a piece of Australian naval history and serves as a fitting tribute to a woman who believed in learning through experience. **Louise Belfield** reports.

An innovative adaptation of a standard split air conditioning system means greater access to a fascinating piece of Australian naval history for young and old.

Sitting proudly in the water and moored alongside the Australian National Maritime Museum (ANMM) in Sydney's Darling Harbour is a relic of the American-Soviet Cold War of 1947–1991 – Australia's HMAS Onslow submarine. Decommissioned in 1999, this vaguely sinister but fascinating sleek, black, 'silent patroller of the deep' clocked up more than 358,000 nautical miles in service before being donated to the ANMM.

The sub is now an exciting and informative experience for young and old alike as they explore the cramped conditions and imagine what life was like for the sailors whose lives were in danger every day they were in it. And while the air quality back in the day was "disgusting ... we were going well over 12 hours a day without fresh air", according to one ex-Navy officer, conditions inside the submarine as a modern tourist attraction have also been less than desirable.

UNSAFE TEMPERATURES

With regular outside summer temperatures of greater than 25°C, temperatures in the submarine cabins were 4–5°C higher. Conditions simply became uncomfortable and unsafe for visitors, volunteers, and staff, says Craig White, the ANMM's building services manager.

Unsurprising really, with a black solid metal hull and deck and very little space inside.

The existing ventilation system, comprising an axial fan, delivered unfiltered and unconditioned air through the air intake shaft within the conning tower into the cabins and was totally unsatisfactory. Tours had to be cancelled.

"We have a number of volunteers and visitors doing regular tours of the sub, but with limited airflow and high temperatures, we had to stop that," White says. "We looked at modifying the sub at one point by piping chilled water to it, but that wasn't going to be viable. It was going to be far more cost effective to install a DX system."

The challenge, however, was getting a system to fit into the tight space and meet the capacity requirements at the same time.

"Because of the very limited space and having also to maintain the historical aspects of the sub, we couldn't just hang a modern aircon unit on the wall," White says.

"Another challenge was getting a fan coil unit to fit into the conning tower [the periscope housing]. Where you would normally put a fan coil system in the ceiling space of a building, the available entry space through an access hatch into the conning tower was only 450w x 600h."

On learning that the tours of the submarine were being cancelled during hot days, including during summer school holidays, Ashakali (Ashak) Nathwani AM, researcher and senior lecturer in HVAC at the University of Sydney stepped in. His late wife Samim had been an early childhood development expert with double master's degrees in this field, before she succumbed to motor neurone disease (MND) in November 2019 [see breakout]. She always said that "children learn through experience". So, to ensure that children could have that experience, and as a tribute to his late wife, Nathwani offered to design and, with the help of his family, cover the costs of the installation of an air conditioning system to ensure year-round access.

TIME FOR SEA CHANGE

Aware that no ordinary split system would do the job, Ashak turned to Aerotherm, a contracting firm that had successfully installed an unusual system designed by him at a Sydney University laboratory namely 'the Indoor Environment Quality (IEQ) laboratory'.

"But that lab is not quite as cramped as the sub," Ashak says. "I asked if we could convert the lab idea into an air con system for a submarine and how big a unit, we could fit in. That took some working out because there was a size constraint. It clearly needed to be custom-made.

"The final design involved the provision of a custom-built split air conditioning system with the air handling unit located in the snorkel mast, replacing the fresh air fan, and the condensing unit located in the chamber below the main cabins.

"The selection of the system involved considering the high ambient dry bulb temperatures together with the high humidity conditions. Considering the corrosive outdoor conditions, consideration also had to be given to the material selection. This required working closely with the contractor and the unit supplier. The unit customisation also ensured that the supply air was filtered with the ASHRAE recommended MERV-13 (to address COVID concerns) air filters.

"While the installation of the air handling component in the air intake within the snorkel mast was straightforward, though a bit awkward for the contractor, the condensing unit had to be brought in on a barge and craned into the chamber below where it was ensured that there was sufficient airflow to facilitate heat rejection."

TRIP HAZARD

Pasquale Belcastro, HVAC contractor and project manager with Aerotherm, agrees that the solution "was all pretty straightforward, really, but it required some careful planning".

"One of the problems we had to consider was recirculation of the cooling air drawn through the condenser within the hull space; we had to ensure the now-heated air could discharge down the hull without turning back on itself and re-entering the condenser, thus causing tripping issues."

To stop this from happening the condenser was simply placed squarely onto the hull so that the condenser cooling fan blows in the fore-to-aft direction, Pasquale says. And while it appears the tripping issue has not eventuated, Aerotherm is monitoring the condenser to see if it needs to be baffled.

"It was essentially about selecting the right size equipment and configuration to do the job. All the stuff is on the market, but ensuring we used the right type of compressor to suit the application was essential. Normally a compressor gets some sort of cooling effect because you have the conditioned air returning from the room already cooled passing over the indoor coil, which gives the system a chance to cope, but when you've got 100 per cent outside air at 35– 40°C constantly on the coil, that puts a big load on the compressor and there is a chance it could fail and trip out.

"So, for this job I went to the next size unit to handle the extra load (but still fit in the cramped conditions)."

A TIGHT SQUEEZE

Physically getting the fan coil unit into the sub was also not without significant issues, considering the extreme summer heat while doing the installation being just one of the added challenges.

"We had to climb in and out numerous times to get the disassembled unit through the access hatch into the conning tower, then climb up a service ladder onto an upper deck, then clamber though the tight passageway of the main support structure to an opening adjacent to the periscope shaft!" Pasquale says.

"Because the indoor unit is basically a box, we had to unscrew the casing panels, take the coil out, take the fan out, then reassemble in situ. We then had to have space for filters and of course have the space to service the unit.

"We found a reasonable opening where we could take all the pieces to and then reassemble it – and it provided enough space for maintenance as well, which was also tricky to find."

The fan coil unit was then connected with a large flexible duct which was woven through the support structure within the conning tower, across to the air intake shaft for final connection.

"Amazingly, the conditioned air just flows down that shaft and then feeds fore and aft right through the submarine and is exhausted on each end of the vessel. It seems to work effectively and is a success – probably a bit too cold, but that's just a matter of relocating the sensor or turning down the fan. It keeps the cabin air dry as well. Nothing out of the ordinary except the challenge of getting materials through the tight spaces and then having to work within them.

"To get the condenser unit inside the hull we had to get the large access hatch on the side of the submarine opened and get the maritime boys to come alongside on a barge with the condenser. Then we were able to crane in and manhandle the condenser onto the upper deck of the sub, and that required a bit of coordination.

"The three-phase electrical supply to the air conditioning unit is via the existing landline power supply. An indoor zone-mounted thermostat maintains the pre-set conditions in the submarine's cabins. And the units were applied with a special epoxy treatment to keep corrosion at bay."

With the easing of COVID-19 restrictions just before Christmas 2021, the HMAS Onslow was allowed to open briefly until it was closed once again in January because of the pandemic. However, it was open for long enough to establish that the system was a winner, Craig says.

"We were getting temperatures of 4-5°C lower than the ambient temperature.

"Honeywell is also looking at how we can automate the system further through the site BMS system, so we can run it without the need for manual on/off controls."

So, thanks to Ashak's interest and innovative approach, there is air-conditioned and filtered fresh air maintaining comfortable conditions in the submarine's cabins, making it far more pleasant for both guides and the general public.

"This will allow the tours to remain open during the hot summer days, COVID restrictions allowing, including school holidays; a peak time for the school-age patrons to 'learn from the experience'."

Challenge met, and objective achieved.

Zayn, Zahra, Kiyan, Amyn, Aydin, Ashak, Azrah, Rehana, Andrew and Nahla-Samim - Nathwani and Weale families, after a tour of Onslow.

The following is reproduced with permission from the National Australian Maritime Museum.

AIR CONDITIONING SOLUTION FOR HMAS ONSLOW

Steve Riethoff – National Australian Maritime Museum

Dr Ashak Nathwani AM designed a new air-conditioning system for HMAS Onslow which will enable the Museum to keep the vessel open to the public on hot summer days and also provide a higher standard of air quality. A donation by the Nathwani family, made in honour of the late Mrs Samim Nathwani, covered the costs of this important work.

The Museum is home to one of Australia's Cold War remnants, the Oberon class submarine HMAS Onslow. It was given to the museum in 1999 and is a major drawcard for museum visitors. Issues arise in the heat and humidity of a Sydney summer, however, when the museum has been forced to close the vessel to the public as conditions inside become uncomfortable.

Onslow's existing ventilation system comprised only an axial fan, which delivered unfiltered and unconditioned air through the conning tower into the submarine's occupied areas. This led to temperatures inside the vessel reaching 4–5°C higher than outside.

Enter Dr Ashak Nathwani AM, Researcher and Senior Lecturer in HVAC (heating, ventilation, and air conditioning) at the University of Sydney. Ashak knew the museum well, having been a designer of its original air-conditioning system in 1991 as a director of leading HVAC consultants Norman, Disney and Young. Ashak was at the museum discussing all things COVID-19 and air conditioning with museum management when he heard about the continual environmental problems with Onslow. Learning that the early closures affected children during school visits and school holidays, he was inspired to design and cover the costs of a new system on behalf of the Nathwani family in honour of his late wife, Samim.

Samim Nathwani was an early childhood development expert with two master's degrees who tragically succumbed to the insidious motor neurone disease (MND) in November 2019. Samim always advocated that children learn through experience and would not have been happy knowing that children were missing out,' said Ashak. 'It struck me that I could provide a solution through my expertise in air conditioning, and the family could provide the funds to make it happen. It seemed like a fitting tribute to her passion.'

Designing and installing the system posed numerous challenges. It had to be custom-made due to size constraints, with options limited due to heritage considerations. In addition, the condensing unit had to be brought in on a barge and craned into the chamber below the main cabins. Getting the fan coil unit into the sub required many trips up and down service ladders and through a tight passageway. The fan coil unit was then connected with a large flexible duct, which was woven through the support structure within the conning tower, across to the air intake shaft for the final connection. Supply air needed to be filtered with MERV-13 air filters (to meet COVID requirements). Conditioned air now flows down the air intake shaft, feeds fore and aft right through the submarine, and then is exhausted at each end of the vessel. The new system has resulted in temperatures of 4–5°C lower than the ambient temperature, allowing Onslow to open fully with happy visitors, volunteers, and staff.

We thank Ashak, Amyn and Rehana Nathwani for their generosity and this wonderful tribute to their wife and mother, Samim. Thank you, Nathwani Family.

18

REFERENCES

REFERENCES

List of peer-reviewed research papers and related publications.

Aghakhani M. & Eslami G. (2012) *Thermal Comfort Assessment of Underfloor vs Overhead Air Distribution System.* Journal of Applied Science **DOI:** 10.3923/jas.2012.473.479

Ahmed K., Kurnitski J. & Sormunen P. (2015) *Demand controlled ventilation indoor climate and energy performance in a high-performance building with air flow rate controlled chilled beams,* Energy and Buildings 109 (2015) 115–126.

AIRAH (1998) – DA09 *Air Conditioning Load Estimation Guide* – published 1998.

Alajmi A. & El-Amer (2010) *Saving energy by using underfloor air distribution (UFAD) system in commercial buildings.* Energy Conversion and Management Vol. 51 August 2010 pp. 1637-1642

Alamdari, F., Butler, D.J.G., Grigg, P.F. & Shaw, M.R. (1998) *Chilled ceilings and displacement ventilation*, Renew. Energy, 15, 300–305.

Allen Consulting Group. (2010). *A review of the contribution that energy efficiency in the buildings sector can make to greenhouse gas emissions abatement.* Retrieved from http://www.asbec.asn.au.

Altomonte, S. & Schiavon, S. (2013). *Occupant satisfaction in LEED and non-LEED certified buildings. Building and Environment, 68* (6), 66-76.

Anton, L.A & Díaz, J. (2014). *Integration of life cycle assessment in a BIM environment.* Procedia Engineering 85, 26e32. https://doi.org/10.1016/j.proeng.2014.10.525.

ARUP (2021) Shand J. *One Bligh Street Wins Award for an extra-ordinary tall building.* https://www.arup.com/news-and-events/winners-awards-of-excellence-for-extraordinary-tall-buildings

ASHRAE (1989) *Handbook--Fundamentals*, chapter 8. Atlanta: American Society of Heating, Refrigerating and Air-Conditioning Engineers, Inc.

ASHRAE (2010) *Thermal environmental conditions for human occupancy*, ASHRAE Standard 55-2010, Atlanta, Georgia, American Society of Heating, Refrigerating and Air-Conditioning Engineers.

ASHRAE (2017) Standard 55. *Thermal environmental conditions for human occupancy*. Atlanta: American Society of Heating, Refrigerating and Air-Conditioning Engineers.

ASTM (1991) ASTM-FI291, *Standard test method for measuring the thermal insulation of clothing using a heated manikin*. Philadelphia: American Society for Testing and Materials.

Azhar S., Carlton W., Olsen D. and Irtishad A. (2010). *Building information modeling for sustainable design and LEED rating analysis*. Journal homepage: www.elsevier.com

Banhidi, L., S. Somogyi, L. Fabo & T. Simon. (1991). *Compensation of asymmetric radiation heat loss to cold walls by different heating systems--Analysis with thermal manikin. Environment International* 17(4): 211- 216.

Bauman F. & Daly A. (2003) *Underfloor Air Distribution (UFAD) Design Guide*. Atlanta, GA: American Society of Heating, Refrigerating and Air Conditioning Engineers; 2003.

Birt, B. & Newsham, G. R. (2009). *Post-occupancy evaluation of energy and indoor environment quality in green buildings: a review*. Paper presented at the 3rd International Conference on Smart and Sustainable Built Environments June 15-19, Delft, the Netherlands.

Canbay, C. S., Hepbasli A. & Gokcen G. (2004). *Evaluating performance indices of a shopping centre and implementing HVAC control principles to minimize energy usage*. Energy and

Chowdhury A., M.G. Rasul M. & Khan M. (2008) *Thermal-comfort analysis and simulation for various low-energy cooling-technologies applied to an office building in a subtropical climate* Applied Energy 85 (2008) 449–462

Colliers International. (2010). *2010 Office Tenant Survey*. Sydney

Davis P. (2006) *Building Procurement Methods*, Report Project No: 2006-034-C-02.

de Dear R. (2004) *Thermal Comfort in Practice.* Indoor Air (2004): 14 (suppl. 7): 32-39

de Dear, R., Nathwani, A. & Cabrera, D. (2012). *The next generation of experientially realistic lab-based research: The University of Sydney's Indoor Environmental Quality Laboratory.* Architectural Science Review, 56, 83–92.

Department of Industry. (2014a). *A Guide to Commercial Building Disclosure: What is Office Space?* Canberra: Commonwealth of Australia.

Didwania, S.K., Rawal, R., Shukla, Y. & Bansal, N.K. (2014) *Relevance of radiant space cooling in Indian context.* 1st International Conference on Energy and Indoor Environment for Hot Climates pp. 17-24

Dilsiz & Nagya (2019) *Embodied versus operational energy in residential and commercial buildings: where should we focus?* Phys. Conf. Ser. 1343 012178

EcoLibrium (2007), *Chilled Beams or Variable Air Volume?* Feature, Issue: September 2007

Fanger, P.O. (1970). *Thermal comfort.* Copenhagen: Danish Technical Press.

Ergonomics, 29:2, 215-235.

Fanger, P.O. (2000). *Indoor air quality in the 21st century: search for excellence.* Indoor Air 2000, 10, 68-73.

Finch, E. F. (1989). *"A Requisite Decision Model for the Selection of Mechanical and Electrical Services in Buildings."* PhD thesis, University of Reading. UK

Fisk, W. J. (2000). *Health and productivity gains from better indoor environments and their relationship with building energy efficiency. Annual Review of Energy and the Environment,* 25(1), 537-566.

Fuller S, Petersen S. (1996). *Life-cycle costing manual for the federal energy management program,* 135. . Washington, DC: National Institute of Standards and Technology (NIST) Handbook; 1996.

Fuller S, Petersen S. (2016). Life Cycle Cost Analysis LCCA). Washington, DC: National Institute of Standards and Technology (NIST) Handbook;

Updated 09.19.2016.

Gabe J. 2016. *Successful greenhouse gas mitigation in existing Australian office buildings*. Building Research & Information. Vol44. No 2. 160-174.

GBCA (2005) Green Building Council of Australia Newsletter – Feature: 30 The Bond – First Chilled Beam System.

GBCA (2013) Green Building Council of Australia. The Value of Green Star – *A Decade of Environmental Benefits*. Sydney (2013).

Harvey, L. (2013). *Recent Advances in Sustainable Buildings: Review of the Energy and Cost Performance of the State-of-the-Art Best Practices from Around the World. Annual Review of Environment and Resources, 38*, 281-309.

Herring, H. (2006). Energy efficiency — a critical view. *Energy, 31*, 10-20.

Hongmei J., Zhanming L., & Weiqiang. (2018) *Research on Optimized Energy Saving Control System of VAV Air Conditioning System*. IOP Conf. Series: Earth and Environmental Science 237 (2018) 042015

Hoyt, T., Arens, E. and Zhang, H. (2014). *Extending air temperature set points: Simulated energy savings and design considerations for new and retrofit buildings*. Building and Environment, 88, 89-96.

Hoyt, T., Schiavon, S., Piccioli, A., Cheung, T., Moon, D. and Steinfeld, K. (2017). CBE *Thermal Comfort Tool*. Center for the Built Environment, University of California Berkeley.

IEA (2012). International Energy Agency. CO2 *Emissions from Fuel Combustion. Beyond 2020 Online Database*, Paris http://data.iea.org

ISO 7730. (2005) *Ergonomics of the Thermal Environment: Analytical Determination and Interpretation of Thermal Comfort using Calculation of the PMV and PPD Indices and Local Thermal Comfort Criteria*. Geneva, Switzerland: International Organization for Standardization; 2005.

IPCC (2021); Intergovernmental Panel on Climate Change (IPCC), Pachauri, R.K.; Meyer, L.

Kang S. Kim H. & Cho Y. (2014) *A study on the control method of single duct VAV terminal unit through the determination of proper minimum air flow*.

Energy and Buildings Volume 69, February 2014, pp. 464-472

Kapoor N, Thakur N S & Nazir S (2019) *Optimising Energy Efficiency in Commercial Buildings through Advanced Building Strategies* DOI:10.47392/IRJAEM.2024.0135

Ke M., Weng K. & Chiang C. (2006) *Performance evaluation of an innovative fan-coil unit: Low-temperature differential variable air volume FCU.* Energy and Buildings Volume 39, 2006, pp. 702-708

Kim Chul-Ho, Lee Seung-Eon, Lee Kwang-Ho and Kim Kang-Soo. (2019) *Detailed Comparison of the Operational Characteristics of Energy-Conserving HVAC Systems during the Cooling Season Energies* 2019, 12, 4160; doi: 10.3390/en12214160

Kim H., Kang S. & Cho Y (2015) *A study on the control method without stratification of single duct VAV terminal units.* A journal of Asian Architecture and Building Engineering 14 (2), pp. 467-474.

Kim J., Braun J. & Tzempelikos A. (2014) 2 *Energy Saving Potential of Passive Chilled Beam System as a Retrofit Option for Commercial Buildings in Different Climates* Vol. 8, 2014 Issue 3

Leaman A., Thomas L. & Vandenberg M. (2007) *'Green Buildings': What Australian Building Users are saying*, EcoLibrium, November 2007.

Leaman A. & Bordass B., (2007). *Are users more tolerant of 'green' buildings?* Building Research and Information 35(6): 662-673.

Liu, G. & Brambley, M.R. (2011) *Occupancy based control strategy for variable-air-volume (VAV) terminal box systems. ASHRAE Trans.* 2011, 117, 244–252.

Lipczynska, A., Schiavon, S. and Graham, L.T. (2018). *Thermal comfort and self- reported productivity in an office with ceiling fans in the tropics.* Building and Environment, 135, 202-212.

Loudermilk, K. (2009) *Designing chilled beams for thermal comfort,* ASHRAE J., 51, 58–64 ,

Nathwani A. (2014) *Thermal comfort in two prayer halls in two continents – a case study.* Proceedings – Windsor Conference 2014, pp 385 – 420

Nathwani A. (2014) *Indoor thermal Comfort in Commercial Buildings Versus Air Conditioning Systems* – Indoor Air 13th International Conference on Indoor Air Quality and Climate, Hong Kong 2014 pp. 320-333

Nathwani A. (2016) *Comfort preferences for Passive Chilled Beams Vs Variable Air Volume Vs Underfloor Air Distribution*. Proceedings – Windsor Conference 2016, pp 264-277

Nathwani A. (2018) *How do Passive Chilled Beams rate compared to Variable Air Volume and Underfloor Air Distribution?* Proceedings – Windsor Conference 2018, pp 176-193

Nilsson H, Holmér I, Bohm M & Norén O (1999a) *Definition and Theoretical Background of the Equivalent Temperature*. Int. ATA Conf, 17-19 Nov, Florence, Italy, 1999A4082.

Palm, J. & Darby, S. J. (2014). *The Meanings of Practices for Energy Consumption – a Comparison of Homes and Workplaces*. Science & Technology Studies, 27(2), 72- 92.

Parameshwaran R., Harikrishnan S. & Kalaiselvam S. (2010) *Energy efficient PCM-based variable air volume air conditioning system for modern buildings* Energy and Buildings. Volume 42, Issue 8, August 2010, pp. 1353-1360

PCA (2012) Property Council of Australia Guide to Office Building Quality Sydney – 2012.

PCA (2019) Property Council of Australia Guide to Office Building Quality Sydney – 2019.

Rawal R., Manu S., Shukla Y., Thomas L. & de Dear R. (2016) Clothing insulation as a behavioural adaptation for thermal comfort in Indian office buildings. Proceedings of 9th Windsor Conference, April 2016

Rawal R., Schweiker M., Kazanci O, Vardhan V., Jin Q. & Duanmu L. (2020). *Personal comfort systems: A review on comfort, energy, and economics*. Energy & Buildings 214 (2020)

Roussac A C, (2017). *A Framework for Presenting Energy Efficiency Feedback to Operators of Buildings*. Thesis (Doctor of Philosophy), University of

Sydney

Shahrestani M, Yao R, Cook G & Clements-Croome D (2018). *Decision-making on HVAC&R systems selection: a critical review. Intelligent Buildings International, Vol. 10, No. 3, 133–153*

Stanescu M, Kajl S & Lamarche L (2013) *Simplified optimization method for preliminary design of HVAC system and real building application*, HVAC&R Research 19:3, 213-229

Tanabe, S., Kimura K. & Inoue. U. (1989). *Proposal of evaluation method with thermal manikin. Annual Meeting of Architectural Institute of Japan, pp. 875- 876. Toda, K. 1958. Thermal manikin and its application for clothing study. Japanese Journal of Hygiene* 13(1): 146.

Taylor S. (2016) *Making UFAD Systems Work* ASHRAE journal March 2016

UNEP (2009) United Nations Environment Program. (2009). *Buildings and Climate Change: Summary for Decision-Makers.* Paris: UNEP Sustainable Building & Climate Initiative.

US EPA, 2022 https://www.epa.gov/system/files/documents/2022-04/ghg_emission_factors_hub.pdf

Wang, E., Shen, Z. & Barryman, C., (2011). A building LCA case study using Autodesk Ecotec and BIM model. In: Paper Presented at the 47th ASC Annual International Conference Proceedings. Omaha, USA.

Wang W., Zhang J., Brambley M. and Futrell B. (2020). *Performance Simulation and Analysis of Occupancy-Based Control for Office Buildings with Variable-Air-Volume Systems. Energies* 2020, 13, 3756

Wang Y., Lian Z. & Brode P. (2012) *A time-dependent model evaluating draft in indoor environment* Energy and Building Vol. 49 2012 pp. 466-470.

Wargocki P. & Wyon D.P. (2016). *Ten questions concerning thermal and indoor air quality effects on the performance of office work and schoolwork* Building and Environment Volume 112, 1 February 2017, Pages 359-366

Wargocki P., Wyon D.P., Sundell, J. & Clausen G. and Fanger P.O. (2000). *The Effects of Outdoor Air Supply Rate in an Office on Perceived Air Quality, Sick Building Syndrome (SBS)*, Indoor Air, 10, 222-236.

Webster T. & Bauman F. (2006) *Modeling of underfloor air distribution (UFAD) systems*, Proceedings of the Third National Conference of IBPSA-USA, 2006.

WGBC (2016) World Green Building Council Report. *Health, Wellbeing & Productivity in Offices – The next chapter for green building.* Published UKGBC 2016. www.worldgbc.org

Younas Muhammad, Muhammad Yaseen, Naveed Farah, Muhammad Arfan-ul-Haq and Shahid Mahmood Khan *A review of changing climate & rising population impacts on agriculture produce: challenges for water & food security and sustainable development.* Published 2016

Zakia A. (2019) *Performance improvement of building heating, cooling and ventilation.* PhD Thesis, Murdoch University, Perth, Australia.

Zheng, D.W. Gao, L. Lin (2013) *Smart meters in smart grid: An overview*, in: IEEE Green Technol. Conf., 2013, pp. 57–64.

Made in the USA
Monee, IL
05 November 2026

67805989R00166